Practice *Planner*

Arthur E. Jongsma, Jr., Series Editor

Helping therapists help their clients...

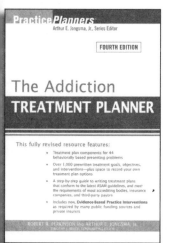

Treatment Planners cover all the necessary elements for developing formal treatment plans, including detailed problem definitions, long-term goals, short-term objectives, therapeutic interventions, and DSM-IV™ diagnoses.

☐ The Complete Adult Psychotherapy Treatment Planner, Fourth Edition........978-0-471-76346-8 / $55.00
☐ The Child Psychotherapy Treatment Planner, Fourth Edition ....978-0-471-78535-4 / $55.00
☐ The Adolescent Psychotherapy Treatment Planner, Fourth Edition ....978-0-471-78539-2 / $55.00
☐ The Addiction Treatment Planner, Fourth Edition.....................................978-0-470-40551-2 / $55.00
☐ The Couples Psychotherapy Treatment Planner, Second Edition..................978-0-470-40695-3 / $55.00
☐ The Group Therapy Treatment Planner, Second Edition..............................978-0-471-66791-9 / $55.00
☐ The Family Therapy Treatment Planner, Second Edition.............................978-0-470-44193-0 / $55.00
☐ The Older Adult Psychotherapy Treatment Planner ....978-0-471-29574-7 / $55.00
☐ The Employee Assistance (EAP) Treatment Planner ....978-0-471-24709-8 / $55.00
☐ The Gay and Lesbian Psychotherapy Treatment Planner ....978-0-471-35080-4 / $55.00
☐ The Crisis Counseling and Traumatic Events Treatment Planner ....978-0-471-39587-4 / $55.00
☐ The Social Work and Human Services Treatment Planner ....978-0-471-37741-2 / $55.00
☐ The Continuum of Care Treatment Planner..978-0-471-19568-9 / $55.00
☐ The Behavioral Medicine Treatment Planner...978-0-471-31923-8 / $55.00
☐ The Mental Retardation and Developmental Disability Treatment Planner...978-0-471-38253-9 / $55.00
☐ The Special Education Treatment Planner...978-0-471-38872-2 / $55.00
☐ The Severe and Persistent Mental Illness Treatment Planner, Second Edition....978-0-470-18013-6 / $55.00
☐ The Personality Disorders Treatment Planner ....978-0-471-39403-7 / $55.00
☐ The Rehabilitation Psychology Treatment Planner ....978-0-471-35178-8 / $55.00
☐ The Pastoral Counseling Treatment Planner...978-0-471-25416-4 / $55.00
☐ The Juvenile Justice and Residential Care Treatment Planner ....978-0-471-43320-0 / $55.00
☐ The School Counseling and School Social Work Treatment Planner ....978-0-471-08496-9 / $55.00
☐ The Psychopharmacology Treatment Planner ....978-0-471-43322-4 / $55.00
☐ The Probation and Parole Treatment Planner...978-0-471-20244-8 / $55.00
☐ The Suicide and Homicide Risk Assessment & Prevention Treatment Planner..978-0-471-46631-4 / $55.00
☐ The Speech-Language Pathology Treatment Planner.................................978-0-471-27504-6 / $55.00
☐ The College Student Counseling Treatment Planner ....978-0-471-46708-3 / $55.00
☐ The Parenting Skills Treatment Planner ....978-0-471-48183-6 / $55.00
☐ The Early Childhood Education Intervention Treatment Planner ....978-0-471-65962-4 / $55.00
☐ The Co-Occurring Disorders Treatment Planner.......................................978-0-471-73081-1 / $55.00
☐ The Sexual Abuse Victim and Sexual Offender Treatment Planner ....978-0-471-21979-8 / $55.00
☐ The Complete Women's Psychotherapy Treatment Planner ....978-0-470-03983-0 / $55.00
☐ The Veterans and Active Duty Military Psychotherapy Treatment Planner...978-0-470-44098-8 / $55.00

The **Complete Treatment and Homework Planners** series of books combines our bestselling *Treatment Planners* and *Homework Planners* into one easy-to-use, all-in-one resource for mental health professionals treating clients suffering from the most commonly diagnosed disorders.

☐ The Complete Depression Treatment and Homework Planner ....978-0-471-64515-3 / $48.95
☐ The Complete Anxiety Treatment and Homework Planner ....978-0-471-64548-1 / $48.95

Over 500,000 Practice*Planners*® sold ...

WILEY

Are You Prepared for Your Next Audit?

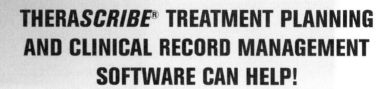

THERA*SCRIBE*® TREATMENT PLANNING AND CLINICAL RECORD MANAGEMENT SOFTWARE CAN HELP!

■ **Standardized language** and **treatment planning** features that conform to the standards of most accrediting bodies (CARF, TJC, NCQA), insurance companies, and third-party payors

■ **Evidence-Based Practice Interventions** and **Progress Notes** that meet the requirements of many public funding sources and private insurers

Easy to learn—generate treatment plans in 15 minutes!

Thera*Scribe*® lets you quickly and easily create effective treatment plans with "point and click" behavioral definitions, *DSM-IV*™ diagnoses, goals, objectives, and therapeutic interventions.

Writing Evidence-Based individualized treatment plans is quick and easy

■ **Robust content**—saves you time with prewritten treatment plan statements—including short-term objectives and long-term goals

■ Organized by **presenting problem** and DSM-IV™ code

Thera*Scribe*® 5.0 Small Practice Edition

■ Developed for practices with more than one practitioner

Thera*Scribe*® Essential 1.0

■ Ideal for solo practitioners   ■ Easy to use and affordable

For more information, call us at 1-866-888-5158 or visit us on the web at www.therascribe.com

WILEY
Now you know.
wiley.com

Get Evidence-Based Psychotherapy Treatment Planning Training!

PURCHASE SEPARATELY OR TOGETHER:
- DVD   • Companion Workbook
- Facilitator's Guide *(for group training)*

■ *Evidence-Based Psychotherapy Treatment Planning Video Series* provides an overview of the empirically supporte[d] treatment interventions available for the most common *DSM-IV*™ disorders and other presenting problems.
   - Introduction to Evidence-Based Psychotherapy Treatment Planning
   - Evidence-Based Treatment Planning for Depression
   - Evidence-Based Treatment Planning for Panic Disorder
   - Evidence-Based Treatment Planning for Social Anxiety Disorder

■ Ideal for individual therapists who want to learn at home or for training mental health clinic staff at any level

Professionally produced DVD series featuring best-selling Practice*Planners*® series authors Drs. Arthur E. Jongsma, Jr. and Timothy J. Bruce. **DVDs offer step-by-step guidance on how to integrate results from psychotherapy research into the entire treatment planning process—increasing the likelihood of client improvement and meeting the expectations of accrediting agencies and funding sources**

Visit **www.wiley.com/go/ebtseries** for complete descriptions and to view the whole series, including video clip[s]

**For more information or to order, call 1-877-762-2974
or visit us online at www.wiley.com/go/ebtseries**

WILEY
Now you know

Earn CE credit—counselors, psychologists, social workers, MFTs, and addiction counselors can earn 1 CE credit per EBT DVD/Workbook in our EB[T] Video Training Program. For more information email mentalhealth@wiley.com • *** *Multiple copy discounts available for in-house training* ***

Veterans and Active Duty Military Psychotherapy Homework Planner

Practice*Planners*® Series

Treatment Planners

The Complete Adult Psychotherapy Treatment Planner, Fourth Edition
The Child Psychotherapy Treatment Planner, Fourth Edition
The Adolescent Psychotherapy Treatment Planner, Fourth Edition
The Addiction Treatment Planner, Fourth Edition
The Continuum of Care Treatment Planner
The Couples Psychotherapy Treatment Planner, Second Edition
The Employee Assistance Treatment Planner
The Pastoral Counseling Treatment Planner
The Older Adult Psychotherapy Treatment Planner
The Behavioral Medicine Treatment Planner
The Group Therapy Treatment Planner
The Gay and Lesbian Psychotherapy Treatment Planner
The Family Therapy Treatment Planner, Second Edition
The Severe and Persistent Mental Illness Treatment Planner, Second Edition
The Mental Retardation and Developmental Disability Treatment Planner
The Social Work and Human Services Treatment Planner
The Crisis Counseling and Traumatic Events Treatment Planner
The Personality Disorders Treatment Planner
The Rehabilitation Psychology Treatment Planner
The Special Education Treatment Planner
The Juvenile Justice and Residential Care Treatment Planner
The School Counseling and School Social Work Treatment Planner
The Sexual Abuse Victim and Sexual Offender Treatment Planner
The Probation and Parole Treatment Planner
The Psychopharmacology Treatment Planner
The Speech-Language Pathology Treatment Planner
The Suicide and Homicide Treatment Planner
The College Student Counseling Treatment Planner
The Parenting Skills Treatment Planner
The Early Childhood Intervention Treatment Planner
The Co-Occurring Disorders Treatment Planner
The Complete Women's Psychotherapy Treatment Planner
The Veterans and Active Duty Military Psychotherapy Treatment Planner

Progress Notes Planners

The Child Psychotherapy Progress Notes Planner, Third Edition
The Adolescent Psychotherapy Progress Notes Planner, Third Edition
The Adult Psychotherapy Progress Notes Planner, Third Edition
The Addiction Progress Notes Planner, Third Edition
The Severe and Persistent Mental Illness Progress Notes Planner, Second Edition
The Couples Psychotherapy Progress Notes Planner, Second Edition
The Family Therapy Progress Notes Planner, Second Edition
The Veterans and Active Duty Military Psychotherapy Progress Notes Planner

Homework Planners

Couples Therapy Homework Planner, Second Edition
Family Therapy Homework Planner, Second Edition
Grief Counseling Homework Planner
Group Therapy Homework Planner
Divorce Counseling Homework Planner
School Counseling and School Social Work Homework Planner
Child Therapy Activity and Homework Planner
Addiction Treatment Homework Planner, Fourth Edition
Adolescent Psychotherapy Homework Planner II
Adolescent Psychotherapy Homework Planner, Second Edition
Adult Psychotherapy Homework Planner, Second Edition
Child Psychotherapy Homework Planner, Second Edition
Parenting Skills Homework Planner
Veterans and Active Duty Military Psychotherapy Homework Planner

Client Education Handout Planners

Adult Client Education Handout Planner
Child and Adolescent Client Education Handout Planner
Couples and Family Client Education Handout Planner

Complete Planners

The Complete Depression Treatment and Homework Planner
The Complete Anxiety Treatment and Homework Planner

PracticePlanners®

Arthur E. Jongsma, Jr., Series Editor

Veterans and Active Duty Military Psychotherapy Homework Planner

James R. Finley

Bret A. Moore

WILEY

John Wiley & Sons, Inc.

ISBN 978-0-470-89052-3 (paper); 978-0-470-93177-6 (ePDF); 978-0-470-93178-3 (eMobi); 978-0-470-93179-0 (ePub)

Printed in the United States of America

10 9 8 7 6 5 4 3 2 1

This book is dedicated to our loved ones, without whose support and encouragement we could not do what we do; to the many colleagues, mentors, and clients who have shared their lives and their wisdom with us through the years; and finally to the brave, skilled, and dedicated men and women in uniform who have been our brothers and sisters in arms past, present, and future.

CONTENTS

PRACTICE*PLANNERS*® SERIES PREFACE

Accountability is an important dimension of the practice of psychotherapy. Treatment programs, public agencies, clinics, and practitioners must justify and document their treatment plans to outside review entities in order to be reimbursed for services. The books and software in the Practice*Planners*® series are designed to help practitioners fulfill these documentation requirements efficiently and professionally.

The PracticePlanners® series includes a wide array of treatment planning books including not only the original Complete Adult Psychotherapy Treatment Planner, Child Psychotherapy Treatment Planner, and Adolescent Psychotherapy Treatment Planner, all now in their fourth editions, but also Treatment Planners targeted to specialty areas of practice, including:

- Addictions
- Co-occurring disorders
- Behavioral medicine
- College students
- Couples therapy
- Crisis counseling
- Early childhood education
- Employee assistance
- Family therapy
- Gays and lesbians
- Group therapy
- Juvenile justice and residential care
- Mental retardation and developmental disability
- Neuropsychology
- Older adults
- Parenting skills
- Pastoral counseling
- Personality disorders
- Probation and parole
- Psychopharmacology
- Rehabilitation psychology
- School counseling
- Severe and persistent mental illness
- Sexual abuse victims and offenders
- Social work and human services

- Special education
- Speech-Language pathology
- Suicide and homicide risk assessment
- Veterans and active military duty
- Women's issues

In addition, there are three branches of companion books which can be used in conjunction with the *Treatment Planners*, or on their own:

- ***Progress Notes Planners*** provide a menu of progress statements that elaborate on the client's symptom presentation and the provider's therapeutic intervention. Each *Progress Notes Planner* statement is directly integrated with the behavioral definitions and therapeutic interventions from its companion *Treatment Planner*.

- ***Homework Planners*** include homework assignments designed around each presenting problem (such as anxiety, depression, chemical dependence, anger management, eating disorders, or panic disorder) that is the focus of a chapter in its corresponding *Treatment Planner*.

- ***Client Education Handout Planners*** provide brochures and handouts to help educate and inform clients on presenting problems and mental health issues, as well as life skills techniques. The handouts are included on CD-ROMs for easy printing from your computer and are ideal for use in waiting rooms, at presentations, as newsletters, or as information for clients struggling with mental illness issues. The topics covered by these handouts correspond to the presenting problems in the *Treatment Planners*.

The series also includes:

- **TheraScribe®**, the #1 selling treatment planning and clinical record-keeping software system for mental health professionals. Thera*Scribe*® allows the user to import the data from any of the *Treatment Planner*, *Progress Notes Planner*, or *Homework Planner* books into the software's expandable database to simply point and click to create a detailed, organized, individualized, and customized treatment plan along with optional integrated progress notes and homework assignments.

Adjunctive books, such as *The Psychotherapy Documentation Primer* and *The Clinical Documentation Sourcebook*, contain forms and resources to aid the clinician in mental health practice management.

The goal of our series is to provide practitioners with the resources they need in order to provide high quality care in the era of accountability. To put it simply: We seek to help you spend more time on patients, and less time on paperwork.

ARTHUR E. JONGSMA, JR.
Grand Rapids, Michigan

PREFACE

Today there is a large and growing population of veterans and active duty military personnel with some unique psychotherapeutic needs. They range from those who are still in their teens to some of their great grandparents who served in World War II and Korea. They are men and women from every sector of society, and they come to us to help them cope with issues such as building new lives with physical disabilities more extensive than ever before, because medicine has advanced so far that doctors can save the lives of Soldiers, Sailors, Airmen, Marines, and Coast Guardsmen who would have died of their wounds in any previous era. Other issues involve their families and the strains of having one and sometimes both parents going overseas multiple times. At the same time, there aren't nearly enough treatment resources to meet the need as well as we wish we could.

The use of therapeutic homework assignments to augment face-to-face sessions with a therapist, social worker, psychologist, or psychiatrist offers great advantages. It serves as a "force multiplier" enabling the clinician to engage the veteran or service member with whom he or she is working in the therapy process every day, rather than only on days they can meet. This allows each professional to help several times as many clients as would be possible if all the work were being done in session. It keeps the therapeutic process in the forefront of the lives of veterans and service members both by engaging their attention and energy daily and potentially in all spheres of their lives. They are able to take the work of therapy into the arenas in life that challenge them, practice what they're learning on the spot, and process the lessons learned when they meet with their clinicians. They are also able to involve their families in their therapy more easily, as they do the homework on their schedule, at the place that works for them.

The homework assignments are provided on a CD-ROM as well as printed in the *Planner*, enabling clinicians to modify them, tailoring each assignment to the situation, coping resources, stages of readiness and insight, and other specifics of each client. They are uniformly cognitive-behavioral in structure, the approach research shows is most effective for psychotherapy in general, with many also containing strong elements of solution-focused brief therapy.

As with other *Homework Planners* in the Practice Planner series, the assignments are closely integrated with the corresponding *Treatment Planner*, *Progress Notes Planner*, and TheraScribe module, being built on the same problem areas. This *Homework Planner* contains 78 homework assignments covering 38 problem areas, with a Therapist's Overview for each assignment. In many cases the Overviews also offer videotherapy recommendations tapping into another Wiley resource, *Rent Two Films and Let's Talk in the Morning,* 2nd ed., by John W. Hesley and Jan G. Hesley.

A final note: Both of us are not only clinicians, we are veterans. We've based a lot of this book on our own experiences on active duty in the U.S. Army and Marine Corps. We have done our best to produce a work that would do as much good for our brothers and sisters in arms as we possibly could. If you have suggestions for ways we can make it better, please contact us via John Wiley & Sons, Inc. We appreciate all the feedback we can get.

ABOUT THE AUTHORS

James R. Finley, MA, LMHC, is a psychotherapist with experience as a therapist, clinical supervisor, and program manager in a variety of military, community, and correctional settings—outpatient and inpatient. He is the author of *Integrating the 12 Steps into Addiction Therapy* and coauthor with Brenda S. Lenz of *The Addiction Counselor's Documentation Sourcebook,* 2nd ed. and *The Addiction Treatment Homework Planner,* 4th Edition, also published by John Wiley & Sons. He is a retired Marine and disabled veteran.

Bret A. Moore, PsyD, ABPP, is a clinical psychologist in San Antonio, Texas. In 2008, he left active duty service in the U.S. Army, where he served as a captain and a clinical psychologist with the 85th Combat Stress Control (CSC) unit based in Fort Hood, Texas. He has extensive experience treating veterans, including two tours of duty in Iraq as an Officer in Charge of Preventive Services and Officer in Charge of Clinical Operations. He is coauthor of *The Veterans and Active Duty Military Psychotherapy Treatment* Planner and *Wheels Down: Adjusting to Life after Deployment.* He is coeditor of *Living and Surviving in Harm's Way: A Psychological Treatment Handbook for Pre- and Post-Deployment of Military Personnel* and *Pharmacotherapy for Psychologists: Prescribing and Collaborative Roles.* He also writes a bi-weekly column for *Military Times* titled Kevlar for the Mind, which deals with mental health issues specific to veterans and service members.

NORMAL REACTIONS TO KILLING

GOALS OF THE EXERCISE

1. Resolve cognitive and emotional conflicts surrounding killing another human.
2. Facilitate reconciliation of spiritual and moral conflicts with killing.
3. Replace negative ruminations with more adaptive thoughts.
4. Reduce anxiety and prepare emotionally for future combat/training missions.
5. Understand how killing another human can impact the mind and create temporary changes in the body's physiology.

ADDITIONAL PROBLEMS FOR WHICH THIS EXERCISE MAY BE USEFUL

- Adjustment to the Military Culture
- Combat and Operational Stress Reaction
- Nightmares
- Posttraumatic Stress Disorder (PTSD)
- Spiritual and Religious Issues

SUGGESTIONS FOR PROCESSING THIS EXERCISE WITH VETERAN/SERVICE MEMBER

The "Normal Reactions to Killing" activity is designed for use with veterans/service members who are experiencing guilt and self-condemnation after combat experiences in which they killed other people, particularly when those emotions are based on conflicts between the act of killing and religious or other moral training received earlier in their lives. Alternately, it may also be useful with veterans/service members who feel "less than" among peers because they (the veterans/service members) perceive themselves as having more trouble making this adjustment than others. The activity seeks to normalize common thoughts and emotions experienced by many people in combat and other situations in which they must kill other human beings, and to help these veterans/service members gain reassurance by seeing that their reactions are healthy and normal. Follow-up for this exercise could include reporting back to the therapist on thoughts and feelings about this assignment and their outcome, as well as bibliotherapy using books suggested in Appendix A of *The Veterans and Active Duty Military Psychotherapy Treatment Planner*.

NORMAL REACTIONS TO KILLING

What is a normal reaction to killing another person? What thoughts and emotions are typical for military men and women in this situation?

First, it's important to realize that there is no one normal reaction. Your response, and anyone else's, is shaped by a combination of childhood lessons about right and wrong, cultural messages, expectations about the experience of fighting and killing, and the specific circumstances in which the experience of killing takes place. There are some common tendencies, though. For many of us, it means we're doing the opposite of what we've been taught, and often of what our instincts tell us. It's also common to find that neither the experience of combat nor our feelings at the time are what we anticipated.

This exercise will help you think through this issue and, hopefully, make more sense of your experience in combat and of your thoughts and emotions about that experience.

1. To start with, what beliefs and values related to killing did you have going into combat, and how do you think those beliefs and values affected your reaction?

    _____

    _____

    _____

2. Some of the common reactions many people have to killing include feeling sick, feeling regret, feeling guilty or ashamed, and other negative emotions. On the other hand, some people feel elated and glad to be alive, and some just feel a sense of satisfaction that they didn't let the other people in their unit down. It doesn't mean there's anything wrong with a person if he or she feels any of these things, or even goes back and forth between some of them. Before your experience of combat and killing, how did you think you would feel, and what did you consider a normal reaction?

    _____

    _____

    _____

3. Now think of a leader you respect deeply, someone you consider both good at accomplishing the mission and a good person in terms of character. How do you suppose that person felt after his or her first experience of combat, death, and killing?

Have you talked with him or her about it, and if not, how do you believe that person would respond if you wanted to have that kind of talk?

_____

_____

_____

_____

4. Although some people are surprised, perhaps even worried about themselves or ashamed, by their reactions to their first experiences of killing, some others are more bothered by the way their feelings about it change with more experience; they may find themselves caring less, feeling hardened, and wondering whether this means they are becoming people with no conscience. Have you experienced anything like this? If you have, please use this space to briefly describe the changes in your feelings and what you think they mean.

_____

_____

_____

5. Now, consider this: Would people who really were without conscience be worried about it, or even think about it at all? In fact, this process of becoming somewhat numb to the experiences of danger, of killing, perhaps of seeing friends killed or wounded, is usually the mind's way of taking care of itself, enabling a person to keep functioning in a harsh environment. We are very adaptable by nature, and human beings have survived in all kinds of extreme situations, in part by adapting mentally. This is a normal and healthy reaction under these extreme and unhealthy conditions, too. What do you think might happen to a person who had to stay in a combat environment and was unable to develop this kind of mental toughness?

_____

_____

_____

6. Finally, people sometimes look at the ways they've reacted to combat and killing and wonder whether they'll be able to readjust to normal life when they return to it. Have you had this concern? If so, what parts of your reaction to war worry you the most?

_____

_____

7. This is a normal concern shared by many people, too; however, most of them make the readjustment to "real world" life successfully, and there are many resources you can go to for information and other tools to help you in the readjustment

process. Please use this space to list three things you can do to make that readjustment as successful as possible for yourself.

_____

_____

_____

Be sure to bring this handout back to your next session with your therapist, and be prepared to discuss your thoughts and feelings about the exercise.

WHEN KILLING IS NECESSARY

GOALS OF THE EXERCISE

1. Resolve cognitive and emotional conflicts surrounding killing another human.
2. Facilitate reconciliation of spiritual and moral conflicts with killing.
3. Replace negative ruminations with more adaptive thoughts.
4. Reduce anxiety and prepare emotionally for future combat/training missions.

ADDITIONAL PROBLEMS FOR WHICH THIS EXERCISE MAY BE USEFUL

- Adjustment to the Military Culture
- Combat and Operational Stress Reaction
- Posttraumatic Stress Disorder (PTSD)
- Spiritual and Religious Issues

SUGGESTIONS FOR PROCESSING THIS EXERCISE WITH VETERAN/SERVICE MEMBER

The "When Killing Is Necessary" activity is designed for use with veterans/service members who are experiencing moral, ethical, and/or spiritual conflict between normal societal values prohibiting killing of other people and the necessity to kill in combat. This activity is best suited for use with veterans/service members who are motivated by spiritual training and concerns about leading socially responsible and ethical lives and are troubled by this conflict, or who respond with feelings of guilt and cognitive dissonance when they find themselves engaged in, preparing to engage in, or remembering combat. Follow-up for this exercise could include reporting back to the therapist/therapy group on thoughts and feelings about this assignment, as well as bibliotherapy using books suggested in Appendix A of *The Veterans and Active Duty Military Psychotherapy Treatment Planner*.

WHEN KILLING IS NECESSARY

Is killing ever right, and if so, when? That may seem like an unrealistic question, but even for some people who have experienced combat and killing, it's hard to answer. However, many people throughout history have struggled with this issue. Each of us must find our own solution, but there are some common realizations that many have found and shared. This exercise will help you think through this question and, hopefully, come to a resolution that truly makes sense for you.

Sometimes it's useful to look at the differences between the situations in which our "normal" values are meant to guide our actions, and the very different situations encountered in combat. Warfare has always created some very hard questions for people who want to do what is right, and it's wise to think through those questions in a calmer situation and, if possible, answer them for yourself before you have to act on your choices. The rest of this assignment will bring up some of those hard questions and ask you to think them through and answer them for yourself now.

1. A useful place to begin is with what we already know or believe. What have you been taught about violence against other people, up to and including killing?

    _____

    _____

    _____

2. What situations have you learned or been taught justified violence against other people, if any—self-defense, defense of another person, and so on?

    _____

    _____

    _____

3. Some people believe killing is always wrong no matter what. That sounds simple and clear, but it doesn't offer an answer when someone is likely to die no matter what you do, and it becomes a choice of who will die—you and your friends, or the enemies you're fighting. If you've held the belief that killing is wrong, period, what do you think the people who taught you that would want you to do when you have to choose between killing to defend yourself and the people depending on you, or

failing to do so and having that result in the deaths of yourself and others in your unit?

_____

_____

_____

4. It's fairly common in some kinds of warfare to encounter situations in which you are confronted with enemies who are not attacking or threatening you at that moment, or not directly, but who will represent a threat if left alone. If a close friend asked your advice, would you tell him or her that killing those enemies was justified—self-defense against a future threat rather than one in the present—and if not, what would you advise your friend to do?

_____

_____

_____

5. Finally, people who have never experienced it may not be able to understand the chaos, confusion, and stress that surround a person making life-and-death decisions in split-seconds in combat; even a belief in the right to self-defense against a clear threat may not guide you when a situation is not clear and failure to act may cause the wounding or death of yourself or other people in your unit, but taking forceful action may cause the deaths of noncombatants due to the confusion and chaos of the moment. Thinking about it now, if that close friend asked your advice again, would you tell him or her that forceful action was justified? If not, what would you recommend that your friend do?

_____

_____

_____

Most people would agree that all you can ask of anyone is that they would do their best in any situation, within the limits of what's going on around them; their mental, emotional, and physical state; and what information they have to act on. Do you agree with that philosophy, and if you do, is that a standard you can meet? If so, as long as you do your best, you'll be making the best of the situation even when none of the possible outcomes are what you might have wished they were. That's not to say you won't be troubled—you may be, depending on what situations you've met in the past or meet in the future. But if you can honestly tell yourself you made the best choices you could given the stressors and time pressure you were under and the limited knowledge of the situation you may have had, you've done all anyone has the right to ask of you. Try to remember not to judge yourself by a higher standard than you'd impose on a friend.

Be sure to bring this handout back to your next session with your therapist, and be prepared to discuss your thoughts and feelings about the exercise.

HOW DID I IMAGINE MY LIFE IN THE MILITARY?

GOALS OF THE EXERCISE

1. Enhance ability to adapt to the structure, expectations, and hierarchical organization of the military.
2. Develop adaptive means for dealing with the physical and mental stress of military service.
3. Identify positive aspects of serving in the military.
4. Develop a trusting and open relationship with a superior within the chain of command.

ADDITIONAL PROBLEMS FOR WHICH THIS EXERCISE MAY BE USEFUL

- Antisocial Behavior in the Military
- Conflict with Comrades
- Diversity Acceptance
- Homesickness/Loneliness

SUGGESTIONS FOR PROCESSING THIS EXERCISE WITH SERVICE MEMBER

Adjusting to military life can be difficult, even for the most well-adjusted individual. The differences between the way service members pictured it before joining and the day-to-day reality of military life can create feelings of disillusionment. Learning to navigate the many sometimes arbitrary, confusing, and counterintuitive rules, customs, and traditions can dampen the spirit of newly minted service members. This exercise allows the service member to develop a greater appreciation for the positive aspects of being in the military as well as identify negative thoughts that may be reinforcing the negative aspects of being in the military. Be mindful that reassurance, patience, and compassion will go a long way in helping service members become accustomed to their new lifestyle. Follow-up for this exercise could include reporting back to the therapist/therapy group on actions related to this assignment and their outcomes, as well as bibliotherapy using books suggested in Appendix A of *The Veterans and Active Duty Military Psychotherapy Treatment Planner* and/or videotherapy using films on the topics of "Friends and Support Systems" and/or "Vocational and Work-Related Issues" recommended in *Rent Two Films and Let's Talk in the Morning*, 2nd ed., by John W. Hesley and Jan G. Hesley, also published by John Wiley & Sons.

HOW DID I IMAGINE MY LIFE IN THE MILITARY?

It's normal to second-guess your choice of joining the military. Nearly every service member has been there at some point. At times, things seem unfair—your life is micromanaged by people you hardly know and you have to ask permission to do the most basic things. But things are not all bad. There are many benefits to being in the military, though it's easy to lose sight of this fact. This exercise will help you focus on the positive aspects of being in the military and get you thinking about ways to overcome the negatives.

1. Most of us find that some parts of military life are not what we expected. We may have pictured it with more drama and glamour, and less stress and boredom. We have become disappointed with this new environment that confronts us with an endless supply of rules, customs, and traditions that are sometimes confusing and don't seem to make sense. If you've found differences between what you expected and what you've experienced, describe those differences here:

    _____

    _____

    _____

2. If you are completing this exercise, it's likely that you are already well-aware of the cons (negatives) of being in the military. Please list some pros (positives) of being in the military:

    a. _____

    b. _____

    c. _____

    d. _____

    e. _____

    f. _____

    g. _____

    h. _____

    i. _____

    j. _____

k. _____

l. _____

3. Choose three of the pros from above and write about why they are important to you. Use three 5×7 note cards and fill up at least the front of each card. Once you've finished them, place the cards in your pocket and review them at least once each day.

4. Now, list three cons of being in the military. List one negative thought that may reinforce negative views of why a "con" situation exists; then list thoughts that explain these situations in more positive ways. (Example: [con] My NCO is always correcting me. [negative thought] He doesn't respect me—he thinks I'm an idiot. [positive thought] He sees my potential and is setting high standards for me because he believes I can meet them.)

A. *Three cons of being in the military*

1. _____

2. _____

3. _____

B. *Negative thoughts* (negative explanations for situation in each con)

1. _____

2. _____

3. _____

C. *Positive thoughts* (positive explanations for situation in each con)

1. _____

2. _____

3. _____

5. Does looking at these "cons" in both negative and positive ways make it easier for you to go through the day in a more positive mood than if you were only thinking about the negatives? Does it make adjusting to military life more manageable? If so, please briefly describe the difference this is making for you:

_____

_____

_____

Be sure to bring this handout back to your next session with your therapist, and be prepared to discuss your thoughts and feelings about the exercise.

ALL FOR ONE AND ONE FOR ALL

GOALS OF THE EXERCISE

1. Identify and implement changes that will reduce the negative emotions brought on by adjustment to military life.
2. Identify and develop activities outside of the military that provide a sense of pleasure and self-worth.
3. Develop friendships with others with similar interests.
4. Use existing supports within the military that assist with the challenges of adjusting to military life.
5. Develop new, or engage in existing, hobbies that are non-military related.

ADDITIONAL PROBLEMS FOR WHICH THIS EXERCISE MAY BE USEFUL

*   Adjustment to the Military Culture
*   Conflict with Comrades
*   Diversity Acceptance
*   Homesickness/Loneliness

SUGGESTIONS FOR PROCESSING THIS EXERCISE WITH VETERAN/SERVICE MEMBER

Joining the military is the first big life decision for many service members. Leaving home and being shipped off to an unfamiliar part of the country or to a foreign land can be intimidating. For many young service members, withdrawal and seclusion are normal reactions to being surrounded by unfamiliar people, places, and things. This exercise will help the service member expand his/her interests and strengthen already existing social supports. It will also help him/her develop new non-military related activities and interests. Follow-up for this exercise could include reporting back to the therapist/therapy group on actions related to this assignment and their outcome, as well as bibliotherapy using books suggested in Appendix A of *The Veterans and Active Duty Military Psychotherapy Treatment Planner* and/or videotherapy using films on the topic of "Friends and Support Systems" recommended in *Rent Two Films and Let's Talk in the Morning*, 2nd ed., by John W. Hesley and Jan G. Hesley, also published by John Wiley & Sons.

ALL FOR ONE AND ONE FOR ALL

For most of us, part of the appeal of military service was the idea of being a member of a tight-knit group—all for one and one for all, as expressed in *The Three Musketeers*. However, when we're uncomfortable with a major life change, we may tend to withdraw from our surroundings. Unfortunately, this limits our interaction with others and keeps us from enjoying places and activities, putting that camaraderie out of reach. In this exercise, list three activities that you enjoy but haven't engaged in since joining the military, and make a plan for how you will get involved in each activity again. In addition to having fun, this is a great way to find friends who share your interests. After you've done that, identify at least five new potential sources of support and friendship that you can explore (e.g., church, singles group, amateur sports team, hobby club, military mentor).

1. Activity #1
    What is the activity? _____
    Plan for getting active in the activity again:

    _____
    _____
    _____
    _____
    _____
    _____
    _____

2. Activity #2
    What is the activity? _____
    Plan for getting active in the activity again:

    _____
    _____
    _____
    _____
    _____

_____

_____

3. Activity #3

    What is the activity? _____

    Plan for getting active in the activity again:

    _____

    _____

    _____

    _____

    _____

    _____

    _____

4. List five new potential sources of support and friendship and when you'll try them out.

    a. _____

    b. _____

    c. _____

    d. _____

    e. _____

    Be sure to bring this handout back to your next session with your therapist, and be prepared to discuss your thoughts and feelings about the exercise.

MOURNING AND ACCEPTANCE

GOALS OF THE EXERCISE

1. Verbalize feelings about the injury.
2. Verbalize an understanding that losing a limb, the ability to walk, stand, or hold a child, and/or bodily disfigurement is a loss that must be grieved.
3. Accept the nature of the injury and understand its psychological and physical consequences.
4. Learn to compensate for any physical, occupational, interpersonal, and/or social limitations that the injury may create.
5. Return to pre-injury levels of self-esteem and confidence.

ADDITIONAL PROBLEMS FOR WHICH THIS EXERCISE MAY BE USEFUL

- Chronic Pain After Injury
- Combat and Operational Stress Reaction
- Nightmares
- Post-Deployment Reintegration Problems
- Posttraumatic Stress Disorder (PTSD)

SUGGESTIONS FOR PROCESSING THIS EXERCISE
WITH VETERAN/SERVICE MEMBER

The "Mourning and Acceptance" activity is designed for use with veterans/service members who, as the problem topic indicates, have experienced severe and long-term/permanent physical injuries. Follow-up or concurrent interventions could include encouraging the veteran/service member to create a personal mourning ritual; assigning the veteran/service member to contact the Disabled American Veterans (DAV) or the Military Order of the Purple Heart (MOPH) for practical assistance in dealing with the Department of Veterans Affairs (VA); bibliotherapy using books listed in Appendix A of *The Veterans and Active Duty Military Psychotherapy Treatment Planner*; videotherapy using *The Waterdance* or another film on the topic of "Chronic Illness and Disabilities" suggested in *Rent Two Films and Let's Talk in the Morning*, 2nd ed., by John W. Hesley and Jan G. Hesley, also published by John Wiley & Sons; encouraging the client to do volunteer work with disabled children or the elderly; and reporting back to the therapist/therapy group on actions related to this assignment and their outcomes.

MOURNING AND ACCEPTANCE

What is the most effective response to the life-changing loss of the function of a part of one's body, or the loss of that body part itself? How do people best adapt to this situation?

It may be useful to think about similar situations, either ones you've encountered or ones experienced by other people whose experiences may serve as a guide. From these sources, you may be able to learn both what strategies will serve you, and what mistakes or mental and emotional traps to avoid. This exercise is designed to help you deal with this issue and, hopefully, find the methods and resources that will enable you to achieve the best quality of life possible.

1. As with any process or journey, to reach your goal you must start with the here and now. No one else can truly know how you feel or what you think about the injuries you've experienced, even if they have suffered similar losses—each person and each situation are unique. The first step is to express to yourself, to your therapist, and to any other people working to help you achieve your goals, your thoughts and feelings about your injury. Please use this space to write down the most important facts and emotions that come to mind for you when you consider your current situation:

    _____

    _____

    _____

    _____

2. Although no one else knows exactly what your thoughts and feelings are about your injury, it's also true that many people have had to deal with similar losses, as noted in this assignment's introduction. Why is this important? Because you may be able to tap into some of the lessons they have learned. Some of those people might not have experienced injuries similar to yours, but may have gone through losses with the same kinds of impacts on their lives, despite the types of injuries or if they happened differently. There are people who may never have had some or all of the things you've lost, or people who have had similar losses but whose losses took place more gradually, as the result of a chronic illness or aging. What

situations come to mind that might present people with parallel challenges to the ones you're dealing with due to your own injury?

_____

_____

_____

_____

3. A common thread running through all these situations and experiences is loss—each of them means that some abilities and experiences are either taken away or were never there for the person involved. To deal with any loss effectively, a person needs to start by acknowledging its reality and letting it sink in—in other words, by mourning. You may have been advised to beware of self-pity, and that is sound advice, because self-pity can be a trap that keeps a person miserable for life—but healthy mourning is not self-pity. Please think of someone you respect and admire, and think of a loss that person has experienced. How did he or she cope with the reality of that loss?

    _____

    _____

    _____

4. There seems to be something in human nature that leads us to create rituals or ceremonies to mark losses and other major life changes, so-called rites of passage. Our society has clear-cut ways of mourning some kinds of losses—a funeral or wake is a good example—but not others. You might find it helps to create a private mourning ritual of your own. Please use this space to describe what that ritual might consist of for you:

    _____

    _____

    _____

5. Now, think about what you've done after other losses in your life, or what you've seen done by others to whom you can relate. The ultimate goal of mourning is not only to accept a loss, but to move ahead with life and regain peace of mind and the ability to be happy. To do this—it helps to bring as much satisfaction into your life as you can—here are three things you can do:

    a. List at least three activities you enjoy that you can still do:

        _____

        _____

        _____

b. List at least three activities you enjoyed at an earlier time in your life but stopped doing, which you can return to and do again:

_____

_____

_____

c. List at least three activities you've always wanted to try but haven't yet, that you can still do:

_____

_____

_____

Choose one activity from each list and make a commitment to yourself and to your therapist that you will engage in those three activities at least once each within the next month.

Be sure to bring this handout back to your next session with your therapist, and be prepared to discuss your thoughts and feelings about the exercise.

WHAT MAKES ME WHO I AM?

GOALS OF THE EXERCISE

1. Accept the nature of the injury and understand its psychological and physical consequences.
2. Learn to compensate for any physical, occupational, interpersonal, and/or social limitations that the injury may create.
3. Verbalize an understanding and acceptance that outer "beauty" is diversely defined and that physical scars do not detract from a person's inner beauty and strength.
4. Return to pre-injury levels of self-esteem and confidence.

ADDITIONAL PROBLEMS FOR WHICH THIS EXERCISE MAY BE USEFUL

- Depression
- Diversity Acceptance
- Nightmares
- Post-Deployment Reintegration Problems
- Social Discomfort

SUGGESTIONS FOR PROCESSING THIS EXERCISE WITH VETERANS/SERVICE MEMBERS

The "What Makes Me Who I Am?" activity is designed for use with veterans/service members who, as the result of severe and long-term/permanent physical injuries, are struggling with problems of self-image based on their former physical capacities or appearance. Follow-up or concurrent treatment activities could include bibliotherapy using one or more of the books listed for this issue in Appendix A of *The Veterans and Active Duty Military Psychotherapy Treatment Planner* and/or videotherapy using *The Waterdance* or another film on the topic of "Chronic Illness and Disabilities" suggested in *Rent Two Films and Let's Talk in the Morning*, 2nd ed., by John W. Hesley and Jan G. Hesley, also published by John Wiley & Sons.

WHAT MAKES ME WHO I AM?

In our mainstream culture today, we tend to be swamped with the message that who we are is based on how we look. If we are young, fit, and attractive, we are meeting the expectations we've been encouraged to set for ourselves, and if we aren't, the message we get is that we are "less than," or not up to the standards of that culture.

Most of us are confronted with this issue sooner or later, normally as we age—and although that is a gradual transition for most of us, giving us quite a bit of time to adjust, many still struggle with accepting the inevitable loss of youthful physical abilities and appearance. For people whose bodies and lives are suddenly and traumatically changed by serious injuries, it's an even harder transition. Still, we're the same people inside no matter how our outward appearances change, and it's vital to our quality of life to find ways to keep that in mind. The purpose of this exercise is to share some ways that many people have succeeded in doing just this.

1. Sometimes, to see where we're going it can help to see where we've been—where we come from. With that thought in mind, please list some important qualities in yourself that have always been part of who you are (e.g., things that make you laugh, things you've always liked and disliked, interests you've held throughout your life):

   _____

   _____

   _____

   _____

2. Think of someone you've admired and respected for much of your life. This could be a family member, a longtime friend, a neighbor, a mentor such as a teacher or the coach of a sports team, a member of the clergy, and so on. Once you have someone in mind, please use this space to list qualities about that person that have been consistent throughout the time you've known him or her and that you can expect to remain constant in the years ahead:

   _____

   _____

   _____

   _____

Do you think that your admiration and respect for this person would change because his or her physical appearance and abilities changed, whether due to age, illness, or injury?

_____

3. If you're like most people, you've thought from time to time about what your own life might be like in old age. When you imagined your long-term future, what kind of life and activities did you picture for yourself, and what parts of that picture could you achieve regardless of the physical limitations resulting from your injuries?

_____

_____

_____

_____

4. There is a saying that has been useful to many people, in many situations, and one that would apply in your situation as it does in a variety of others:

I am not my thoughts; I am the person who thinks the thoughts, but even when those thoughts change, I will remain who I am.

I am not my emotions; I am the person who feels the emotions, but even when those emotions change, I will remain who I am.

I am not my actions; I am the person who takes the actions, but even when those actions change, I will remain who I am.

To this we can add:

I am not my body; I am the person who lives in this body, but even when this body changes, I will remain who I am.

With this in mind, what do you see in yourself today that remains the same, regardless of any changes in your thoughts, in your emotions, in your actions, and in your body?

_____

_____

_____

_____

5. To complete this exercise, look at your answers to questions 1, 3, and 4, and use this space to list the items from those answers that you think will continue to be true in the years ahead—regardless of any physical changes:

_____

_____

_____

_____

_____

Be sure to bring this handout back to your next session with your therapist, and be prepared to discuss your thoughts and feelings about the exercise.

ANGER AS A DRUG

GOALS OF THE EXERCISE

1. Develop an awareness of current angry behaviors, clarifying origins of, and early warning signs of, aggressive behavior.
2. Refrain from physically and emotionally abusive behavior against significant other.
3. Come to an awareness and acceptance of angry feelings while developing better control and more serenity.
4. Become capable of handling angry feelings in constructive ways that enhance daily functioning.
5. Learn to self-monitor and shift to a thinking and problem-solving mode rather than a reactive mode when anger is triggered.

ADDITIONAL PROBLEMS FOR WHICH THIS EXERCISE MAY BE USEFUL

- Antisocial Behavior in the Military
- Borderline Personality
- Conflict with Comrades
- Physiological Stress Response—Acute
- Post-Deployment Reintegration Problems
- Posttraumatic Stress Disorder (PTSD)
- Separation and Divorce

SUGGESTIONS FOR PROCESSING THIS EXERCISE WITH VETERANS/SERVICE MEMBERS

The "Anger as a Drug" activity may be especially useful with angry veterans/service members who have also responded to stressful situations by engaging in substance abuse or other addictive behaviors. It is suggested for use with veterans/service members who have some insight into their own feelings or are willing to be introspective. Follow-up can include bibliotherapy using books suggested for this problem in Appendix A of *The Veterans and Active Duty Military Psychotherapy Treatment Planner* and/or videotherapy using films recommended on the topic of "Communication and Conflict Resolution" in the book *Rent Two Films and Let's Talk in the Morning*, 2nd ed., by John W. Hesley and Jan G. Hesley, also published by John Wiley & Sons. Another good exercise is journaling about experiences using alternative behaviors to cope with situations that trigger anger.

ANGER AS A DRUG

Does it seem strange to call anger a drug? We usually think of drugs as substances like alcohol, cannabis, cocaine, and heroin. We talk about being addicted to a drug if we find it hard to quit and keep using it even when the consequences are more bad than good. People also behave addictively with activities like gambling, sex, eating, spending, and work, and with some emotions. Addictive activities and emotions can cause as much trouble as any substance.

What do these things have in common? They can change the way we feel, quickly, on demand. Physically and emotionally, we can use them to block pain or to feel great. We can become addicted to anything that makes us feel good quickly and easily.

Anger can feel good. If we're anxious or depressed, we may feel weak, uneasy, and ashamed. When we get angry, we're more likely to feel strong and sure of ourselves. Anger can also make us feel more alert, awake, and energetic, so we may use anger to cope with uncomfortable feelings. Once this pattern is established, a feeling of fear, anxiety, or shame can trigger anger so fast we may not even realize that the first feeling was there before the anger.

Like other drugs, anger has negative consequences. It leads to destructive actions and can damage the immune system and raise the risk of cancer or heart disease. It may also destroy our relationships with the people who matter most to us. In this exercise, you'll look at your anger to see if you've used it as a drug and to find better ways to handle painful feelings.

1. When you've been very angry, in a rage, have you felt weak or strong? Uneasy or sure of yourself? How does anger feel to you?

    _____

    _____

    _____

2. Next think about a time when you got very angry. What happened just before that feeling?

    _____

    _____

    _____

3. When you think about what was going on before the anger, how did it make you feel? If your anger came up so fast that you didn't have time to be aware of other feelings, what painful emotions such as anxiety, fear, hurt, or shame would be natural in that situation?

_____

_____

_____

_____

4. Another characteristic of drug use is a rebound effect when they wear off. You may have found that when the anger wore off painful emotions returned. What rebound effects have followed your anger?

_____

_____

_____

_____

5. Some powerful natural mood-lifting and pain-relieving chemicals are produced in the brain by cardiovascular exercise, by meditation, and by laughing hard. Please list some ways you can try to feel happy and energetic or to cope with emotional pain without using anger or another drug.

_____

_____

_____

_____

6. The next time painful emotions start to trigger your rage, how can you redirect that reaction to something that gives you better results? If other people can help, what can they do? List two people who can help and describe when and how you'll ask them to help you.

_____

_____

_____

_____

_____

_____

_____

Be sure to bring this handout back to your next session with your therapist, and be prepared to discuss your thoughts and feelings about the exercise.

BEING WHO I WANT TO BE

GOALS OF THE EXERCISE

1. Decrease overall intensity and frequency of angry feelings, and increase ability to recognize and appropriately express angry feelings as they occur.
2. Develop an awareness of current angry behaviors, clarifying origins of, and variations in, aggressive behavior.
3. Refrain from physically and emotionally abusive behavior against significant other.
4. Become capable of handling angry feelings in constructive ways that enhance daily functioning.
5. Learn and implement problem-solving and/or conflict resolution skills to manage interpersonal problems.

ADDITIONAL PROBLEMS FOR WHICH THIS EXERCISE MAY BE USEFUL

- Borderline Personality
- Depression
- Physiological Stress Response—Acute
- Post-Deployment Reintegration Problems
- Posttraumatic Stress Disorder (PTSD)
- Separation and Divorce

SUGGESTIONS FOR PROCESSING THIS EXERCISE WITH VETERANS/SERVICE MEMBERS

The "Being Who I Want to Be" activity is designed for use with veterans/service members who exhibit out-of-control angry and aggressive behaviors, particularly when they find themselves recreating abusive dynamics from their own childhoods. This is for veterans/service members who are motivated to make positive changes and who have at least some insight into their own dysfunctional patterns. Follow-up or concurrent treatment activities could include bibliotherapy using one or more of the books listed for this issue in Appendix A of *The Veterans and Active Duty Military Psychotherapy Treatment Planner* and/or videotherapy using films on the topic of "Communication and Conflict Resolution" suggested in *Rent Two Films and Let's Talk in the Morning*, 2nd ed., by John W. Hesley and Jan G. Hesley, also published by John Wiley & Sons.

BEING WHO I WANT TO BE

When does anger become a serious problem? Most people would say that when a person's anger had jeopardized or caused harm to that person's health, safety, freedom, employment, and/or important relationships, it had become a problem. Often the person who has the problem with anger knows it, but can't seem to keep it under control. In many cases, angry people also feel shame and guilt because when they look at their own behavior they see a resemblance to negative actions of their parents, possibly things they'd sworn as children they'd never do when they grew up. If any of this relates to your own life and experiences, this activity will help you start making the changes that will break the pattern of destructive anger and hurt to yourself and others around you.

1. What do you think is needed to gain control of angry impulses and keep you from losing your temper and being physically or verbally abusive? What unfilled need or needs have blocked your efforts to change up until now?

   _____

   _____

   _____

   _____

2. In this assignment we talk about several methods and insights that have helped countless people overcome the same kinds of problems so that they could look in their mirrors and see the people they really wanted to be. The first important skill is to understand the roots of your anger. We all tend to get angry if we feel fear or hurt; it's the fight part of the fight-or-flight reaction that's normal when you feel threatened. For prehistoric people who lived a hunting and gathering life this helped them survive. The dangers and hurts in their lives were mainly physical, so there were things they could either fight or run from, and their anger and/or fear helped them fight harder or run faster. List a couple of situations where you got angry because you felt threatened or hurt (not necessarily a physical threat—anything that endangers our relationships, status, or self-esteem can trigger the same reaction)?

   _____

   _____

Did your anger, however you did or did not express it, improve the situation? If so, how?

_____

3. This is valuable information to understand about yourself, because it enables you to anticipate when situations might push your buttons and threaten to make your anger erupt. If you were already prepared and knew that anger might come up, how could you handle the situation differently? Here are some approaches that have worked for many people.

    First, if you can just avoid the situation without that causing a big problem, avoid it.

    Second, find a good friend and spend some time "venting" with him or her and getting feedback before the situation arises. It also helps to set a time to talk again after you get through the stressful situation.

    Third, have your own transportation, so that if you find the situation to be more than you can handle you can leave without depending on someone else for a ride.

    Fourth, bring a trusted friend or relative with you if you can, for support and to remind you of what you're trying to do.

    Fifth, if you're going to be facing a stressful situation, have a HALT plan—HALT stands for Hungry, Angry, Lonely, or Tired. If you're in any of these conditions and go into a trying situation, your chances of maintaining self-control go way down.

    Sixth, if you know you're going to be dealing with things that may trigger your anger, don't go into the situation with any drugs in your system that may interfere with impulse control and/or judgment, alcohol in particular.

    Please list some situations from your own life where you could use these methods to maintain your self-control even when it's hard to do:

    _____

    _____

    _____

4. Up to now we've worked on knowing how to avoid blow-ups so that it is safe for our families and friends to be close to us. That's only half of the task at hand, though. People trying to break behavior patterns generally fail if all they're doing is focusing on *not* doing whatever harmful thing they've had problems with. The second part, the part that makes you more likely to succeed in being the person you

want to be, is having positive patterns to replace the negative ones. Here are some good ways to avoid blow-ups:

- Know your own early warning signs, so that when you start to get angry you can redirect yourself while it's still easy and you haven't said or done anything to regret. Make a list of the sensations you feel when your anger is rising; use them as cues to break the pattern.

- Identify the trigger. Ask yourself, "Where's the threat, or the hurt?" When you've figured that out, ask yourself whether it's a real threat—if not, you can relax; if it is, you'll respond more effectively if you're thinking rather than just exploding.

- If your anger is being triggered by someone else's actions, you can approach that person and tell him or her calmly, clearly, and firmly how their behavior is affecting you, and then ask them to change their actions.

Please try these methods between now and your next therapy session and briefly describe how they did or did not work for you:

_____

_____

_____

_____

Be sure to bring this handout back to your next session with your therapist, and be prepared to discuss your thoughts and feelings about the exercise.

WHAT WAS I THINKING?

GOALS OF THE EXERCISE

1. Accept responsibility for own behavior and keep behavior within the acceptable limits of military rules and regulations.
2. List relationships damaged by disrespect, disloyalty, aggression, and/or dishonesty.
3. Indicate steps to be taken to make amends or restitution for past behaviors.

ADDITIONAL PROBLEMS FOR WHICH THIS EXERCISE MAY BE USEFUL

- Anger Management and Domestic Violence
- Borderline Personality
- Conflict with Comrades
- Financial Difficulties
- Separation and Divorce
- Substance Abuse/Dependence

SUGGESTIONS FOR PROCESSING THIS EXERCISE WITH VETERANS/SERVICE MEMBERS

The "What Was I Thinking?" activity is intended to lead the veteran/service member to answer that literal question related to antisocial behavior, face up to its impact on others, and make amends as appropriate. Minimization and denial are predictable, being traits that often accompany antisocial behavior. This exercise is designed to increase sensitivity to the ways antisocial behaviors may cause pain to others. It is also intended to help the service member attempt to correct any damage done to his/her military career. Confrontation may be necessary to challenge the veteran's/service member's minimization, denial, and tendency to blame others for his/her behavior. Follow-up could include reporting back to the therapist/therapy group on actions related to this assignment and their outcomes, as well as bibliotherapy using books listed in Appendix A of *The Veterans and Active Duty Military Psychotherapy Treatment Planner* and/or videotherapy using films recommended for the topics of "Communication and Conflict Resolution" and "Values and Ethics" in *Rent Two Films and Let's Talk in the Morning*, 2nd ed., by John W. Hesley and Jan G. Hesley, also published by John Wiley & Sons.

WHAT WAS I THINKING?

We are capable of hurting others in a variety of ways. This assignment will help you become more aware of those behaviors which have a negative impact on others, including the habit of thinking that make it easier for us to justify or excuse our behavior to ourselves when we treat people in ways we wouldn't want them to treat us. It will also help you become more sensitive to others' feelings, make you aware of the impact your hurtful behavior has on others, and help you get started in repairing any damage to your military career your behavior may have caused.

1. Please review the list of hurtful behaviors below and put a check mark next to those that you have engaged in and that have resulted in pain for others. Resist the urge to minimize or refuse acknowledgment of your behaviors:

_____	Dishonesty (Lying)	_____	Gossiping
_____	Verbal attacks	_____	Unfaithfulness (Cheating)
_____	Threatening	_____	Sexual abuse
_____	Physical assault	_____	Weapon use
_____	Stealing	_____	Irresponsibility
_____	Illegal acts	_____	Name calling
_____	Drug or alcohol abuse	_____	Insensitivity
_____	Blaming others	_____	Unkept promises

2. Please describe three situations where you have hurt others by engaging in one of the behaviors listed above. Choose at least one situation that has negatively impacted your military career (e.g., Article 15, demotion, etc.), if that has happened.

    Situation #1:

    _____

    _____

    Situation #2:

    _____

    _____

Situation #3:

_____

_____

3. Describe how your behavior affected others. How were they hurt?

Situation #1:

_____

_____

Situation #2:

_____

_____

Situation #3:

_____

_____

4. What might you do to make amends to the people you hurt in these three situations?

Situation #1:

_____

_____

Situation #2:

_____

_____

Situation #3:

_____

_____

5. For the situation(s) that negatively impacted your military career, list three specific things you can do to overcome these consequences:

a. _____

b. _____

c. _____

Be sure to bring this handout back to your next session with your therapist, and be prepared to discuss your thoughts and feelings about the exercise.

MENTORSHIP AND RESPECT

GOALS OF THE EXERCISE

1. Accept responsibility for own behavior and keep behavior within the acceptable limits of military rules and regulations.
2. List relationships that have been damaged because of disrespect, disloyalty, aggression, and/or dishonesty.
3. List steps to make amends or restitution for past behaviors.

ADDITIONAL PROBLEMS FOR WHICH THIS EXERCISE MAY BE USEFUL

- Anger Management and Domestic Violence
- Borderline Personality
- Conflict with Comrades
- Separation and Divorce
- Substance Abuse/Dependence

SUGGESTIONS FOR PROCESSING THIS EXERCISE WITH VETERANS/SERVICE MEMBERS

The "Mentorship and Respect" activity is designed for veterans/service members who seem open to forming mentorship relationships with others who will be good influences and teach more functional interpersonal and problem-solving strategies. Hurtful behavior toward others is easily minimized or denied by those who engage in the behavior. This assignment tasks the veteran/service member with finding a mentor he/she respects, such as a senior he/she sees as fair and dependable; then, with the guidance of that mentor, taking the first step of admitting his/her wrongdoings, increasing sensitivity to harm caused by his/her actions, and when appropriate, making amends for his/her behavior. As projection is a common tactic for placing blame on someone or something else, gentle—or direct, though not judgmental—confrontation may be needed to help the veteran/service member complete the assignment. Follow-up could include reporting back to the therapist/therapy group on actions related to this assignment and their outcomes, as well as bibliotherapy using books from Appendix A of *The Veterans and Active Duty Military Psychotherapy Treatment Planner* and/or videotherapy with films on the topics of "Substance Abuse" and/or "Values and Ethics" listed in *Rent Two Films and Let's Talk in the Morning*, 2nd ed., by John W. Hesley and Jan G. Hesley, published by John Wiley & Sons.

MENTORSHIP AND RESPECT

If you've been given this handout, it's probably because something you did got you into some kind of trouble—legal, disciplinary, or some other kind. The way this exercise works is different from any others you may have done. First it asks you to choose a mentor and get that person's input on your situation and the best way to improve it. What is a mentor? A role model, someone fair and depenxdable, and someone with wisdom; usually someone older with more life experience who may have learned some things that could help you avoid getting into trouble or doing things that hurt people.

When you have someone in mind, tell your therapist who it is, then talk about how to bring this up with that person and what comes next. It's useful to put things down on paper to help you see the situation more clearly. Use this handout as a guide to help you talk with your mentor about ways to do things that give you better results and don't hurt others.

Admitting the pain we've caused others by our behavior is the first step. The next step is to make amends. Many times saying "I'm sorry" is not enough. People want us to treat them with respect and consideration, and they may still feel hurt and angry. But it's a start. It can mean a lot to someone just to see that you realize you hurt them and you respect their right to be treated the same way you want them to treat you. You'll feel better about yourself no matter how they respond. This assignment asks you to describe three incidents where you have hurt others, then write a brief letter of apology for each incident—your mentor and your therapist can help.

1. *Three Hurtful Incidents*: Please describe what you did, who was hurt, how they felt about it, how you feel about it now, and how you could have acted more kindly.

   Incident #1: _____

   _____

   _____

   Incident #2: _____

   _____

   _____

   Incident #3: _____

   _____

   _____

2. *Apology*: Write a short letter of apology to each person you hurt in the three incidents. Include a description of what you did, how your actions affected them, how you feel today about your actions, and what you could have done instead of the hurtful behavior. Once you've done that, go over the letters with your mentor and therapist before you give them to the people you hurt. Once you do give them the letters, describe that situation, how they felt about it, and how you felt afterward:

    Incident #1: _____
    _____
    _____
    _____
    _____

    Incident #2: _____
    _____
    _____
    _____
    _____

    Incident #3: _____
    _____
    _____
    _____
    _____

Once you've done this, be sure to bring this handout back to your next session with your therapist, and be prepared to discuss your thoughts and feelings about the exercise.

ACTION, COPING SKILLS, AND ACCEPTANCE

GOALS OF THE EXERCISE

1. Reduce overall frequency, intensity, and duration of anxiety so that daily functioning is not impaired.
2. Stabilize anxiety level while increasing ability to function on a daily basis.
3. Enhance ability to effectively cope with the full variety of life's responsibilities.
4. Learn and implement calming skills to reduce overall anxiety and manage anxiety symptoms.

ADDITIONAL PROBLEMS FOR WHICH THIS EXERCISE MAY BE USEFUL

- Combat and Operational Stress Reaction
- Depression
- Panic/Agoraphobia
- Physiological Stress Response—Acute
- Posttraumatic Stress Disorder (PTSD)
- Pre-Deployment Stress

SUGGESTIONS FOR PROCESSING THIS EXERCISE WITH VETERANS/SERVICE MEMBERS

The "Action, Coping Skills, and Acceptance" activity is designed for use with veterans/ service members who exhibit levels of anxiety that significantly impair their quality of life and ability to perform their military duties. It is designed to reduce anxiety by guiding the veteran/service member in correcting cognitive distortions and learned helplessness and shifting from a primarily external to a more internal locus of control. The techniques used in this activity are compatible with the evidence-based Cognitive Processing Therapy (CPT) model currently in use within the Department of Veterans Affairs. Follow-up or concurrent treatment activities could include bibliotherapy using one or more of the books listed for this issue in Appendix A of *The Veterans and Active Duty Military Psychotherapy Treatment Planner* and/or videotherapy using films suggested for the topic of "Emotional and Affective Disorders" in *Rent Two Films and Let's Talk in the Morning*, 2nd ed., by John W. Hesley and Jan G. Hesley, also published by John Wiley & Sons.

ACTION, COPING SKILLS, AND ACCEPTANCE

Anxiety is one of the most uncomfortable emotions we can feel, but no one's life is completely free of it. In many cases it has survival value, so being without anxiety would not be in a person's best interests anyway—however, it's also clear that when anxiety gets too intense it can cause great suffering and prevent people from functioning effectively; it has even been linked to increased risk for several kinds of medical problems due to its negative impact on the immune system. So what each of us needs is a happy medium—enough anxiety to keep us from taking foolhardy risks, but not so much that it becomes a mental and emotional prison. Fortunately, there are some simple tools nearly anyone can use to help us tell the difference between useful anxiety and the unrealistic kind. This exercise will help you learn and practice some of these tools.

1. What methods have worked for you to control and cope with anxiety in the past? How about methods you've seen other people use, especially people with whom you have a lot in common?

    _____

    _____

    _____

2. One of the things that we all tend to do is to let our thinking get distorted, and that can cause a lot of useless or needless worrying. In this exercise, we'll look at two of the most common problems. The first is the habit sometimes called "negative filtering." Another way to put it might be that a person sees all the thorns but none of the roses, and although nearly every situation has both good and bad elements, they focus on the bad and overlook the good. They also tend to see the world as a much more negative place than if they had paid equal attention to all of it. Can you think of a recent example of negative filtering, either in your own thinking or in that of someone else? What was it about, and what good things were overlooked?

    _____

    _____

    _____

One good way to get out of this mental trap is to make a "gratitude list." It might sound dumb, but it works, and as the old saying goes, "If it's dumb but it works, then it isn't dumb." To make a gratitude list, sit down in a quiet place where you can write without being interrupted and start writing a list of all the things in your life that you would miss if they were gone. This can include everything from physical health to important relationships to things like a song you enjoy every time you hear it or a favorite meal. If you make a regular habit of this, you'll find yourself noticing more of the good things in life as you go through your day and you'll probably have less anxiety because the world won't seem like such a dark and painful place.

3. Another mistake in thinking we often make that increases our anxiety levels is to underestimate our own strength and ability to cope with unpleasant experiences. Even when we're making the first mistake and catastrophizing about a situation, we tend to forget to ask ourselves the next logical question: "And if that worst-case outcome does happen, can I handle it? Do I have strengths and skills I could use to get through it? Have I coped with equally painful situations before?" To that question, if we think for a moment, the answer is nearly always, "Yes, it might be a very unpleasant experience, but I could cope with that event if it did happen." Please briefly describe a situation in which something really bad happened and you struggled, got through it, and were able to keep functioning and go on with life:

    _____

    _____

    _____

4. Finally, we want to think briefly about acceptance. There will always be some things in our lives we would change if we could, but they're beyond our power to affect. People often misunderstand the meaning of acceptance in regard to bad situations, and get angry if others suggest that they need to practice acceptance. The truth is that if I am practicing acceptance about a situation, it doesn't mean that I like the situation. It doesn't mean that I think it will always be the way it is, or that I won't try to improve it. All acceptance really means, if we use the word in the right way, is that I am acknowledging the way things are in the present moment. It's just being realistic instead of trying to live in a fantasy world, and we are free to use that present reality as a starting point from which to work at making things better. Acceptance can often bring a decrease in anxiety and an increase in our peace of mind; it helps us to think about our situations and possible courses of action more calmly and realistically; and to take actions that give us better results.

    Please think of a situation that has caused you a lot of anxiety and worrying, either in the present or past, and use this space to briefly describe the situation. Describe what you were afraid would happen, explain what did happen, and describe how you handled that event:

_____

_____

_____

_____

The more times you go through this process with different harsh experiences from different times in your life, the more you'll see that the worst possibility doesn't happen most of the time, and that when it does you are tougher, more resourceful, and more of a survivor than you've probably given yourself credit for.

Be sure to bring this handout back to your next session with your therapist, and be prepared to discuss your thoughts and feelings about the exercise.

GETTING AWAY FROM CATASTROPHIZING

GOALS OF THE EXERCISE

1. Reduce overall frequency, intensity, and duration of anxiety so that daily functioning is not impaired.
2. Stabilize anxiety level while increasing ability to function on a daily basis.
3. Enhance ability to effectively cope with the full variety of life's responsibilities.
4. Learn and use calming skills to reduce anxiety and manage its symptoms.
5. Verbalize an understanding of the role that cognitive biases play in excessive irrational worry and persistent anxiety symptoms.

ADDITIONAL PROBLEMS FOR WHICH THIS EXERCISE MAY BE USEFUL

- Borderline Personality
- Combat and Operational Stress Reaction
- Depression
- Panic/Agoraphobia
- Physiological Stress Response—Acute
- Posttraumatic Stress Disorder (PTSD)
- Pre-Deployment Stress

SUGGESTIONS FOR PROCESSING THIS EXERCISE WITH VETERANS/SERVICE MEMBERS

The "Getting Away from Catastrophizing" activity is created for veterans/service members with significant levels of anxiety focused on unrealistically dire anticipations of future events. It is designed to reduce anxiety by teaching the veteran/service member to recognize catastrophizing in his or her thinking and replace the worst-case view with a more balanced and realistic one. This activity is compatible with the evidence-based Cognitive Processing Therapy (CPT) model currently in use within the Department of Veterans Affairs. Follow-up or concurrent treatment could include bibliotherapy using books listed for this issue in Appendix A of *The Veterans and Active Duty Military Psychotherapy Treatment Planner* and/or videotherapy using films suggested for the topic "Emotional and Affective Disorders" in *Rent Two Films and Let's Talk in the Morning*, 2nd ed., by John W. Hesley and Jan G. Hesley, published by John Wiley & Sons.

GETTING AWAY FROM CATASTROPHIZING

What is catastrophizing? It's the mental and emotional habit of extreme pessimism, always anticipating the most disastrous possible future, having worst-case expectations like Chicken Little thinking the sky was falling or Eeyore from the *Winnie the Pooh* stories. Catastrophizing is a problem because it keeps a person constantly fearful, anxious, and obsessed with awful possibilities. It can make people unable to function in the military, in their jobs, or in their family lives; contributes to depression; and can even endanger a person's physical health through its weakening effect on the immune system. Fortunately, it's also a problem with a clear solution that anyone can apply if they want to change. This exercise will help you learn to identify and correct catastrophizing in your thinking.

1. Can you think of an example of catastrophizing that you've seen recently, either in your own thinking or in someone else's? If so, briefly describe the catastrophic event that you or the other person were afraid would happen, then describe what actually happened:

    _____

    _____

    _____

2. A wise person once said that every problem starts out as the solution to another problem, and catastrophizing is no exception. We need the ability to recognize possible future dangers so that we can prepare and survive them—as long ago, in prehistoric times—usually by either fighting or running away. The ability to anticipate that falling asleep in the open might result in being eaten by a leopard would have been useful for survival. The problem is that what should be a reasonable degree of caution—just one part of our world—has outgrown its proper size and is dominating our minds and crowding out other kinds of thinking. It can be very much like the way a person with posttraumatic stress disorder (PTSD) may feel the need to always be on guard, anticipating that they might be attacked at any moment. Please list some situations or life experiences other than serving in combat that you think might cause a person to get in the habit of catastrophizing:

    _____

    _____

    _____

3. Now for the solution—this is a simple solution, and although it helps to do it in writing at first, with some practice it becomes easier and easier until it's almost an automatic response. To start with, think for a moment about the situation you or another person has been catastrophizing about—briefly describe it on paper, then write down the worst-case outcome that the catastrophizing is predicting.

4. Now write down a range of four or five other possible outcomes ranging from not quite as bad as the catastrophizing up to the best possible turn of events.

   Imagine that you have to place bets on what is most likely to happen in the situation—if you had 20 dollars, would you bet it all on that catastrophized worst-case outcome? Or if you divided your 20 dollars and bet parts of it on several or all of the possibilities, which would you bet the most money on? This is a good way to figure out what you really expect to happen, at a deeper level than the anxiety. Please use this space to record a brief description of the situation, a list of the possible outcomes you thought of, and how you placed your bets. If it's a real-world event in the near future you can come back to this page later and see how accurately you analyzed the situation.

   _____

   _____

   _____

5. Finally, there's a second part to catastrophizing—our belief that if that worst-case event happened we would be unable to cope. Usually, though, we're under-estimating ourselves as badly as we're overestimating the likelihood of the catastrophic outcome. Along with putting the catastrophe in its place as just one possible outcome among several, and maybe not the most likely, we need to ask ourselves, "Okay, if that worst possible event did happen, could I cope with it?" And the best guide to answer that "what if" question about the future is to look to the past. To personalize it for yourself, think about some of the worst experiences you've had in your life, and reflect on the fact that you did get through them, even ones you wouldn't have believed you could handle if you'd known they were going to happen; please briefly describe one or two of those situations—what happened, and how you got through it:

   _____

   _____

   _____

   _____

   The more times you go through this process with different harsh experiences from different times in your life, the more you'll see that the worst possibility doesn't happen most of the time, and you'll see that when it does, you are tougher, more resourceful, and more of a survivor than you've probably given yourself credit for.

Be sure to bring this handout back to your next session with your therapist, and be prepared to discuss your thoughts and feelings about the exercise.

STAYING FOCUSED

GOALS OF THE EXERCISE

1. Increase levels of attention/concentration in all settings.
2. Minimize impact of attention/concentration deficits in daily life through the use of effective coping skills.
3. Improve overall satisfaction with periods of personal time and extracurricular activities.
4. Implement problem-solving strategies that will mitigate work problems caused by attention/concentration deficits.
5. Learn and implement skills to reduce the disruptive influence of distractibility.

ADDITIONAL PROBLEMS FOR WHICH THIS EXERCISE MAY BE USEFUL

- Combat and Operational Stress Reaction
- Mild Traumatic Brain Injury
- Social Discomfort

SUGGESTIONS FOR PROCESSING THIS EXERCISE WITH VETERANS/SERVICE MEMBERS

The "Staying Focused" activity is designed for use with veterans/service members whose levels of attention and concentration deficits are significantly interfering with their functioning in their military duties or other job responsibilities, family and marital roles, and other life responsibilities requiring sustained focus. The approach of the activity is to teach the veteran/service member techniques to help him/her compensate for these deficits. The techniques used in this activity are consistent with solution-focused therapy models and as such may be mastered by the veteran/service member within a few sessions. Follow-up or concurrent treatment activities could include bibliotherapy using one or more of the books listed for this issue in Appendix A of *The Veterans and Active Duty Military Psychotherapy Treatment Planner*.

STAYING FOCUSED

When we have difficulty staying focused, it can create problems in any area of life. When we have trouble completing tasks, staying engaged in conversations, and sustaining focus in other ways, it can create conflict with other people who don't understand why we seem bored and uninterested. But just as people can learn to overcome other difficulties, we can learn methods to overcome these problems. This assignment will introduce you to some of these methods and help you gain more control over your life.

1. When we get distracted from tasks at work, school, and around the house, it's often the same kinds of distractions that divert our attention time after time. Please think of some recent situations in which you were working on something and got sidetracked, and list the kinds of things that tend to distract you most often—some examples might be interactions with other people, the TV or music, having trouble finding all the items needed for the task, or noticing something else that needs to be done.

    _____

    _____

    _____

2. A large part of staying focused can be as simple as removing distractions from our surroundings, or removing ourselves from distracting surroundings. For example, if you have found that you lose focus because of distractions from the TV or music, you might be able to remove that distraction by turning them off (easier if you live alone or at least have a fair amount of time alone) or by going somewhere quiet, like a library, where they won't intrude. Would this work in any of the situations in which you often get distracted? If it would mean getting away from the distractions, where are some places you could go?

    _____

    _____

    _____

3. Similarly, if you're being interrupted by people, you may be able to solve the problem by explaining that you need to stay focused and asking them not to interrupt your concentration, going somewhere else, or working on the task when

they aren't around or are asleep. In some workplaces, a person can close an office door, but in many, that option doesn't exist; if so, a supervisor may be willing to let you work somewhere else for certain tasks if you explain the situation, or help you find another way to adapt your work to this need (if you've been diagnosed with Attention Deficit Disorder (ADD), you have the right to reasonable accommodation for that condition in the workplace under the Americans with Disabilities Act (ADA)). Do any of these—reducing distractions, asking people not to interrupt, shutting the interruptions out, or going to a quieter place—sound like things that would work for you? If so, how could you use them?

_____

_____

_____

4. The techniques listed in question 3 often help, but they won't always be available. Here are some methods we can use when we have fewer choices in our environment. Begin by going step-by-step when we're starting a task.

    The first step is to collect all the things we'll need—such as tools, materials, books, other information sources, and so on. It's much easier to stay focused if we don't have to stop what we're doing to go get something we need for the next step. Making a list of those items helps, in the same way a grocery list helps make sure we get home from the supermarket with everything we need for dinner that night.

    Two more techniques go with working step-by-step: one is decluttering. It's much easier to collect the things we need for tasks, without delay, when they aren't lost in the midst of clutter. There are all kinds of guidelines people use to declutter, but they all boil down to getting rid of what you don't need. For example, one rule of thumb might be that if you've read a magazine and know you don't normally go back and reread it, it's best to toss it in the recycling bin. You can figure out what works for you.

    The last technique is having a specific place to put each item when we aren't using it, and always putting it there; for example, a tray where you put your keys when you get home. It helps when we don't have to wonder where we left things we reuse and need—it's tough to remember at first but it gets easier with practice.

    What are some tasks that will be easier if you do these three things—collect the things you need before starting a task, declutter, and put things away in the same places when you use them?

_____

_____

_____

5. Another simple strategy is to change the way you organize your time. You may actually find it works better to switch tasks every 15 to 20 minutes, rather than try to stick to one for a long time. How could you use this approach?

    _____

    _____

    _____

6. Finally, other people can help us as well as get in the way. In the classroom, a teacher may ask a fellow student to help someone who has trouble staying focused—you can do the same for yourself. The helper can share activities, like studying together or teaming up on projects, or just remind us every so often of what we're working on. Who could you ask to do this, and how would you ask them? Your therapist may be able to help you with this plan.

    _____

    _____

Be sure to bring this handout back to your next session with your therapist, and be prepared to discuss your thoughts and feelings about the exercise.

STRUCTURING MY LIFE

GOALS OF THE EXERCISE

1. Minimize impact of attention/concentration deficits in daily life through the use of effective coping skills.
2. Increase perceived level of effectiveness in work, academic, and social arenas.
3. Improve overall satisfaction with periods of personal time and extracurricular activities.
4. Implement problem-solving strategies that will mitigate work problems caused by attention/concentration deficits.
5. Learn and implement skills to reduce the disruptive influence of distractibility.

ADDITIONAL PROBLEMS FOR WHICH THIS EXERCISE MAY BE USEFUL

- Adjustment to the Military Culture
- Combat and Operational Stress Reaction
- Financial Difficulties
- Mild Traumatic Brain Injury

SUGGESTIONS FOR PROCESSING THIS EXERCISE WITH VETERANS/SERVICE MEMBERS

The "Structuring My Life" activity is designed for use with veterans/service members who report having chaotic or disorganized lives and who frequently overlook or forget tasks like paying bills, keeping appointments, and so on. The activity takes the approach of guiding veterans/service members in creating schedules, checklists, and other structuring techniques to help them reduce the disorder and resulting stress in their lives. The techniques used in this activity are consistent with solution-focused therapy models and as such may be mastered by the veteran/service member within a few sessions. Follow-up or concurrent treatment activities could include bibliotherapy using one or more of the books listed for this issue in Appendix A of *The Veterans and Active Duty Military Psychotherapy Treatment Planner*.

STRUCTURING MY LIFE

When our lives feel chaotic and overcomplicated, it can seem stressful and overwhelming just to wake up in the morning and think about the day ahead. It can also result in our often running late, losing things, and forgetting to take care of responsibilities and commitments. However, there are some strategies that anyone can use to reduce these problems a great deal, making life easier and simpler. These strategies consist of ways to structure our lives—it makes sense, because when we create an element of structure, we are making a decision once instead of having to make that decision over and over. As an example, if a person always goes to bed at the same time, he or she doesn't have to decide when to do that; the same idea applies in many of the activities of our daily lives. This activity will guide you in creating some of these structures so that you can reduce the stress and complexity in your life.

1. Most of us have quite a few activities in our lives that we repeat over and over—and yet we may forget them or get to them late, leaving us (and others) wondering why we didn't get to them on time. Often we can make life easier by making a simple schedule, writing down the things we need to do and choosing a time to do each of them every day. For example, if a person always leaves for work at 8:00 A.M., he or she doesn't have to think about it and make a decision about it every day. If we keep finding that we meant to do something but somehow didn't get to it—like going to the gym—we can do a better job of making it happen by being sure to include it in that daily schedule. It helps keep us from overcommitting ourselves, too. What are the things that you do every day and could put on a daily schedule?

     _____

     _____

     _____

2. Another way to use structure to make daily life easier is to use checklists. One of the most common is to put a list on the inside of the front door, listing things we want to be sure we did before leaving—the kinds of things we may otherwise worry about or have to come back to check, like turning off the coffeepot or being sure we

have wallet or keys with us. What would go on your inside-the-door checklist, and where else could a checklist like this be useful for you?

_____

_____

_____

3. All of us have other tasks or commitments to keep track of that don't belong on a daily list, but either come up weekly, monthly, or yearly, or are not on a regular schedule but need to be tracked and taken care of, like medical appointments. There are two ways we can make life much easier when it comes to things like these. First, standardize the times as much as possible, as with daily activities—for example, a person might always do laundry on Sunday afternoon, or pay the bills the first Saturday after pay day. Second, carry a notebook with a calendar in it and list those events on the calendar. Any office supply store sells organizers of different sizes with calendars in them, or you can use a 3-ring binder and a calendar template on a word-processing program like Microsoft Word. How have you previously kept track of events like these, and would these two tools—standardized times and a calendar—work better? What items would be on your calendar for this week?

_____

_____

_____

4. Another benefit of structuring our time this way is that it can help us see how we're spending it, so we can make sure that we're really treating the things that matter most as priorities. One example would be a piece of advice often heard in relationship counseling, which is for a couple to schedule a date night every week. We can take the same approach to making sure we spend time with our children, or get together with other family members or friends. If we have goals that will take regular effort over time—going back to school, working on a major home renovation—we can use the calendar to make room for those in our lives, too. What relationships and goals that are important to you might this help you with?

_____

_____

_____

5. Finally, beyond the ideas in this activity, there is a wide range of other ways to organize and structure parts of our lives—any good-sized library or bookstore will have books on this subject, and there are businesses that do nothing but sell and/or install storage and organizing systems for closets and garages. Why not look up some books, in person or via the Internet, and look for ideas? Your therapist may

be able to help you plan this. Please use this space to list places you can check for information on structure and organization for your everyday life.

_____

_____

_____

_____

Be sure to bring this handout back to your next session with your therapist, and be prepared to discuss your thoughts and feelings about the exercise.

COMMEMORATING LOST FRIENDS AND FAMILY

GOALS OF THE EXERCISE

1. Accept the loss and return to previous level of social and occupational functioning.
2. Think and talk about the individual without experiencing significant negative emotions and physical symptoms.
3. Verbalize feelings of sadness to trusted individuals.
4. Express feelings and thoughts that were not expressed while the fallen comrade was alive.
5. Develop a memorial to the fallen comrade.

ADDITIONAL PROBLEMS FOR WHICH THIS EXERCISE MAY BE USEFUL

- Combat and Operational Stress Reaction
- Depression
- Nightmares
- Posttraumatic Stress Disorder (PTSD)
- Survivor's Guilt

SUGGESTIONS FOR PROCESSING THIS EXERCISE
WITH VETERANS/SERVICE MEMBERS

The "Commemorating Lost Friends and Family" activity is designed for use with veterans/service members experiencing significant unresolved grief over the loss of fellow veterans/service members or others to whom they were emotionally close. Its approach is to help the veteran/service member move ahead with his/her grieving and create a formal rite of passage acknowledging both the loss and the good that the relationship brought to the veteran/service member's life. Follow-up or concurrent treatment activities could include bibliotherapy using one or more of the books listed for this issue in Appendix A of *The Veterans and Active Duty Military Psychotherapy Treatment Planner* and/or videotherapy using films on the topics "Death and Dying" and "Grief and Loss" suggested in *Rent Two Films and Let's Talk in the Morning*, 2nd ed., by John W. Hesley and Jan G. Hesley, also published by John Wiley & Sons.

COMMEMORATING LOST FRIENDS AND FAMILY

No two of us experience grief exactly the same way, but there are some common elements. When we lose people close to us, the emotional pain can seem unbearable—often it can actually hurt physically; the word "heartache" describes what many people feel in a way that's all too real. The closer the relationship, the harder it hits us, and the bonds we form in combat are often as close as those in marriage or between family members. On top of that, when people die suddenly, it's usually more of a blow than an expected death due to illness or old age.

At the time the loss happens, we are often unable to stop and let ourselves feel the pain, because we have to keep functioning and sometimes because there are so many losses in such a short time that we'd be overwhelmed. So we compartmentalize our minds and put those feelings aside to deal with them later. We may be tempted to keep them set aside forever for fear we'll be overwhelmed and lose control if we let ourselves start to feel them, but sooner or later we're left feeling the grief either for that particular loss or as a generalized depression. On the other hand, some try to speed up the process of getting through the pain by wallowing in it, so to speak, but that doesn't seem to work for most of us either—bereavement goes on in each of us at its own pace. And not only does that mean we can't usually postpone it forever or rush through it, it means that no one has any right to tell someone else how long they should mourn and when they should "get over it."

Although we can't control the time span of grief, formal ceremonies can help by both providing an acknowledgment by the unit, the family, or the circle of friends of what has happened, and by bringing together those left behind for mutual comfort. This is why every culture seems to have some form of funeral ritual. Sometimes, though, we can find ourselves "stuck" in our grief and feeling as if we need to resolve it somehow. Many people, in and out of the military, have found that commemorating the person who has died in a personal way of their own helps them to find peace with their losses, to honor their lost friends or family members in a way that feels right to them, and to start healing and going ahead with life. The purpose of this activity is to help you create a commemoration of this kind, either just for yourself or for a small group of the people closest to the one who has died.

1. When you think of a funeral or memorial service, what thoughts and images come to mind for you? Do those thoughts and images feel right and are they effective in helping you deal with the sadness you feel?

_____

_____

_____

2. If a funeral or memorial took place and left you feeling like it didn't help, or if you were unable to attend, or if none was held, do you have a clear idea of what kind of ceremony would feel fitting to you, and if so what would it consist of?

_____

_____

_____

3. If you're having trouble thinking of ideas, it may help to consider some things others have found helpful. We list several here—please mark any that seem fitting to you.

    a. Writing a letter, a poem, or a song to him or her;

    b. Choosing a souvenir of your relationship with this person—a photo, a piece of a uniform, or something related to a shared interest;

    c. Visiting the person's grave or marker, telling him or her anything you might have wanted to say if you had the chance, and leaving the letter, poem, souvenir, or other item there;

    d. Alternatively, taking your letter, poem, or souvenir, spending some quiet time thinking about your relationship with your friend or family member, and then burning it;

    e. Planting a tree in honor of the memory of the person you've lost;

    f. Donating money or time to a worthy cause you know he or she would support.

    There are half a dozen ideas here, but you can create more if you wish. The key is that it helps you, and maybe others who share in your loss, with the grieving process.

4. Two final considerations that may help you are: First, if your friend or family member who has died was suffering, his or her pain has ended. The second thing to think about is not only what you would say to this person if you could, as mentioned in item 3.c., but considering what he or she might say to you. One way to do this is with an exercise called the empty chair—it may feel awkward at first, but it has worked very well for many people. To do this, you simply position two chairs facing each other. Sit in one of the chairs and visualize the person who has died sitting in the other chair facing you, and say the things you'd say to him or her if you could. Once you've done that, get up, sit down in the other chair, and try to put yourself in his or her place, then say whatever you feel that person would say to you in response to what you've said. Please use this space to write down a brief summary of what you said, and what you feel the other person would have said in reply.

You: _____

_____

_____

The person you've lost: _____

_____

_____

Be sure to bring this handout back to your next session with your therapist, and be prepared to discuss your thoughts and feelings about the exercise.

HOW DO I WANT TO BE REMEMBERED?

GOALS OF THE EXERCISE

1. Accept the loss and return to previous level of social and occupational functioning.
2. Verbalize feelings of sadness to trusted individuals.
3. Express feelings and thoughts that were not communicated while the fallen comrade was alive.
4. Reflect on the purpose and meaning of life.

ADDITIONAL PROBLEMS FOR WHICH THIS EXERCISE MAY BE USEFUL

- Combat and Operational Stress Reaction
- Depression
- Nightmares
- Posttraumatic Stress Disorder (PTSD)
- Spiritual and Religious Issues
- Suicidal Ideation
- Survivor's Guilt

SUGGESTIONS FOR PROCESSING THIS EXERCISE WITH VETERANS/SERVICE MEMBERS

The "How Do I Want to Be Remembered?" activity is designed for use with veterans/ service members struggling with existential anxiety after the death of a comrade, other close friend, or family member. The activity's aim is to help these veterans/service members, by guiding them to contemplate the meaning they seek in their own lives, and to perceive that in the lives of the people they have lost. By considering how they themselves would want their own friends and families to move on after mourning them and regain happiness in their lives, this activity is also meant to help clients who may be "stuck" in their grief and, perhaps, feel that it would be disloyal to the people they've lost to let go. Follow-up or concurrent treatment activities could include bibliotherapy using one or more of the books listed for this issue in Appendix A of *The Veterans and Active Duty Military Psychotherapy Treatment Planner* and/or videotherapy using films suggested for the topics "Death and Dying" and "Grief and Loss" in *Rent Two Films and Let's Talk in the Morning*, 2nd ed., by John W. Hesley and Jan G. Hesley, also published by John Wiley & Sons.

HOW DO I WANT TO BE REMEMBERED?

The death of someone for whom we care deeply is always painful, and it is healthy and natural to feel grief, sadness, and sometimes anger, confusion, or despair. We may find our feelings changing often between these and other emotions, and we all have our own unique ways of experiencing bereavement. There is no right or wrong way to mourn and no correct timetable for grief.

However, we sometimes find that we can't seem to get over these losses, that they continue to feel intensely painful well after the tragic events; we feel "stuck." We may also be unable to find an understanding of the meaning of the life of the person who has died, or a reason that makes sense for his or her death.

This exercise will guide you through some thought processes that have helped many people overcome this situation and reach a more peaceful emotional state, one in which you can remember your lost friend or family member with happiness for the good things you shared when he or she was alive.

1. We often feel unsettled emotions and have unanswered questions when someone close to us dies. We may find ourselves having feelings we don't understand and wondering about the meaning and value of life. If you have been experiencing this, what emotions have you been feeling and what thoughts have you had about the meaning of life and death?

    _____

    _____

    _____

    _____

    _____

    _____

2. It can help us clarify some of these things to consider the lives we know best—our own—and our own deaths sometime in the future. Have you also had thoughts or questions like these about your own life, as many people do at a time of loss? If so, please use this space to record the things you want most to understand about this subject:

    _____

    _____

_____
_____
_____
_____

3. Many find that it comforts them and helps them move through their grief to consider the question in the title of this activity: How do I want to be remembered? This simple question is complicated to answer. Here are some basics that can help you get started:

   a. What qualities about my relationships with the people who mean the most to me would I want them to think of when they remember me?

   b. What values have I tried hardest to live by?

   c. What achievements in my life have been the most important to me?

   d. What would I want to be the difference I have made in the world during my life?

   e. What would I want my close friends and family to think and feel when they remember me—what emotions would I want to inspire in their lives?

   The answers to the first four questions, 3.a. through 3.d., vary widely among people, which is what we would expect given the near infinite range of people's interests, passions, and personalities. However, most people answer the last question, 3.e., the same way. They want the people they care about most to remember them with affection, and over time they want the pain and grief those people feel about their deaths to fade and be replaced by pleasant memories of the good things in life they shared—happy occasions, meaningful accomplishments, and/or shared hardships they overcame together. And whether they imagine their deaths as being sudden or slow, painless or painful, people indicate that they would not want their memory to be a source of suffering for others. They would want people to remember that after death, they were freed of whatever earthly pain and anguish they may have felt as their lives ended, that they would be at peace, and that they would want the people who cared about them to be at peace with their memories, too. Use the space below to record the most important things you want to be remembered for and how you hope the people close to you will feel when they remember you.

_____
_____
_____
_____

_____

_____

_____

_____

Be sure to bring this handout back to your next session with your therapist, and be prepared to discuss your thoughts and feelings about the exercise.

AM I COMPARING MY INSIDES WITH OTHER PEOPLE'S OUTSIDES?

GOALS OF THE EXERCISE

1. Replace dichotomous thinking with the ability to tolerate ambiguity and complexity in people and issues.
2. Learn and practice interpersonal relationship skills.
3. Come to an awareness and acceptance of angry feelings while developing better control and more serenity.
4. Become capable of self-monitoring, identification of cognitive distortions (e.g., all-or-nothing thinking, catastrophizing, and unrealistic perceptions of self and others), and replacement of these distorted thoughts with more accurate and constructive cognitions leading to reduction of self-destructive behaviors.

ADDITIONAL PROBLEMS FOR WHICH THIS EXERCISE MAY BE USEFUL

- Adjustment to the Military Culture
- Anger Management and Domestic Violence
- Conflict with Comrades
- Social Discomfort
- Substance Abuse/Dependence

SUGGESTIONS FOR PROCESSING THIS EXERCISE WITH VETERANS/SERVICE MEMBERS

The "Am I Comparing My Insides with Other People's Outsides?" activity may be especially useful with veterans/service members who display borderline tendencies rooted in distorted perceptions or expectations about themselves and others in relationships, leading to self-sabotaging and self-destructive behaviors. Follow-up can consist of bibliotherapy using books suggested in Appendix A of *The Veterans and Active Duty Military Psychotherapy Treatment Planner* and/or videotherapy using films suggested for the topic "Substance Abuse" in *Rent Two Films and Let's Talk in the Morning*, 2nd ed., by John W. Hesley and Jan G. Hesley, also published by John Wiley & Sons.

AM I COMPARING MY INSIDES WITH OTHER PEOPLE'S OUTSIDES?

This exercise is about patterns that many of us have in our interactions with other people, patterns that don't work very well for us and may make it difficult or impossible for us to have stable, rewarding relationships. The same patterns may also make it harder for us to maintain our own emotional stability and lead us to self-destructive behavior of many kinds. These patterns are the results of distorted ways of thinking too negatively about ourselves and more idealized than is realistic about others. By working through this exercise, you can become more skilled at identifying and testing your judgments about yourself and others, testing those judgments to see whether they're really accurate, and correcting them if necessary.

1. You may or may not have heard the phrase in this exercise's title. Please take a moment to think about it and what it might mean. What do you think it would mean to compare your insides with other people's outsides?

    _____

    _____

    _____

2. It's a term some people use for the habit of seeing other people as being calm, confident, and secure in interpersonal situations or in crises, while they see themselves as nervous, clumsy, and tongue-tied in the same situations. Please think of a recent personal experience such as this and briefly describe it—when and where did it take place, what was going on, and with whom were you comparing yourself?

    _____

    _____

    _____

3. What terms would you use to describe how you felt, and how you perceived the other person?

    Yourself: _____

    The other person: _____

4. What evidence did the other person's behavior, expression, and body language give you to tell you how he or she was actually feeling—what did you see and hear?

_____

_____

5. What do you think you would have been feeling and thinking about yourself if you had been in his or her place in the same situation?

_____

_____

6. Now think of a situation in which you felt scared, embarrassed, confused, insecure, and/or overwhelmed, but on the outside, to others, you looked confident, relaxed, and competent. Briefly describe that situation and what you were doing to give people that impression:

_____

_____

Do you think that sometimes other people are doing the same thing, that they look good on the outside but feel pretty miserable on the inside?_____

7. Take a moment to think about a person in your life that you admire and respect, and then think of a situation in which he or she was experiencing all of those painful thoughts and judgments about himself or herself. What was the situation, and what did he or she do about it? Do you respect this person less because he or she has sometimes felt this way?

_____

_____

8. If the person you respect used an effective strategy to cope with painful thoughts and feelings about himself or herself, could you use the same strategy? How would you do that?

_____

_____

To change these patterns, it helps to work at becoming your own friend rather than your own meanest critic. To do this, monitor what you feel and say to yourself—try carrying a small notepad, and when you feel bad about yourself, stop and write down four things: (1) what the situation is, (2) what you're saying to yourself, (3) whether it's accurate, and (4) whether you'd say the same thing to a friend who was in your situation. If the answer to (4) is "no," write down what you would say to your friend instead. Often we mix up a negative judgment about an action with a negative judgment about ourselves, and it's important not to mix up what we do with who we are.

Be sure to bring this handout back to your next session with your therapist, and be prepared to discuss your thoughts and feelings about the exercise.

I CAN'T BELIEVE EVERYTHING I THINK

GOALS OF THE EXERCISE

1. Replace dichotomous thinking with the ability to tolerate ambiguity and complexity in people and issues.
2. Develop and demonstrate anger management skills.
3. Learn and practice interpersonal relationship skills.
4. Reduce the frequency of maladaptive behaviors, thoughts, and feelings that interfere with attaining a reasonable quality of life.
5. Identify, challenge, and replace biased, fearful self-talk with reality-based, positive self-talk.

ADDITIONAL PROBLEMS FOR WHICH THIS EXERCISE MAY BE USEFUL

- Anger Management and Domestic Violence
- Anxiety
- Conflict with Comrades
- Phobia
- Social Discomfort
- Suicidal Ideation
- Survivor's Guilt

SUGGESTIONS FOR PROCESSING THIS EXERCISE WITH VETERANS/SERVICE MEMBERS

The "I Can't Believe Everything I Think" activity is designed for use with veterans/service members who present with the cognitive distortions, emotional lability, and difficulty in relationships common to people suffering from borderline personality traits. The approach this exercise uses is the classic method found in cognitive-behavioral therapy (CBT), rational emotive behavior therapy (REBT), and cognitive processing therapy (CPT). Follow-up or concurrent treatment activities could include bibliotherapy using one or more of the books listed for this issue in Appendix A of *The Veterans and Active Duty Military Psychotherapy Treatment Planner* and/or videotherapy using films suggested for the topic of "Emotional and Affective Disorders" in *Rent Two Films and Let's Talk in the Morning*, 2nd ed., by John W. Hesley and Jan G. Hesley, also published by John Wiley & Sons.

I CAN'T BELIEVE EVERYTHING I THINK

Most of us find ourselves getting upset—angry, worried, or depressed—over things that happen in our day, and we tend to assume that the events caused the feelings. That can also leave us feeling vulnerable and helpless, with our happiness and peace of mind at the mercy of people and situations beyond our control. That's not quite how it really works, though—the process is a bit more complex—and by gaining an understanding of how our experiences, thoughts, and feelings *really* work, we can have much more power over our quality of life. This activity will walk you through a strategy to take charge of your own emotional life.

1. The most important fact in this process is this: The events in our lives do not lead directly to our emotional responses. There is a step in between, and that step is the thought we have about the event or the situation—the thoughts are what generate the emotions, and a lot of unhappiness is caused by mistakes in those thoughts. When you've completed this exercise, you will have a handy way to check for those mistakes, correct them, and improve your quality of life. Here's an example: Suppose Person A is entering a grocery store and sees a friend, Person B, coming out. A smiles, nods to B, and starts to greet him, but B walks past A without acknowledging him and is already walking down the sidewalk before A has a chance to say hello. What would Person A's immediate reaction be?

    _____

    For a lot of people, the reaction would be for Person A to feel angry and hurt at being given the cold shoulder by Person B. But notice the way that this is being expressed—the anger and hurt is a response to being deliberately ignored by the friend.

    But is that what really happened? The truth is, with the information from this event, it's impossible to be sure. What are some other reasons that might be behind the behavior of Person B in this scenario?

    _____

    _____

    _____

2. It probably wasn't hard for you to come up with some alternative explanations: what if Person B had lost his contact lenses and just didn't recognize Person A? What if Person B had just gotten a call on his cell phone telling him a family member had been in a car crash and was in the emergency room? What if he had a migraine headache and was in enough pain to keep him from noticing Person A? None of those would be reason for Person A to be angry or hurt at all. Those emotions actually came from a couple of thinking mistakes: in this case, the mistakes were jumping to a conclusion and assuming that Person B's behavior was about, or focused on, Person A, when in reality it might have had nothing to do with him.

3. There are many other common thinking mistakes, or as they're also called, cognitive distortions. Here are some that most of us engage in at times:

   a. All-or-nothing, good-or-bad thinking—this is when we think of a person or a situation as unrealistically idealized or terrible. This in turn sets us up to form unrealistic expectations and be surprised and upset when people we had idealized turn out to be flawed and only human. People and situations are always a mix of good and bad.

   b. Emotional reasoning—we make this mistake when we listen to our emotions and accept how we feel about ourselves, other people, or situations as reality. For example, if a person has failed at one task and is feeling humiliated, that person might believe that he or she is completely incompetent, or feel that others see him or her that way.

   c. Overgeneralizing—for example, meeting a person from New York who is pushy and loud, and deciding that all New Yorkers are pushy and loud.

   d. Mind-reading—assuming we know what others are thinking or feeling, especially their motives for their actions or what they think of us.

   e. Fortune-telling—predicting future events, or future actions by other people, when we don't really know what will happen.

4. Those are some of the mistakes but there are quite a few more. The important thing is to recognize that all human beings are prone to these kinds of thinking errors. We need to dig out the thoughts underlying our emotions and see whether they really make sense. To analyze any situation divide a sheet of paper into six columns. In Column 1 describe what happened; in Column 2, write any thoughts you had about the event in Column 1; and in Column 3, write the emotion or emotions you felt as a result of the thought in Column 2, rating the emotion's intensity from 1% to 100%.

   In Column 4, list any mistakes or distortions you can see in the thought in Column 2 as it relates to the event in Column 1. In Column 5, write a more realistic thought that is solidly based on the facts you have (this thought will often be neutral or positive when the thought in Column 2 was negative). And in Column 6, write the emotions you now feel after filling out Columns 4 and 5, and again rate the intensity of the emotion from 1% to 100%. Here's an example, using the scenario from earlier in this activity:

Event	Thought	Emotion based on thought	Thinking mistake(s)?	More realistic thought	Emotion based on new thought
Person B walks past Person A without saying hello.	"He just gave me the cold shoulder!"	Anger, 80% Hurt, 90% Confusion, 50%	Jumping to a conclusion, taking things personally, mind-reading	"I wonder why he didn't say hello? I hope he's okay. I'll check with him."	Curiosity, 75% Concern, 33%

For most of us, the emotions in the last column will cause much less distress. So try practicing this at least once a day, and you may find you like the results enough that it will be habit-forming.

Be sure to bring this handout back to your next session with your therapist, and be prepared to discuss your thoughts and feelings about the exercise.

STAYING IN TOUCH WITH REALITY

GOALS OF THE EXERCISE

1. Obtain a complete history, including the type and severity of psychotic symptoms.
2. Strengthen treatment alliance so that psychotropic medication is taken as prescribed.
3. Report decrease or elimination of positive psychotic symptoms (i.e., hallucinations and delusions).
4. Eliminate or adequately control positive and negative psychotic symptoms so that independent functioning can resume.

ADDITIONAL PROBLEMS FOR WHICH THIS EXERCISE MAY BE USEFUL

- Combat and Operational Stress Reaction
- Depression
- Mild Traumatic Brain Injury
- Performance-Enhancing Supplement Use
- Phobia

SUGGESTIONS FOR PROCESSING THIS EXERCISE
WITH VETERANS/SERVICE MEMBERS

The "Staying in Touch with Reality" activity is designed for use with veterans/service members who are newly experiencing psychotic symptoms in the immediate aftermath of a severely traumatic or shocking experience and are trying to understand what is happening to them. The rapid onset of psychotic symptoms is extremely disturbing, especially to individuals who have never experienced them before. Questions such as "Am I crazy?" "Will I be like this the rest of my life?" or "Will I be able to stay in the military?" should be expected. This exercise will help the veteran/service member gain some perspective on his/her illness and engage in reality testing to regain more sense of control in his/her life. It will also help the therapist identify any precipitating factor(s) leading up to the psychotic break and assist the therapist with mitigating risk factors that may exacerbate current symptoms. Follow-up for this activity can include bibliotherapy using books suggested in Appendix A of *The Veterans and Active Duty Military Psychotherapy Treatment Planner.*

STAYING IN TOUCH WITH REALITY

Symptoms such as hearing voices others don't hear, seeing things others don't see, and believing that people are plotting against you can be very distressing, especially if you've never experienced them before. These symptoms can seem very real even when they aren't. If they become long-lasting or permanent, they are considered evidence of a disorder called psychosis (also known as schizophrenia), which means that a person sees, hears, smells, feels, or tastes things that aren't really there, or that he or she has strong beliefs about situations when the available evidence doesn't support those beliefs.

However, sometimes after experiencing a traumatic or shocking event, a person can experience something called a brief reactive psychotic episode, in which these symptoms appear suddenly, but fade out within a month or so with medications and do not turn into a long-term problem.

This exercise will help you gain a greater understanding of these symptoms, learn ways to tell when things you experience are not real, and help you and your therapist develop a plan to help you get better.

1. Have you recently begun to have strange sensory experiences that people around you aren't having—hearing voices other people don't hear, seeing people or objects that other people aren't seeing, or having any other kinds of sensory experiences other people around you don't have—smells, tastes, or physical sensations? _____ If you have, briefly describe these experiences, including when they started, any important events that happened before they started, and the following additional information:

    a. What kinds of events happened shortly before these experiences started, and when?

    _____

    _____

    _____

    b. If you've heard voices, say whether you recognize them as people you know, what they say to you, and whether they try to get you to do anything:

    _____

    _____

    _____

c. If you see people or objects, briefly describe them; if they are people, do you know them? What do you see them doing?

_____

_____

_____

d. If you have other sensory experiences that other people don't—smells, tastes, or physical sensations—briefly describe them:

_____

_____

_____

e. On a scale of 1 to 10, with 1 being the least and 10 the most, how much do these experiences bother you? _____

f. If there are events, situations, or things that you do that cause them to start, increase, or become more upsetting, what are those events, situations, or actions?

_____

_____

_____

g. If there are events, situations, or things that you do that cause them to stop, decrease, or become less upsetting, what are those events, situations, or actions?

_____

_____

_____

2. Have you recently begun having thoughts that people want to hurt you or are secretly planning to hurt you? Yes _____ No _____. If you have, briefly describe these thoughts, including what they are, when they started, any important events that happened before they started, and whether there are ways you can tell they are or aren't true:

_____

_____

_____

a. What kinds of events happened shortly before these thoughts started, and when?

_____

_____

_____

b. On a scale of 1 to 10, how much distress do the thoughts cause you? If you can tell when they aren't really true, does that lower your stress level? _____

c. If there are events, situations, or things that you do that cause these thoughts to start, increase, or become more upsetting, what are those events, situations, or actions?

_____

_____

_____

d. If there are events, situations, or things that you do that cause them to stop, decrease, or become less upsetting, what are those events, situations, or actions?

_____

_____

_____

3. Have you noticed anything about any of these sensory experiences or thoughts that enables you to tell whether they are real or not? _____ If so, describe how you can tell:

_____

_____

4. If you've identified ways to tell when any of these kinds of experiences aren't real, does it make it less stressful to know that you can still tell the difference between things that are real and those that aren't? _____ Does it make these experiences less stressful when you know that when they suddenly start the way they did in your situation, they usually go away within a month after the trauma or shock that caused them? _____ Please keep working with your therapist on ways to cope with these experiences.

Be sure to bring this handout back to your next session with your therapist, and be prepared to discuss your thoughts and feelings about the exercise.

REALITY CHECKS

GOALS OF THE EXERCISE

1. Report decrease or elimination of positive psychotic symptoms (i.e., hallucinations and/or delusions).
2. Take psychotropic medications as prescribed.
3. Eliminate or adequately control positive and negative psychotic symptoms so that independent functioning can resume.

ADDITIONAL PROBLEMS FOR WHICH THIS EXERCISE MAY BE USEFUL

- Combat and Operational Stress Reaction
- Depression
- Mild Traumatic Brain Injury
- Performance-Enhancing Supplement Use
- Phobia

SUGGESTIONS FOR PROCESSING THIS EXERCISE WITH VETERANS/SERVICE MEMBERS

The "Reality Checks" activity provides the veteran/service member with information about the formation of hallucinations and delusional beliefs in both transient and chronic thought disorders; this exercise is primarily aimed at veterans/service members experiencing brief reactive psychotic episodes, and thus is aimed at a fairly well-organized and high-functioning person whose sensory and cognitive processes are mostly normal and are expected to fully return to normal in a short time. Follow-up for this activity can include bibliotherapy using books suggested in Appendix A of *The Veterans and Active Duty Military Psychotherapy Treatment Planner*.

REALITY CHECKS

Most of us go through life, most of the time, taking it for granted that our physical senses and our thought processes are working properly. If you're in traffic and see a blue station wagon in front of you, it probably never crosses your mind to wonder whether it's really there, or whether it's really blue. We also trust our logic and ability to tell fact from fantasy. However, you may be finding that as a result of a recent traumatic experience your senses and thinking have become less dependable. You can assume pretty safely that this is a short-term result of that recent trauma, because if this was a more serious and chronic problem, you wouldn't have ever gotten into the military in the first place, or would have failed to complete basic training or OCS. Still, even knowing it won't last, it's nerve-wracking, like living in a minefield, to have to constantly wonder about the reality of what we see, hear, think, or remember.

However, there are tools you can use to handle this while your brain is recovering from its recent shock. This exercise will show you some of those tools.

1. The title of this exercise, "Reality Checks," is often used to describe a situation in which someone finds out that something he or she believed isn't true, often in some way that is costly, embarrassing, or painful. Here we mean it literally, though, as in checking the reality of things, to avoid those situations. Another phrase used more seriously for the same kind of thing is "reality testing," and it applies to both sensory experiences and the thoughts that interpret them. What do you think would be some effective ways to test the reality of things you see and hear?

   _____

   _____

   If you saw the film *A Beautiful Mind*, you may remember a scene in which John Nash, the mathematician whose story the film tells, is teaching at a university after decades of struggling with a mental illness that caused him to hallucinate (in his case, he sometimes saw people who weren't actually there) and suffer from delusions (beliefs that are not based on fact and are often bizarre). A man stops him in the hallway at the school and tells him that he, John Nash, has just been awarded the Nobel Prize for his work. Nash stops a passing student, points to the man from the Nobel committee, and asks the student, "Can you see him?" When the student says he can, Nash accepts that this is real, but his first thought is that he might be hallucinating—so he gets a second opinion. Obviously, he couldn't do this with everything he saw or heard. So he would first ask himself if what he perceived was consistent with the way the world and his life normally operated. The more out of the ordinary something was, the more likely it wasn't real. Having a stranger walk up and tell him, out of the blue, that he had won a prize that would make him rich and world-famous was definitely not part of his average day, so the first thing he did was get an independent check. We all do this at times: Can you remember a situation where you saw something strange or unusual enough that you said to whoever was with you, "Did you see that?" or something similar, or had someone say it to you? What was the situation?

_____

_____

_____

2. The point of presenting this example is to show you that you already have a lot of practice at reality testing when it comes to your senses. Since you experienced your recent trauma, have you seen, heard, smelled, tasted, or felt things that turned out not to be real? What were they, and how did you find out that your senses were playing tricks on you?

_____

_____

3. Beyond asking someone nearby whether he or she can see or hear the thing you're wondering about, another option for testing might be to take a picture of it, maybe with a camera built into your cellular phone, then show the picture to other people later and ask them to tell you what they see. Would this work for you? _____

4. What sensory illusions or hallucinations have you experienced recently, if any, and did they have characteristics you could watch for that would make it possible to tell them from things that are real? If so, describe the hallucinations and the qualities that let you know they weren't real:

_____

_____

5. Are there people who could help you with this kind of reality testing, like the student in the hallway in the film? Who are they, and how can you ask for that help?

_____

_____

6. The other positive symptom of a psychotic episode—positive means that something's happening that shouldn't (a negative symptom is the absence of something that should be present)—is delusional thinking. As we said above, this means a belief in something that contradicts obvious facts. Again, it's impossible to go through life checking the validity of every thought that drifts through your

mind, so the best strategy is to test thoughts that seem weird based on our knowledge of the world in general. What delusional thoughts have you had, if any, since your recent shocking experience?

_____

_____

Is there a pattern in those thoughts you could use to check the reality of future thoughts? If you see a pattern, what is it?

_____

_____

7. Finally, can the people who could help you check for hallucinations also help you check for delusions, or can someone else? Again, who are they and how can you ask for that help?

_____

_____

Be sure to bring this handout with you to your next therapy session, and be prepared to discuss your thoughts and feelings about this exercise.

ALTERNATIVE METHODS FOR MANAGING PAIN

GOALS OF THE EXERCISE

1. Develop nonpharmacological pain management skills.
2. Alleviate pain to a degree that allows a return to previous level of social and occupational functioning.
3. Increase aerobic and anaerobic fitness.
4. Accept that some level of pain and limitations may be lifelong.

ADDITIONAL PROBLEMS FOR WHICH THIS EXERCISE MAY BE USEFUL

- Amputation, Loss of Mobility, Disfigurement
- Depression
- Mild Traumatic Brain Injury
- Opioid Dependence
- Posttraumatic Stress Disorder (PTSD)
- Substance Abuse/Dependence

SUGGESTIONS FOR PROCESSING THIS EXERCISE WITH VETERANS/SERVICE MEMBERS

The "Alternative Methods for Managing Pain" activity is intended to provide veterans/service members suffering from severe and/or chronic pain with alternatives to the use of potentially addictive medications to manage that pain. The exercise offers several alternative approaches to managing pain and restoring quality of life without running the risk of addiction or a relapse which may accompany either use of traditional pain medications or trying to "gut it out" and cope with pain through willpower, risking relapse via self-medication. Follow-up may include assignments to investigate local service providers or support groups, as well as investigation of online resources including the support groups identified in the handout; bibliotherapy using books listed in Appendix A of *The Veterans and Active Duty Military Psychotherapy Treatment Planner,* and/or films suggested for the topics of "Chronic Illness and Disabilities" and "Substance Abuse" in *Rent Two Films and Let's Talk in the Morning*, 2nd ed., by John W. Hesley and Jan G. Hesley, also published by John Wiley & Sons.

ALTERNATIVE METHODS FOR MANAGING PAIN

If you suffer from severe or chronic pain but are concerned about addiction and need ways to manage pain other than narcotic pain medications, this exercise will help you find some ways.

1. How does the chronic pain you experience affect your daily life?

    _____

    _____

2. Please identify any professionals with whom you're working to manage your pain.

    _____

    _____

    Do those professionals know of your concerns about addiction? Are they experienced and qualified in working with people who suffer from addictions? _____

3. What other methods of pain management have you tried, and what worked best for you?

    _____

    _____

4. Here are some nonaddictive ways of managing pain. Please talk with your doctor and your therapist about each of these approaches, investigate whatever opportunities your community offers you to try, and briefly write about what you find.

    a. *Over-the-counter (OTC) pain medications.* These are relatively mild pain-relieving drugs with no mind-altering effects. The most common are aspirin, ibuprofen, naproxen, and acetaminophen, all of which go by various brand names. All of these except acetaminophen are classified as non-steroidal anti-inflammatory drugs, or NSAIDs. If you use these medications, be careful not to exceed safe dosages. Excessive amounts can damage the stomach lining, liver, and kidneys, and in extreme cases cause death. Other pain-relieving medications stop the pain of acid reflux and heartburn (and also lower your risk for cancer of the esophagus.)

b. *Other non-mind-altering medications.* This category includes medications for joint pain called *glucosamine chondroitin* and *MSM*. They help the body's natural healing processes rebuild damaged cartilage and connective tissues.

c. *Topical (external) medications.* These are ointments that can provide relief for pain from musculoskeletal problems including arthritis and joint injuries. They include pain-relieving ingredients, and some also have anti-inflammatory ingredients which reduce swelling and soreness. Some contain steroid compounds, and some contain capsaicin, the same chemical that makes pepper spray burn. You should check with your doctor before using these medications.

d. *Diet modifications.* Sometimes pain is caused by unhealthy elements or deficiencies in a person's diet. Other problems may be due to food allergies—these can cause heartburn, headaches, rashes, and other problems. As part of a medical workup, you should get an allergy screening. You may want to work with a dietician or nutritionist.

e. *Acupuncture.* Acupuncture has been proven to give fast and effective relief of pain in many cases. If you use acupuncture, work only with a qualified professional.

f. *Therapeutic massage.* This is another technique that, provided by trained professionals, can give quick and lasting relief for many cases of chronic musculoskeletal pain.

g. *Hypnosis.* This is very effective for many people—as with other types of treatment, be sure to work with a professional with the right training, credentials, and experience.

h. *Meditation.* Many pain sufferers find that meditation, especially guided imagery, can help them detach from their pain. Soothing music can increase the effectiveness of meditation and people undergoing surgery respond better to anesthesia and recover more quickly afterward if they listen to soothing music before, during, and after surgery.

i. *Stretching and progressive muscle relaxation.* Be careful not to push the stretch too far and cause more pain or injury. This is good for back and neck pain and headaches.

j. *Moderate cardiovascular exercise.* If you can exercise, 20 to 30 minutes of moderate cardio workout (enough to make you sweat, but not to cause shortness of breath) will relieve your pain by increasing the brain's levels of neurotransmitters that act as natural pain relievers. Before you start an exercise program, talk with your doctor to make sure it's safe and to ask how to get the most benefit from your workouts.

k. *Laughter.* Hearty or prolonged laughter boosts levels of the same neurotransmitters as cardiovascular exercise, and affects pain and emotional distress the same way. Laughter also strengthens your immune system, improving your resistance to illness.

l. *Pet therapy.* Spending time with an affectionate animal also provides some relief from physical and emotional distress. Hospitals often include pet therapy in treatment.

m. *Spiritual and/or religious activity.* Many find comfort in prayer and the company of others who share their spiritual beliefs. This can reduce the isolation that often comes with intense pain and help people make sense of an experience that seems senseless.

n. *Pain management support groups.* You may find advice and support in these groups. They may be listed in local newspapers or magazines, and hospitals often have groups. You may find one by checking there. There are also pain management groups online. You can find current information via the Internet. Some active sites as of summer 2010 are:

American Chronic Pain Association: www.theacpa.org

Back Pain Support Group: www.backpainsupportgroup.com

Chronic Pain Support Group: www.chronicpainsupport.org

National Chronic Pain Outreach Association, Inc.: www.chronicpain.org

Which of these are available for you?

_____

_____

5. Briefly describe your plan to cope with pain using nonaddictive methods:

_____

_____

_____

Be sure to bring this handout back to your next therapy session, and be prepared to discuss your thoughts and feelings about the exercise.

COPING WITH ADDICTION AND CHRONIC PAIN

GOALS OF THE EXERCISE

1. Alleviate pain to a degree that allows a return to previous levels of social and occupational functioning.
2. Follow through with medical recommendations.
3. Take medication as prescribed.
4. Strengthen support network.

ADDITIONAL PROBLEMS FOR WHICH THIS EXERCISE MAY BE USEFUL

- Depression
- Insomnia
- Opioid Dependence
- Performance-Enhancing Supplement Use
- Physiological Stress Response—Acute
- Substance Abuse/Dependence

SUGGESTIONS FOR PROCESSING THIS EXERCISE WITH VETERANS/SERVICE MEMBERS

The "Coping with Addiction and Chronic Pain" activity is designed for use with veterans/ service members who, as the title indicates, suffer from both addiction and severe and persistent pain. It addresses the perceived dilemma many pain sufferers face of reconciling participation in 12-Step recovery programs with the need to use prescribed medications that have a high potential for addiction, as well as noting other sources of emotional and practical support. It is helpful for the psychotherapist to coordinate work on this issue with any other health care providers from whom the veteran/service member is receiving services, after ensuring that you and the other providers have each received the veteran's/service member's consent to share treatment information. Follow-up or concurrent treatment activities can include referral to one or more of the chronic pain support groups cited in the exercise and bibliotherapy using one or more of the books listed for this issue in Appendix A of *The Veterans and Active Duty Military Psychotherapy Treatment Planner* and/or videotherapy using films on the topic of "Chronic Illness and Disabilities" recommended in *Rent Two Films and Let's Talk in the Morning*, 2nd ed., by John W. Hesley and Jan G. Hesley, also published by John Wiley & Sons.

COPING WITH ADDICTION AND CHRONIC PAIN

Some people suffer from both substance abuse problems and chronic pain. This puts them in a dilemma, as normal treatments for pain use narcotics or other strong drugs with potential for addiction. Often, the pain may be what led these people to begin using addictive drugs. On the other hand, some doctors are reluctant to prescribe these drugs, for fear of their patients getting addicted. Either way, you need to achieve and maintain a life free of both addiction and ongoing pain. Fortunately, there are solutions. This exercise will help you find some of those solutions.

1. How does chronic pain impact your daily life? Describe the relationship between your problems with alcohol or other drugs and with pain management.

    _____

    _____

    _____

2. Do your medical providers specialize in pain management and addiction? If not, can they give you a referral to a pain management specialist? As part of this exercise, please check on this and let your therapist know. Also, have you told them about your addiction history? If not, what keeps you from sharing that information?

    _____

    _____

3. In recent years the medical profession has found that even drugs that are usually highly addictive do not result in addiction for pain patients if they take no more than is needed, and for no longer than needed, to control the pain. If you and your doctor plan to manage your pain this way, how will you avoid taking more than you need and switch to something safer and not so strong as soon as appropriate, to avoid getting hooked?

    _____

    _____

4. Another fact about pain medications: When they are taken before pain gets severe, it takes less to block the pain and keep the patient comfortable. This is why hospitals sometimes give people their pain medications on a regular schedule even when they aren't too uncomfortable. How do you feel about the idea of taking pain medications on a schedule?

_____

_____

_____

5. Many alcoholics and other addicts have found that when they used narcotics or equivalent drugs, even if they didn't get addicted to those drugs, their judgment and inhibitions were affected, and they relapsed into drinking or using other drugs. How will you avoid this trap?

    _____

    _____

6. Medical professionals have a central part in pain treatment, but other people also have key roles to play in helping you manage this situation (e.g., your recovery sponsor, family, and friends). How can they help you avoid falling into addictive thinking and behaviors when you're using potentially habit-forming drugs to manage your pain?

    _____

    _____

7. If you are participating in a 12-Step program, you need to know your program's philosophy about the use of prescribed medications. The position of Alcoholics Anonymous is that if your doctor knows your history and is experienced working with people with addictions, and you're taking the medications as prescribed, you're doing what you need to do to stay sober. Other programs have similar views. If others in your group challenge this, they don't know their program well enough. If you have questions, check the official literature. Do you know others in 12-Step programs that have had to take powerful prescribed medications? How have they avoided falling into the trap of substance abuse?

    _____

    _____

8. In addition to 12-Step or other recovery programs focused on addictions, you may find help from support groups specifically for chronic pain, either local groups which you may be able to find through local media (many newspapers publish lists of support groups of all kinds) or online groups like the following (these are current in mid-2010, but with time these sites may disappear and others appear—for current info, use an Internet search engine).

    a. American Chronic Pain Association: www.theacpa.org

    b. Back Pain Support Group: www.backpainsupportgroup.com

    c. Chronic Pain Support Group: www.chronicpainsupport.org

    d. National Chronic Pain Outreach Association, Inc.: www.chronicpain.org

9. Have you had any contact with any of these or other groups, either local or online? If so, please identify the groups and a brief note about your experience with each. If not, please look into them and talk with your therapist about what you learn.

    _____

    _____

    _____

10. Please list the methods and resources you will use to cope with addiction and chronic pain.

    _____

    _____

    _____

Be sure to bring this handout back to your next session with your therapist, and be prepared to discuss your thoughts and feelings about the exercise.

HELPING MYSELF BY HELPING OTHERS

GOALS OF THE EXERCISE

1. Alleviate pain and allow a return to previous levels of functioning.
2. Resolve any negative feelings about the injury responsible for the pain.
3. Develop an understanding that thoughts and behaviors affect the pain experience.
4. Describe ways to take an active role in pain control.
5. Strengthen support network.

ADDITIONAL PROBLEMS FOR WHICH THIS EXERCISE MAY BE USEFUL

- Amputation, Loss of Mobility, Disfigurement
- Bereavement Due to Loss of a Comrade
- Borderline Personality
- Depression
- Homesickness/Loneliness
- Post-Deployment Reintegration Problems
- Posttraumatic Stress Disorder (PTSD)
- Spiritual and Religious Issues
- Substance Abuse/Dependence
- Suicidal Ideation

SUGGESTIONS FOR PROCESSING THIS EXERCISE
WITH VETERANS/SERVICE MEMBERS

The "Helping Myself by Helping Others" activity is designed for veterans/service members at greater risk of unhealthy patterns of isolation and brooding or self-pity, or those with strong religious or spiritual beliefs. It is based on studies of the beneficial effects of altruism ranging from Victor Frankl's *Man's Search for Meaning* to the more recent work of Paul Pearsall (*The Pleasure Prescription,* 1996), Larry Dossey (*Meaning & Medicine,* 1991), and Allan Luks and Peggy Payne (*The Healing Power of Doing Good,* 1991), as well as the 12-step principle that the best way to maintain one's own recovery is to help others with theirs. Follow-up can include bibliotherapy using books listed for this issue in Appendix A of *The Veterans and Active Duty Military Psychotherapy Treatment Planner* and/or videotherapy using films on the topics "Friends and Support Systems," "Inspiration," "Substance Abuse," and "Values and Ethics" listed in *Rent Two Films and Let's Talk in the Morning,* 2nd ed., by John W. Hesley and Jan G. Hesley, published by John Wiley & Sons.

HELPING MYSELF BY HELPING OTHERS

Like the medical problems that cause it, chronic pain can be complicated. People living with serious injuries or illnesses must deal with not only the physical pain, but often with depression, anxiety, or uncertainty about the future. So we may find that although the pain medications and physical therapy prescribed by our health care providers help, they don't help enough, and they don't address the mental and emotional parts of our pain as well as the physical.

This is a problem people have known about for ages, and for just as long, people have discovered and rediscovered that we can find further relief for our suffering by helping others with their problems. In recent times there have been a number of scientific studies that confirm what many people have known for thousands of years, and explain how this works.

This exercise will guide you in learning about the benefits people gain in their own healing and quality of life by helping other people and exploring the ways you can take advantage of this in your own life.

1. One of the first benefits is a positive change in brain chemistry. To sum it up, the act of extending our caring to other people somehow increases the brain's levels of endorphins. These are natural chemicals that function to relieve pain, increase pleasure, lift our mood, and increase our feelings of energy and well-being. The same chemicals are responsible for what is called a "runner's high,"—a feeling of elation that long-distance runners often experience after they've reached a certain level of exhaustion—and for the temporary blocking of pain we may feel for a short time after an injury. Some have called this effect the "helper's high." Do you know anyone who often does kind things for others and always seems unusually happy and healthy? Have you ever experienced this, and if so how?

    _____

    _____

    _____

2. Another benefit, which seems like common sense once we think about it, is that doing good things improves the way we feel about ourselves. In Alcoholics Anonymous, there's a saying: "If you want to have self-esteem, do esteemable things." Again, think of your own experiences and describe a time when you've

done something unselfish and made someone else's life a bit better, and found that you felt better about yourself, too. Would this help when you're having trouble with depression, discouragement, or anxiety?

_____

_____

_____

3. Some other facts about human psychology seem to help explain the benefits of doing good things for other people. First, one of the main elements in depression— even suicide—is a feeling of isolation and lack of emotional connection to other people, a feeling that we don't matter to anyone else. It's easy to see that when one person reaches out and helps another, that sense of isolation and not mattering would be reduced in both of them. Another part of depression is a feeling of being powerless over what happens in our lives, and when we take action to make the world better for someone else we're proving to ourselves that we aren't powerless after all. Again, please think of your own experiences and briefly note a time when you might have felt depressed and found that your mood improved when you did something kind for another person, or when someone did something caring for you:

_____

_____

_____

4. Another fascinating piece of news from several research studies, on the effects of kindness and unselfishness, is that it actually improves the functioning of the immune system, helping us to resist illness, relieve the symptoms of chronic illnesses like arthritis, and speed recovery from injuries or surgeries. This news is clearly important for anyone living with chronic pain due to wounds, injuries, or illness. Are you interested in trying this out, and if so, how will you do so? What can you do to test it, and how can you keep track of your results?

_____

_____

_____

5. Here's another possible benefit. In the book _Flow_, a psychologist named Mihaly Csikszentmihalyi reports on a systematic study he completed to discover what makes people happy. He learned that we are happiest when we're doing something in which we get so absorbed that we forget about everything else for a while, and that the people who spend the most time in activities like that were the ones who were happiest overall. For a lot of us, that's how it feels when we help someone, especially if the help takes the form of sharing an activity we love with them. How could you try this out and see how it works for you?

_____

_____

_____

6. What other ideas do you have about ways you can put this idea to use and help yourself by helping others?

_____

_____

_____

_____

Be sure to bring this handout back to your next session with your therapist, and be prepared to discuss your thoughts and feelings about the exercise.

NORMAL REACTIONS IN EXTREME SITUATIONS

GOALS OF THE EXERCISE

1. Describe the various symptoms that have developed in response to the combat/operational stress.
2. Return to full mission capability.
3. Restore confidence in combat abilities.
4. Acknowledge that combat/operational stress symptoms are transient and that full recovery is expected.

ADDITIONAL PROBLEMS FOR WHICH THIS EXERCISE MAY BE USEFUL

- Adjustment to Killing
- Anxiety
- Insomnia
- Nightmares
- Physiological Stress Response—Acute
- Posttraumatic Stress Disorder (PTSD)

SUGGESTIONS FOR PROCESSING THIS EXERCISE WITH SERVICE MEMBERS

The "Normal Reactions in Extreme Situations" is designed for use with service members experiencing combat and operational stress reactions (COSRs) as the result of trying events in combat, training, or other duties. COSRs are a common occurrence in service members who are faced with difficult and dangerous jobs. Unlike psychiatric disorders, COSRs are generally viewed as transient and an expected consequence of serving in a hostile or dangerous environment. Therefore, focus in treatment should be on the transient nature of the symptoms and helping the service member normalize his or her reactions with the expected outcome of a return to previous level of functioning. It is crucial that the service member not be placed into the role of "patient." This only reinforces the symptoms and halts the service member's natural process of recovery and adjustment. Follow-up for this activity could include a reading assignment from Appendix A of *The Veterans and Active Duty Military Psychotherapy Treatment Planner*.

NORMAL REACTIONS IN EXTREME SITUATIONS

Being exposed to difficult and dangerous situations in either deployed or garrison settings can put you at risk of experiencing a combat and operational stress reaction (COSR). This is a normal, expected, and predictable emotional, physical, and behavioral reaction to a stressful event. Although generally viewed as a consequence of serving in a war zone, COSRs may also develop during training operations, peacekeeping missions, and/or humanitarian missions. Symptoms of the COSR can range from mild to severe. However, in most situations, the symptoms will disappear on their own or with some brief help from a mental health professional, chaplain, or leader within your chain of command. The important message to take from this is that you can expect this to pass. This exercise will help you identify and understand the typical symptoms associated with COSRs and help get you back on track.

1. Please circle the different reactions you've been experiencing since the stressful event:

Physical	Emotional	Behavioral
Fatigue	Anxiety	Indecisiveness
Jumpiness	Grief	Inattention
Difficulty sleeping	Inability to concentrate	Carelessness
Irregular heartbeats	Nightmares	Hyper-alertness
Dizziness	Self-doubt	Lack of motivation
Nausea, vomiting, or diarrhea	Anger	Irritability
Slow reaction time	Excessive concern with minor issues	Crying
Muscle tension	Loss of confidence in self and unit	Argumentative
Weakness and paralysis		Fighting
Impaired vision, hearing, and touch	Loss of trust in superiors	Tardiness
	Loneliness	

2. Listed below are some ways to address these responses that many others have found helpful. In addition to these, you can probably think of some more ideas that will work well for you. Please use the empty lines to list things you'll do during the next week:

Addressing physical reactions: Exercise moderately, stretch, get some extra sleep (relax and rest if you have trouble sleeping), take a hot shower, hydrate, eat something you like. For nausea, vomiting, or diarrhea, see a medic/corpsman.

a. _____

b. _____

c. _____

d. _____

e. _____

f. _____

Addressing emotional reactions: Talk to trusted friends and/or a chaplain or counselor; remember past stressful times and how you got through them; watch a comedy or talk with a friend who makes you laugh; pray; write in a journal; remind yourself this will pass; remember your accomplishments and skills; engage in a hobby; read something interesting; listen to upbeat music; think about plans for five years from now; meditate.

a. _____

b. _____

c. _____

d. _____

e. _____

f. _____

Addressing behavioral reactions: Look for ways to stay organized; focus on practical tasks and do them as well as possible; acknowledge feelings and thoughts to yourself and/or a trusted friend, chaplain, or counselor but remind yourself that you choose how to act on them; use methods friends have used to cope with temporary upsets (though not drinking or using other mood-altering substances, except under a doctor's instructions.)

a. _____

b. _____

c. _____

d. _____

e. _____

f. _____

3. (Answer this question one week after the first two questions.) Please answer the following:

    a. How many of the activities you chose in question 2 did you end up doing during the past week?

    _____

    b. Which ones do you think were most useful in helping you relax and feel better?

    _____

    _____

    _____

    c. What changes do you see in the reactions you circled for question 1?

    _____

    _____

    _____

Be sure to bring this handout back to your next meeting with your counselor or chaplain, and be prepared to discuss your thoughts and feelings about the exercise.

HEALTHY WAYS TO HANDLE STRESS FAST

GOALS OF THE EXERCISE

1. Return to full mission capability.
2. Restore confidence in combat abilities.
3. Eliminate physical and emotional factors that impede mission performance.

ADDITIONAL PROBLEMS FOR WHICH THIS EXERCISE MAY BE USEFUL

- Adjustment to Killing
- Anger Management and Domestic Violence
- Anxiety
- Borderline Personality
- Brief Reactive Psychotic Episode
- Insomnia
- Nightmares
- Panic/Agoraphobia
- Phobia
- Physiological Stress Response—Acute
- Posttraumatic Stress Disorder (PTSD)
- Pre-Deployment Stress
- Separation and Divorce
- Sexual Assault by Another Service Member
- Suicidal Ideation

SUGGESTIONS FOR PROCESSING THIS EXERCISE
WITH VETERANS/SERVICE MEMBERS

The "Healthy Ways to Handle Stress Fast" activity is designed for service members experiencing combat and operational stress reactions (COSRs). The best "treatments" for COSRs are simple stress-reduction strategies and staying active in a stable and structured routine. These approaches, especially when integrated, help limit the impact COSR symptoms have on the service member and bolster confidence in his/her abilities. Remember to set an expectation of rapid recovery for service members and not lead them to see themselves as patients. Follow-up can include reading assignments from Appendix A of *The Veterans and Active Duty Military Psychotherapy Treatment Planner*.

HEALTHY WAYS TO HANDLE STRESS FAST

This exercise has two parts. First is a list of ways to handle stress fast; the second part is about making sure we actually use those stress-management strategies by including them in a structured schedule for our daily routine (and having more structure is a stress reduction strategy in itself). When you're going through a combat and operational stress reaction, these will help you get through it and back to your usual self as quickly as you can. For the scheduling portion, please ask your chaplain or counselor to make seven copies of the daily schedule for you so that you can fill out one for your routine each day of the week.

1. *Stress management tools*: Basically, we'll divide these into different categories depending on whether they're activities that take more than one person or ones you can do solo and whether they're mainly physical or mainly mental. This handout lists some in each category, but you'll think of more that work well for you and add them to this list.

With Other People—Mainly Physical	Solo—Mainly Physical
Team sports	Stretching
Running	Running
Working out	Working out
	Sleep
	Hot shower

With Other People—Mainly Mental	Solo—Mainly Mental
Conversation	Reading
Watching a comedy	Writing in a journal
Games—cards, chess, etc.	Watching a comedy
Computer/video games	Computer/video games
	Listening to music
	Playing music
	Calling, emailing, or writing home
	Meditation
	Prayer

2. *Scheduling and structure*: Following is a sample page for your daily schedule. Please ask your chaplain or counselor to make enough copies to cover a week.

Be sure to bring this handout back to your next meeting with your counselor or chaplain, and be prepared to discuss your thoughts and feelings about the exercise.

Day/Date _____

Time	*Activity*	*Completed?*
0500 to 0530		
0530 to 0600		
0600 to 0630		
0630 to 0700		
0700 to 0730		
0730 to 0800		
0800 to 0830		
0830 to 0900		
0900 to 0930		
0930 to 1000		
1000 to 1030		
1030 to 1100		
1100 to 1130		
1130 to 1200		
1200 to 1230		

Time	Activity	Completed?
1230 to 1300		
1300 to 1330		
1330 to 1400		
1400 to 1430		
1430 to 1500		
1500 to 1530		
1530 to 1600		
1600 to 1630		
1630 to 1700		
1700 to 1730		
1730 to 1800		
1800 to 1830		
1830 to 1900		
1900 to 1930		
1930 to 2000		
2030 to 2100		
2100 to 2130		
2130 to 2200		
2200 to 2230		
2230 to 2300		
2300 to 2330		
2330 to 2400		
2400 to 0500		

COMMUNICATION AND CONFLICT MANAGEMENT SKILLS

GOALS OF THE EXERCISE

1. Eliminate verbal and physical confrontations with military peers and/or superiors.
2. Develop problem-solving and interpersonal skills to manage conflicts.
3. Develop an increased awareness of his/her role in conflicts.
4. Learn to recognize escalating behaviors that lead to conflicts.

ADDITIONAL PROBLEMS FOR WHICH THIS EXERCISE MAY BE USEFUL

- Adjustment to the Military Culture
- Anger Management and Domestic Violence
- Antisocial Behavior in the Military
- Borderline Personality
- Separation and Divorce

SUGGESTIONS FOR PROCESSING THIS EXERCISE WITH VETERANS/SERVICE MEMBERS

The "Communication and Conflict Management Skills" activity is designed for use with veterans/service members who lack adequate skills in these areas but are motivated to learn those skills and reduce conflicts with those around them in military, family, and social environments. This assignment fits extremely well into a treatment plan that is based on cognitive-behavioral therapy (CBT) or Cognitive Processing Therapy (CPT) and lends itself well to role-playing approaches in individual, couples, or group counseling. This can be valuable for veterans/service members who are in recovery from addictions and at risk for stress-related relapse, as relationship conflict is one of the most common stressors reported as leading to relapse. Follow-up or concurrent treatment activities can include bibliotherapy using one or more of the books listed for this issue in Appendix A of *The Veterans and Active Duty Military Psychotherapy Treatment Planner* and/or videotherapy using films suggested for the topics of "Communication and Conflict Resolution," "Divorce," "Intimate Relationships," "Marriage," and/or "Parent-Child Relationships" in *Rent Two Films and Let's Talk in the Morning*, 2nd ed., by John W. Hesley and Jan G. Hesley, also published by John Wiley & Sons.

COMMUNICATION AND CONFLICT MANAGEMENT SKILLS

Saying what you mean, clearly and respectfully to both others and yourself, is a skill that must be learned. So is listening to what others are trying to tell you. Effective communication takes two basic skills: (1) expressing yourself clearly, and (2) listening actively. In this exercise you will learn how to communicate more effectively, and how to teach these skills to others.

1. A good place to start is with communication styles and how they work. Here are four styles—we may use them all, but we each have a favored style we use most. As you read, please think about your communication habits and those of others in your life.

   a. *Aggressive.* Expressing yourself with little regard for others' rights, thoughts, or feelings. Aggressive communication can be abusive and judgmental. It may include name-calling, yelling, interrupting, sarcasm, ridicule, and hostile body language.

   b. *Passive-aggressive.* Not expressing yourself openly. Hinting; talking behind others' backs; sarcasm; constant complaining; expecting others to know what you think, feel, or want without telling them; refusing to talk even when others can see you're upset.

   c. *Passive.* Not expressing yourself in ways you fear might upset others, or possibly any way at all. Giving short, uninformative answers; agreeing with whatever others say.

   d. *Assertive.* Expressing your thoughts, feelings, and wishes clearly without ignoring those of others; being able to say "no" in a way that respects both others and yourself.

   Which of the styles described above best describes your style of communication? Please choose one and give some examples of how you use this style.

   _____

   _____

2. In your relationships with family members, friends, and coworkers, what happens most often when you disagree with someone or they disagree with you? What styles are used?

_____

_____

3. Think about the last time you disagreed with someone close to you. How did you handle the situation, and how did the other person? What styles were used? What was the result?

_____

_____

4. Now we'll look at specific techniques of effective communication and how to use them:

   a. *Avoid mind-reading.* Don't try to tell other people what they think and feel or what their reasons are for the things they do. No one likes it when others do this, and it often triggers arguments. Think of a time when someone did this to you. Describe that situation, how you felt, and how it affected your communication:

   _____

   _____

   b. *No name-calling.* When we're upset with others it is because of what they did or didn't do: in other words, their actions. Calling people names is not referring to their actions, it's labeling who and what they are—actions can be changed, but who we are we can't, so name-calling is really an attack on our identity. It's one of the surest ways to turn a discussion into a fight. Think about a time when someone called you names. Describe the situation, how you felt, and how it affected your communication:

   _____

   _____

   c. *No interrupting/No long speeches.* These two go together. When we cut others off or finish their sentences for them, the message they hear is, "What you have to say is not important enough for any more of my time." Also, when we finish people's sentences, we're often wrong about what they were going to say, and it can trigger a fight. Of course, for one person to let another talk uninterrupted, they both have to know that they'll also have a chance to speak. That's why long speeches cause problems. Think about a time when someone went on and on in a conversation, or kept interrupting you. Describe the situation, how you felt, and how it affected your communication:

   _____

   _____

   d. *Be specific.* When we say "You always _____" or "You never _____" we're wrong. Nobody is that consistent. If we tell others they always or never do things, they'll just think of the exceptions. They'll probably feel angry that we don't recognize those exceptions. This leads to a fight about the "always/never" statement, instead of a useful talk about changing behavior. Think about a time when someone did this to you; describe the situation, how you felt, and how it affected your communication:

_____

_____

e. *Talk about one thing at a time.* We may have many problems with a person, but if we bring them all up at once he/she will feel overwhelmed. Most of us want to get along with others and are willing to change some of our actions, but if we feel that there is no way to please the other person, it turns into a fight. When we start bringing up one issue after another, it is sometimes called "kitchen-sinking" because it seems as if we are throwing everything at them including the kitchen sink. Think about a time when someone "threw the kitchen sink" at you by piling issue upon issue. Describe the situation, how you felt, and how it affected your communication:

_____

_____

f. *Take responsibility for your own feelings and actions.* A near-guaranteed way to pick a fight is to blame someone for your own feelings or actions, by saying "You made me (mad, depressed, etc.)" or "You made me do_____." Other people can't make us do anything, unless they use physical force. They can't make us feel or think a certain way. Do you want to be blamed for someone else's actions and feelings? It works better to say things like "When you did (*action*), (*result*) happened, and I felt (*emotion*)." Think about the last time someone blamed you for their feelings or actions. Describe the situation, how you felt, and how it affected your communication:

_____

_____

g. *Respond to both the spoken and unspoken parts of the message.* As well as listening to other people's words, we need to respond to the emotions they express through facial expressions, body language, and tone of voice. It always helps if others see we are paying attention and trying to understand them. Think about a time someone acknowledged your feelings as well as your words. How did they let you know? How did you feel about it?

_____

_____

5. These techniques can seem awkward at first but will get easier with repetition. It helps to practice with important people in our lives. Part of this exercise is to talk about this with at least two important people in your life, practice these skills with

them, and talk about the results with your therapist and/or your therapy group. After practicing these communication techniques, what questions/challenges do you have about continued improvement of your communication skills?

_____

_____

_____

_____

Be sure to bring this handout back to your next therapy session, and be prepared to discuss your thoughts and feelings about the exercise.

UNDERSTANDING SOURCES OF CONFLICT

GOALS OF THE EXERCISE

1. Eliminate verbal and physical confrontations with military peers and/or superiors.
2. Develop problem-solving and interpersonal skills to manage conflicts.
3. Report elimination or decrease in disciplinary actions related to conflicts.
4. Develop an increased awareness of his/her role in conflicts.
5. Learn to recognize escalating behaviors that lead to conflicts.

ADDITIONAL PROBLEMS FOR WHICH THIS EXERCISE MAY BE USEFUL

- Adjustment to Military Culture
- Anger Management and Domestic Violence
- Antisocial Behavior in the Military
- Borderline Personality
- Separation and Divorce

SUGGESTIONS FOR PROCESSING THIS EXERCISE WITH VETERANS/SERVICE MEMBERS

The "Understanding Sources of Conflict" activity is designed to help the veteran/service member assess patterns in conflicts (e.g., topics of conflict, times conflicts are likely to happen, and with whom). It guides the veteran/service member in looking at initiation or maintenance of a conflict as something in which he/she has an active part, assisting him/her in taking active steps to resolve conflict in healthy ways. This assignment fits extremely well into a treatment plan that is based on cognitive-behavioral therapy (CBT) or Cognitive Processing Therapy (CPT) and lends itself well to role-playing approaches in individual, couple, or group counseling. This can be valuable for veterans/service members who are in recovery from addictions and at risk for stress-related relapse, as relationship conflict is one of the most common stressors reported as leading to relapse. Follow-up or concurrent treatment activities can include bibliotherapy using one or more of the books listed for this issue in Appendix A of *The Veterans and Active Duty Military Psychotherapy Treatment Planner* and/or videotherapy using relevant films suggested in *Rent Two Films and Let's Talk in the Morning*, 2nd ed., by John W. Hesley and Jan G. Hesley, also published by John Wiley & Sons.

UNDERSTANDING SOURCES OF CONFLICT

Conflict in any group of people is inevitable, whether it's a military unit, a family, or a civilian work team, and it can either weaken or strengthen that group. On one hand, resolving conflict in negative ways (e.g., ignoring, being physically or emotionally abusive, refusing to admit wrongs, blaming others, leaving) creates more problems and further isolates people from each other. On the other, resolving conflict in positive ways helps teamwork and relationships grow stronger. To manage conflict in a positive way, we have to look at our roles in starting, maintaining, and resolving conflicts, and be willing to change our behavior as well as asking others to change theirs. This exercise asks you to gather information about what conflict looks like in your life to help you find patterns you can correct and get better results.

1. For each conflict event in your life for the next two weeks, please write down the following:

    *   Date and time.
    *   Intensity of the conflict (1 = very low to 10 = very high).
    *   Situation.
    *   Who was present?
    *   Your actions during the conflict.
    *   The actions of the other person(s) involved.
    *   What did you want to have happen as the outcome of the conflict?
    *   What was the outcome?

    After two weeks, please review your conflict journal and answer the following questions:

2. What themes or patterns did you notice about the conflicts you recorded?

    _____

    _____

    _____

3. What times of the day were conflicts or arguments most likely to occur (e.g., upon waking, at breakfast, during the work day, bedtime, after work/school)?

    _____

    _____

4. If any conflict situations came up more than once, what were they?

_____

_____

5. What role(s) did you most often play in the conflicts you recorded (e.g., instigator, victim, peacemaker, rescuer, defender, etc.)?

_____

_____

6. If any of these conflicts ended with positive results, how were they different based on the factors we asked you to list in item 1? From those that ended badly, what was different about the situation, who was involved, what were they about, how did people behave, and so on?

_____

_____

_____

7. Do you tend to see arguments as right/wrong, win/lose, or as situations where the best result is a compromise everyone can live with? Either way, how do you think this view affects the conflicts in which you're involved?

_____

_____

8. What problems came up repeatedly and made it harder to resolve conflicts?

_____

_____

9. What do you feel needs to change to reduce negative conflict in your life?

_____

_____

10. Do you tend to get into conflicts with some members of your family more often than others? If so, why do you think this is?

_____

_____

11. Talk with someone you trust who usually gets along with people really well, and ask him or her about the ways they deal with conflict in their lives and get positive results. Record their answers here:

_____

_____

_____

_____

12. Write down one thing you can begin to work on in the next week to approach conflict in your unit, family, or workplace differently.

_____

_____

Be sure to bring this handout with you to your next therapy session, and be prepared to discuss your thoughts and feelings about the exercise.

CHALLENGING DEPRESSIVE ILLUSIONS

GOALS OF THE EXERCISE

1. Verbally identify, if possible, the source of depressed mood.
2. Alleviate depressed mood and return to previous level of effective functioning.
3. Develop healthy cognitive patterns and beliefs about self and the world that lead to alleviation of depression and help prevent relapse into depressive symptoms.
4. Identify and replace cognitive self-talk that is engaged to support depression.
5. Verbalize more hopeful and positive statements regarding self, others, and the future.

ADDITIONAL PROBLEMS FOR WHICH THIS EXERCISE MAY BE USEFUL

- Amputation, Loss of Mobility, Disfigurement
- Anxiety
- Bereavement Due to the Loss of a Comrade
- Borderline Personality
- Chronic Pain After Injury
- Homesickness/Loneliness
- Separation and Divorce
- Suicidal Ideation
- Survivor's Guilt

SUGGESTIONS FOR PROCESSING THIS EXERCISE WITH VETERANS/SERVICE MEMBERS

The "Challenging Depressive Illusions" activity teaches veterans/service members to reality-test depressive perceptions and correct those that are not accurate. This activity is oriented toward Cognitive-Behavioral Therapy (CBT) or Cognitive Processing Therapy (CPT). In addition to therapeutic homework, this activity is suitable for discussion and use in individual or group therapy sessions. Follow-up concurrent treatment can include bibliotherapy using books listed for this issue in Appendix A of *TheVeterans and Active Duty Military Psychotherapy Treatment Planner* and/or videotherapy using films suggested for "Emotional and Affective Disorders" in *Rent Two Films and Let's Talk in the Morning*, 2nd ed., by John W. Hesley and Jan G. Hesley, published by John Wiley & Sons.

CHALLENGING DEPRESSIVE ILLUSIONS

When we suffer from depression, our views of ourselves, other people, our situations, and our futures usually become systematically distorted in ways that feed into the depression, until we are living in a world of negative illusions instead of seeing the world as it really is. This exercise will help you learn to catch these illusions when they creep into your thinking and replace them with more accurate ways of seeing things.

There are several kinds of depressive illusions. Let's look at how they work, ask how you may see them in your life, and what more accurate kinds of beliefs we can replace them with.

1. *All or nothing thinking.* We see things as completely good or bad (usually bad when we're depressed) or perfect or awful—perfectionism fits into this kind of illusionary thinking. When we make mistakes we see ourselves as idiots; with the self-talk inside our minds, we are far meaner to ourselves than we would be to anyone else.

    One way I see this in my life:

    _____

    Corrective thought: Life is never all good or bad, nor are we or anything we do. Look for exceptions to this illusion and write one or two here:

    _____

2. *Predicting negative outcomes for uncertain situations.* We leap to conclusions about the future, usually in a negative way. We put definite and negative interpretations on events or actions that don't have clear meanings, such as thinking people are mad at us when they don't act happy. We don't check to see whether our interpretations are right before we accept them as true.

    One way I see this in my life:

    _____

    Corrective thought: The future is uncertain, and lots of things could happen. Let me focus my energy on what I can do to raise the chances of a good outcome. One action is:

    _____

3. *Emotional reasoning.* We assume that our emotions or suspicions reflect the way things really are: "If I feel it, it must be true."

One way I see this in my life:

_____

Corrective thought: When I'm upset, I know I can misinterpret things—the sky is probably not really falling; I need to get some feedback from a level-headed person I trust, namely:

_____

4. *Lots of "should" statements.* We guide our actions by what we think we should or shouldn't do, and beat ourselves up with guilt and shame whenever we fail to meet those standards (which are usually impossible). We may also do this to other people, getting angry and judgmental when they don't do what we think they should, even if we have no business demanding anything from them or we never told them what our expectations were.

    One way I see this in my life:

    _____

    Corrective thought: Says who? Is that "should" reasonable?

    _____

5. *Judgment and labeling.* We use negative outcomes or actions as a basis to judge ourselves and others instead of judging just the outcomes or actions. If we lose at something, we call ourselves losers; if another person fails at something, we see him or her as a failure.

    One way I see this in my life:

    _____

    Corrective thought: We all have many successes and many failures in our lives—to judge myself or anyone else on the basis of one success or failure is unreasonable and oversimplified. For the negative label I just listed, here's a piece of evidence that points to the opposite conclusion about myself or someone else:

    _____

6. *Taking things personally.* We see other people's actions as being aimed at us, and we feel responsible for things we can't control.

    One way I see this in my life:

    _____

    Corrective thought: Whatever other people choose to do is under their control, not mine, and is about them, not me.

7. Another strategy to correct distorted thinking is to check it out with someone you trust. When you're upset about a situation, talk with someone wise and trusted

who isn't emotionally involved. Tell them what happened—only what you actually saw and heard, not what you believe others were thinking or feeling. Ask this person what he or she thinks, and share your thoughts and feelings. Ask them if it seems as if you're making one of the mistakes listed above. Please try this and describe what happens:

_____

_____

_____

Be sure to bring this handout back to your next session with your therapist, and be prepared to discuss your thoughts and feelings about the exercise.

FROM ACCEPTANCE TO APPRECIATION

GOALS OF THE EXERCISE

1. Identify and replace cognitive self-talk that supports depression.
2. Use behavioral strategies to overcome depression.
3. Recognize and verbalize ways in which your situation has improved and elements in your life situation for which you are grateful.

ADDITIONAL PROBLEMS FOR WHICH THIS EXERCISE MAY BE USEFUL

- Amputation, Loss of Mobility, Disfigurement
- Anxiety
- Borderline Personality
- Chronic Pain after Injury
- Financial Difficulties
- Homesickness/Loneliness
- Separation and Divorce
- Suicidal Ideation

SUGGESTIONS FOR PROCESSING THIS EXERCISE WITH VETERANS/SERVICE MEMBERS

The "From Acceptance to Appreciation" activity is designed to help veterans/service members who have already achieved at least a moderate degree of acceptance of the challenges in their lives. The purpose of this activity is to help these veterans/service members make further progress to alleviate depression by appreciating the positive aspects of their life situations and by seeing ways in which their problems are less difficult than those of some other people. Follow-up or concurrent treatment activities can include encouragement to engage in volunteer work in community programs assisting others; bibliotherapy using one or more of the books listed for this issue in Appendix A of *The Veterans and Active Duty Military Psychotherapy Treatment Planner*; and/or videotherapy using films suggested for the topic "Emotional and Affective Disorders" in *Rent Two Films and Let's Talk in the Morning*, 2nd ed., by John W. Hesley and Jan G. Hesley, also published by John Wiley & Sons.

FROM ACCEPTANCE TO APPRECIATION

In working to overcome depression and other challenges in your life, you may have come to a point where you are able to clearly see the sources of your problems, the resources and methods you can use to cope with those problems, and to accept those facts as they are, rather than engaging in denial or wishful thinking. You may have reached an understanding of the meaning of acceptance as simply acknowledging the way things are and not as necessarily liking those realities, and as seeing that accepted reality as a starting point for change rather than as the way things will stay. This is a great deal of progress and insight, more than many people ever achieve. If you've reached this point you may have more awareness of your power to solve problems and attain goals and have greater hope than you had in the past, and thus have good reason to feel hope and optimism. However, at this point—one of insight, acceptance, and empowerment—happiness and satisfaction with life may still appear to be more hope than reality. The purpose of this exercise is to guide you in continuing your progress and finding greater happiness by seeing more of the positive aspects of your current situation in comparison to the past, in terms of the possibilities it offers, and by comparison to the problems some other people live with.

1. There's an old story about the nature of good and bad luck which you may have heard. In the story, a farmer's horse escapes from its stable and runs away.

   A neighbor felt bad for him and said, "I'm sorry your horse is gone—that was an unlucky event for you," to which the farmer replied, "Oh, I don't know, it might not be so bad."

   The following week the horse returned, and following it were three more horses in the prime of health. The farmer's neighbor congratulated him on this stroke of luck, but the farmer said, "I don't know, it might not be such good fortune—we'll see."

   The farmer's son really liked one of the new horses, so the farmer gave it to him, but when the son saddled the horse and set out for a ride, the horse threw him and he broke his leg. The neighbor shook his head and offered the farmer (and the farmer's son) consolation over this injury, but the farmer shrugged and said, "Well, it might not be such a bad thing."

The following week, the emperor sent officials to the village to draft all the young men into the army, but the farmer's son was excused because of his broken leg. Not long after, the village got word that all the young men that had been drafted had died in a battle.

The farmer's neighbor stopped jumping to conclusions about whether events were lucky or unlucky, seeing that the future is unknown and what seems like misfortune may turn out to be good luck and vice versa.

After reading this, what is an example from your life, or that of someone you know, of an event that seemed unlucky but turned out in time to be a blessing, or the other way around?

_____

_____

2. The message of this assignment is not that anyone's challenges and losses are not real and difficult; that would be insulting and also untrue. However, there's a reason for clichés like "a blessing in disguise" and "every cloud has a silver lining." One way this is shown is in the benefits we gain from the work our problems force us to do, such as better understanding of other people and ourselves, problem-solving skills, and confidence in our ability to cope with whatever life throws at us. Please list some benefits like this that you appreciate most:

_____

_____

3. Another result of experiencing trying situations is that it can "stretch your yardstick." By this we mean that everyone has a sort of mental yardstick they use to measure how good or bad something is by comparing events to others they've experienced. When we've gone through genuine crises, lesser problems don't cause us as much stress and anxiety as they would if we'd never dealt with serious problems. Please list a couple of events or situations that stretched your yardstick:

_____

_____

4. It is also true that regardless of what problems we have, we can almost always think of someone else whose troubles look worse to us, someone we wouldn't want to trade places with. For example, in a recent conversation with a veteran whose body is paralyzed from the chest down, he expressed gratitude that he has the use of his arms and hands, and mentioned another patient in the same VA hospital who is paralyzed from the neck down. Are there problems that you see others struggle with that you are grateful not to have? If so, can you provide some examples?

_____

_____

5. A good way to get a more rounded viewpoint on life is to find ways we can help other people coping with their own challenges. Doing good things for other people benefits us in many ways including lifting our moods, improving self-image, and relieving pain. But in relation to this exercise, we're focusing on two main benefits: the first is allowing us to see ways other people may be successfully overcoming their problems, and the second is giving us a chance to see that there are a lot of people in this world dealing with hardships of all kinds. What kind of volunteer work would you be interested in doing?

_____

_____

Once again, we want to say as clearly as we can that the message of this exercise is not to imply that your challenges, or anyone's, are not real, serious, and difficult, or to sound as if the work you're doing to overcome them is not tough and sometimes painful. But every situation looks better from some viewpoints than from others. Our goal is to help you look at your situation from some different angles, with the idea of sharing a tool you can use to avoid discouragement and depression and gain a better quality of life.

Be sure to bring this handout with you to your next therapy session, and be prepared to discuss your thoughts and feelings about this exercise.

DIFFERENT PEOPLE, DIFFERENT STRENGTHS

GOALS OF THE EXERCISE

1. Become more accepting of, and cooperative with, others from different cultural, racial, ethnic, and religious backgrounds.
2. Develop an appreciation for people that are dissimilar.
3. Actively seek out knowledge about different cultures, races, ethnic groups, and religions.
4. Develop a friendship with someone from a different background.

ADDITIONAL PROBLEMS FOR WHICH THIS EXERCISE MAY BE USEFUL

- Adjustment to Military Culture
- Antisocial Behavior in the Military
- Conflict with Comrades
- Social Discomfort
- Spiritual and Religious Issues

SUGGESTIONS FOR PROCESSING THIS EXERCISE WITH VETERANS/SERVICE MEMBERS

The "Different People, Different Strengths" activity is designed for work with veterans/ service members who exhibit discomfort, intolerance, or judgmental behavior toward others based on cultural, racial, ethnic, or religious characteristics. The goal of this activity is to heighten awareness that no two people are exactly alike, and that because their strengths and weaknesses are different, people with marked differences complement one another and can form a team that is better rounded and has more strengths and skills to call on than any one individual, or even a group of individuals who are all from similar backgrounds. Follow-up activities could include administration of the Myers-Briggs Type Indicator (MBTI) personality-type instrument, followed by group discussion, comparison of results, and a discussion of tasks for which various types have more or less aptitude; bibliotherapy using one or more of the books listed for this issue in Appendix A of *The Veterans and Active Duty Military Psychotherapy Treatment Planner*; and videotherapy using *The Waterdance*, *Powder*, and/or other films pertaining to issues of alienation and prejudice.

DIFFERENT PEOPLE, DIFFERENT STRENGTHS

It's a natural human tendency to feel cautious and uncomfortable around what we don't understand, and that includes people who belong to groups that we may not have much experience with—these groups can be cultural, racial, ethnic, religious, or national. For a person living in an environment where he or she doesn't encounter anyone from outside groups, this trait may never cause discomfort, but that's not what the military is like. When we entered the service, most of us found ourselves among people from many different backgrounds, more than we'd ever encountered before in our lives. And in the military, it's critical to develop trust and confidence in the people with whom we serve—not only because we live and work together and interact constantly, but because our lives may literally depend on them and vice versa.

If we feel discomfort with others who are different from us, the solution is to get to know them better so that they are no longer people we don't understand. An additional reason for us to learn as much as we can about each other is so that we can get a better understanding of our own strengths and weaknesses and those of the people with whom we serve. Then we can make the best use of everyone's abilities by giving each task to the person or people best suited to it. This exercise will guide you in exploring ways to get more comfortable with people who may initially seem strange, to understand them better, and to identify their strengths and what they can contribute to the mission of whatever organization you find yourself in with them.

1. Think of a person with whom you work, someone who is from a background very different from your own. In what ways are you and this person different from each other, and what parts of his or her background are least familiar to you?

    _____

    _____

2. What concerns do you have, if any, about serving beside this person? If there are important areas in which you don't know what to expect from him or her, or if you believe that this person is less knowledgeable and capable than you are, list them below.

    _____

    _____

3. In what areas do you feel confident that this person is as skilled and trustworthy as you are, or even more so? Are there situations where you would be glad he or she was there to help accomplish the mission, and if so what are they?

_____

_____

4. Now let's turn this around. Put yourself in the place of the person we've been thinking about, the one who is different from you. In what areas do you think he or she might not be sure what to expect from you, and in what other areas do you think he or she would have full confidence in you?

_____

_____

_____

5. As we get to know the people we serve or work beside, we tend to find that we differ from each other not only in the ways that are easy to spot—like race, ethnicity, or gender—but also in personality. We may be very different from people who look just like us and come from the same backgrounds we do. All this difference is good, not bad, for the effectiveness of the organization, and in the military that can mean it improves our chances of surviving and winning in combat. Each different background and each mix of personality traits creates a unique set of strengths and weaknesses. If a unit was made up of people who were all alike, it would be at risk, because they would all have the same blind spots—the same gaps in their knowledge, the same weaknesses in their skill sets. And because they had those same blind spots, they might not even realize it. In an organization with a mix of people, the group is less likely to have blind spots, because whatever is a weakness for one member is likely to be a strength for another. In fact, and ironically, the more glaring the qualities we see as other people's weaknesses, the more effective as teammates those people are likely to be for us and us for them. For example, some people have a great ability to carry out detailed instructions with great attention to detail; others are more adept at spotting patterns in situations and do better if they are given general instructions—such as what end result is needed—and left to figure out how to get it done on their own. There will be situations calling for each of these types, in which the other type would not do as well, so they balance each other. This is the kind of mix and balance that makes a military unit or other organization stronger. Looking back at your answers to questions 2, 3, and 4, what are some tasks that you would probably do better at than the other person you were thinking about?

_____

_____

6. What are some tasks that this other person would probably do better at than you would?

_____

_____

7. Finally, consider this—are the differences you looked at in questions 5 and 6 based on culture, race, ethnicity, or religion, or are they based more on personality? If the same differences might exist between you and someone with the same background as you, they're most likely a matter of personality and not the more obvious factors.

_____

_____

Be sure to bring this handout with you to your next therapy session, and be prepared to discuss your thoughts and feelings about the exercise.

WE'RE MORE ALIKE THAN WE LOOK: SEEING PAST THE SURFACE

GOALS OF THE EXERCISE

1. Become more accepting of, and cooperative with, others from different cultural, racial, ethnic, and religious backgrounds.
2. Base judgments about others on their actions instead of their cultural, racial, ethnic, and religious backgrounds.
3. Demonstrate trust and respect toward others who come from different backgrounds, and show that trust in military duty assignments as well as social contacts.
4. Verbalize more realistic cognitive reframes of beliefs about people from other cultures, races, ethnicities, and religions.
5. Identify, challenge, and replace negative biases about individuals from different cultural, racial, ethnic, and religious backgrounds.

ADDITIONAL PROBLEMS FOR WHICH THIS EXERCISE MAY BE USEFUL

- Adjustment to Military Culture
- Antisocial Behavior in the Military
- Conflict with Comrades
- Social Discomfort
- Spiritual and Religious Issues

SUGGESTIONS FOR PROCESSING THIS EXERCISE WITH VETERANS/SERVICE MEMBERS

The "We're More Alike than We Look: Seeing Past the Surface" activity complements the "Different People, Different Strengths" activity. It is designed for veterans/service members who exhibit discomfort, intolerance, or judgmental behavior toward others based on culture, race, ethnicity, or religion. This activity highlights the common qualities and needs present in all human beings, and encourages the veteran/service member to get to know people from other backgrounds and find common interests and qualities. Follow-up could include bibliotherapy using books listed for this issue in Appendix A of *The Veterans and Active Duty Military Psychotherapy Treatment Planner* and videotherapy with films such as *The Waterdance*, *Powder*, and/or other films presenting issues of alienation and prejudice.

WE'RE MORE ALIKE THAN WE LOOK: SEEING PAST THE SURFACE

We start forming impressions about everyone around us at first sight; part of that process is comparing them to what is familiar and what we see as being like us or different from us. Naturally, the first things we may notice about other people is whether they look like us or different in obvious and conspicuous ways like physical appearance, speech, off-duty dress, and religious practices. Based on those differences, we often gravitate toward people who seem more familiar—we are more confident that we'll know how to talk with them, what to expect, and so on. However, if we choose to find out more about the people who seem strange to us, we often find that beneath the obvious differences we have much in common, and we can form enjoyable, and sometimes, lifelong friendships and learn valuable information that increases our understanding of people and life in general. In a military unit in particular, it's vital to take that step and get to know the people with whom we serve because our lives may depend on their competence and character. In that respect, it is good that in combat units in particular we live in close quarters—it is difficult *not* to get to know someone. This exercise will guide you in getting better acquainted and finding common interests and qualities with people who don't look like you on the surface.

1. Take a few moments and think about what makes you unique. What are the most important things that make you who you are? Give a thumbnail description of yourself, the way you think a member of your family or your best friend would describe you:

    _____

    _____

2. Most often, people's answers to the question above relate to their personalities and interests. A person might describe himself or herself as outgoing or shy, liking dancing or movies, athletic or mechanically inclined—more than about things like culture, race, and so on. Of course, this varies. If we're surrounded by people who resemble us in those surface factors, we focus on the inside things, and if we're around people who are externally different, then we are more conscious of those differences. The military tends to throw us into a mix of people from many different backgrounds, and this can make us more conscious of those surface differences

than we were before we put on the uniform. Did you experience this when you entered the service?

3. What basic human needs and goals do you share with people from different backgrounds with whom you serve or work?

4. Most of us find that the military itself is a separate culture in many ways, one very different from the ones we grew up in and from mainstream society. A couple of the key differences are that you are among a tiny minority of Americans—only around 1%—who volunteer to serve in uniform. Consistent with that fact is that the military is a culture where the good of the group is a higher value than individualism, while mainstream American society is one of the most individualistic cultures that has ever existed. Has this been your experience, and if so, what other differences have you found between the culture of the military (and within it, of your own branch and specialty) and the one you knew before you joined?

5. If you and the other people in your unit have gotten used to living within the military's culture, you may find that in some ways you feel out of place in civilian society; the longer you've served and the more intense the experiences you've shared, the more likely this is to be true. So as time passes, you and the other people with whom you serve come more and more to belong to the same culture, no matter how different the ones you started from. Think about a person in your unit from a very different background from your own. Are there meaningful ways in which you have more in common with that person than with, for example, people you went to high school with? If so, what are they?

6. What other things do you think you might have in common with people in your unit who came to the military from different backgrounds that might serve as a basis for friendships with some of those people?

_____

_____

_____

7.   Finally, consider how having more friendships, including some with people you
     probably would never have gotten to know if you hadn't gone into the military,
     could make your life more interesting. What benefits do you think you might gain,
     and what is one step you can take this week to get to know a potential friend from
     a different background better?

_____

_____

_____

Be sure to bring this handout with you to your next therapy session, and be prepared
to discuss your thoughts and feelings about the exercise.

MONEY MANAGEMENT SKILLS

GOALS OF THE EXERCISE

1. Establish a realistic budget that effectively balances income and expenses.
2. Consistently apply effective money management techniques.
3. Keep weekly spreadsheets of all expenditures and income.
4. Explore means of decreasing debt and expenditures.
5. Explore means of increasing level of income.

ADDITIONAL PROBLEMS FOR WHICH THIS EXERCISE MAY BE USEFUL

- Anxiety
- Depression
- Parenting Problems Related to Deployment
- Post-Deployment Reintegration Problems
- Separation and Divorce

SUGGESTIONS FOR PROCESSING THIS EXERCISE WITH VETERANS/SERVICE MEMBERS

The "Money Management Skills" activity is designed for work with veterans/service members experiencing stress, relationship challenges, and/or legal problems related to poor financial management. This activity takes a skill-building approach aimed at helping the veteran/service member gain control of his/her personal finances and achieve financial stability. Follow-up activities could include bibliotherapy using one or more of the books listed for this issue in Appendix A of *The Veterans and Active Duty Military Psychotherapy Treatment Planner*.

MONEY MANAGEMENT SKILLS

We all have to manage money, but many of us have little or no training or knowledge in this when we enter adult life. It doesn't help that entire industries are built on exploiting people's lack of that knowledge, or that our society is oriented toward getting what we want right away. Luckily, the skills aren't complicated and the information is available if you know where to look. This exercise will guide you in getting started on taking control of this important part of your life.

1. The first thing to look at is budgeting. This means having your income and your expenses in balance, or having more income than expenses. Many people believe the key to financial peace is more income, but it's often more about reducing expenses. What did you learn about this growing up, either from your family, at school, or from other sources?

    _____

    _____

2. A budget is just a matter of simple arithmetic. A spreadsheet program like Microsoft Excel can be handy to track it but isn't necessary. To create one, we need to capture as complete a picture as we can of our income, and of where and how we spend it. Sources of income include whatever we are paid for work plus what we get from any other source. What sources of income do you have right now?

    _____

    _____

3. The other half of the budget is what we spend. Our expenses vary widely depending on our situations—usually there are some we can reduce or eliminate, and others we can't. What kinds of expenses do you have right now?

    _____

    _____

4. For many, it's hard to find complete answers. When we add up our incomes and subtract our expenses, we find we should have more left than we do. This means we're spending money in ways that we're forgetting. We need a complete picture of our finances. We can do two things to get a clearer picture of where our money goes: first, pay for things with a checking account or debit card instead of cash,

because that gives us a record of all those expenses. Notice we said debit card, not credit card. They look the same, but every use of a credit card is a loan, often at a high interest rate. A debit card is tied to a checking account and purchases with the card are immediately deducted from that account—no borrowing, no increase of debt. Some people keep credit cards for emergencies or pay the balances in full every month; used those ways, credit cards don't make the financial situation worse. To use checking or either kind of card, we need to know how to manage them. You can probably find classes on this fairly easily—a bank or credit union may offer a free class, or you may be able to find one through an agency on or off base. If you need training on how to use these tools and a budget, where will you look for it?

_____

5. The second thing we can do is track our cash spending by getting receipts when we pay cash for anything, or writing down what we spent if a receipt is unavailable (from a vending machine, for example). If you get a notebook and record your daily cash spending and then add it up, you may be surprised at the end of the month by how much you spend on small items—vending machine snacks, fast food, and so on. You may decide it's worth the bother to pack a lunch instead of grabbing a burger combo (and probably healthier, too!). What kinds of small items do you think you spend a fair amount of cash on and how much do you estimate that is?

_____

_____

6. There may not be much you can do to increase your income, but depending on your situation and income, you may qualify for food stamps or other financial assistance. This can make a big difference, paying for hundreds of dollars in groceries every month. Please talk with your therapist about how you can look into this. Also, you or someone in your family may qualify for grants or loans for education. Is anyone in your family taking college classes? _____ You may also be able to add a part-time job to your schedule. If this is an option, where could you get a job, what would it pay, and how much time would you put into it every month? A look at the numbers will tell you whether this option is worth pursuing.

_____

_____

7. Look at other ways to cut costs: Try buying generic products instead of brand names, buying simpler versions of products like electronics, and spending less on holiday gifts. What other ways can you think of to spend less without sacrificing too much quality of life?

_____

_____

8. There's no way to cover this topic in one exercise, but there's one more area to look at as a start—managing credit. We touched on it with credit cards, but it also includes "rent to own" deals on furniture, car loans, home loans, and so on. Anytime you're thinking of buying something on credit, there are two main questions: do I need/want this too badly to wait while I save up to get it, and how much will this really cost? Part of a class on managing money may be figuring out what a loan will really cost to pay off, and you may be surprised; the rule of thumb is to get the lowest interest rate (fixed, not variable) and shortest payoff time you can. What loans do you have or are you considering? Can you save by skipping, refinancing, or speeding up the final payoff on any of them?

_____

_____

Be sure to bring this handout with you to your next therapy session, and be prepared to discuss your thoughts and feelings about the exercise.

SPENDING AS A DRUG

GOALS OF THE EXERCISE

1. Regain sense of self-worth independent of material goods owned.
2. Gain insight into dynamics related to impulsive and irresponsible spending (e.g., family modeling, low self-esteem), leading to termination of poor money management.
3. Identify personal traits that make irresponsible spending possible.
4. Use cognitive-behavioral methods in controlling spending.

ADDITIONAL PROBLEMS FOR WHICH THIS EXERCISE MAY BE USEFUL

- Anxiety
- Depression
- Parenting Problems Related to Deployment
- Post-Deployment Reintegration Problems
- Separation and Divorce
- Substance Abuse/Dependence

SUGGESTIONS FOR PROCESSING THIS EXERCISE WITH VETERANS/SERVICE MEMBERS

The "Spending as a Drug" activity is designed for work with veterans/service members who are experiencing legal, disciplinary, and/or marital problems due to compulsive spending. This may also be useful with veterans/service members who are newly clean and sober from substance dependence or abuse, due to the risk of switching their addictive patterns from ingesting substances to reckless spending or gambling. Follow-up activities could include bibliotherapy using one or more of the books listed for this issue in Appendix A of *The Veterans and Active Duty Military Psychotherapy Treatment Planner*.

SPENDING AS A DRUG

What is a drug? In one sense, it's a substance that people eat, drink, smoke, inject, and so on, and that affects their moods, senses, or thinking. However, we can also think of a drug as anything else that has that effect, that changes how we feel or think, especially if it does so quickly and with little or no effort on our part. If it makes us feel better by reducing pain and discomfort or by increasing pleasure, we're more likely to get in the habit of turning to it. If it becomes something we rely on to feel okay, we can get psychologically dependent on it. And if it has long-term costs that eventually outweigh the short-term benefit, but we feel we can't give it up because we need that short-term benefit—at that point it has become an addiction. There are a lot of people who never take so much as an aspirin who are still seriously addicted to things that can wreck their lives. Those addictions can include gambling, unsafe sex, overexercising, workaholism, and of course, overspending. Spending money can make us feel happy, excited, and content; if it's at a level we can afford and doesn't create problems for us, it isn't a problem. But when we spend at a level we can't afford it can quickly get out of control. The purpose of this activity is to guide you in deciding for yourself whether you use spending as a drug, and if you do and want to change that, what you can do about it. We'll start by looking for addictive spending patterns. An easy way to do this is by looking at the same factors used to diagnose chemical dependence, except that we'll translate them into terms of spending. There are seven of them and here they are translated from chemical to financial:

1. *Tolerance*: With chemicals, this means that it takes a larger dose to get the same effect, or that the same dose gives less effect. For example, many people find that the first time they try alcohol, one drink leaves their heads spinning; for a person who's never tried caffeine before, one cup of coffee is super-energizing. With more use, tolerance develops and it may take several drinks or a pot of coffee to get the same effect. If you use spending to lift your mood or distract you from problems, does it take spending more to improve your mood by the same amount as was once the case? If so, can you give an example?

   _____

   _____

2. *Withdrawal*: When a person is dependent on a chemical, he or she may experience unpleasant physical consequences after suddenly stopping its use. The most familiar examples for most people are probably the migraine-like headache a constant coffee

drinker gets if he or she goes too long with no caffeine, or the craving a smoker feels after a few hours (or less) without any tobacco. In terms of spending, this would take the form of a restless feeling and a growing urge to go somewhere (or get online) and buy something. Have you experienced this? If you have, briefly describe that situation:

_____

_____

3. *Loss of control*: With substances this is defined as taking it in larger amounts or over a longer period than was intended. To turn to alcohol again as an example of this, we might see someone who stops at a bar planning to have one drink and chat with friends for 20 minutes, and ends up getting drunk and passing out or staying for hours. It's easy to guess what loss of control of spending looks like: spending more than we planned or can afford. Do examples come to mind in your life? If so, describe one:

_____

_____

4. *Failed attempts to quit or cut back*: Most who are addicted, whether to chemicals or behaviors, know they have problems and have tried again and again to control those problems. A lot of problem drinkers have tried making different rules about drinking, or tried to quit, but found that those strategies didn't work for long. In terms of spending, this might take the form of failed budgets, staying away from places where spending has caused problems, avoiding buying certain kinds of things, only buying them at certain times, and so on. As with other symptoms, give an example if this has happened to you:

_____

_____

5. *Time spent*: With alcohol or another chemical, this means spending a lot of time getting the drug, using it, or recovering from the effects of use. Time thinking and talking about use counts, too. With spending, we wouldn't count all work time as spent getting the "substance," but we'd count work time that went to earn money spent compulsively. Do you find that spending absorbs a lot of your time, attention, and energy? If so, give an example here:

_____

_____

6. *Other important activities sacrificed*: Giving up or reducing an important activity because it conflicts with drinking is a sign of a drinking problem. If you find yourself sacrificing an important social, work, or recreational activity due to spending, please describe that here:

_____

_____

7. *Continued use despite resulting problems*: A person who has emphysema and keeps smoking has a nicotine addiction; a drinker who doesn't quit despite liver damage has a drinking problem. Have you had problems due to reckless spending but continued anyway? If so, briefly describe that problem and how it has affected your life:

_____

_____

One incident of any of these doesn't make it a pattern. Still, with a chemical, if three or more of the seven are patterns for a year or longer, it qualifies as an addiction. If you do have a spending addiction, you don't have to fight it alone. Talk with your therapist about the resources available.

Be sure to bring this handout with you to your next therapy session, and be prepared to discuss your thoughts and feelings about the exercise.

MAKING THE BEST OF WHEREVER I AM

GOALS OF THE EXERCISE

1. Reduce thoughts of home, family, and friends to a level that is not distressing.
2. Increase comfort and contentment with the new environment.
3. Reduce feelings of homesickness/loneliness.
4. Increase social contacts and new friendships.
5. Maintain contact with family and friends back home, while recognizing the importance of limits.

ADDITIONAL PROBLEMS FOR WHICH THIS EXERCISE MAY BE USEFUL

- Adjustment to Military Culture
- Anxiety
- Borderline Personality
- Depression
- Separation and Divorce

SUGGESTIONS FOR PROCESSING THIS EXERCISE WITH SERVICE MEMBERS

The "Making the Best of Wherever I Am" activity is intended for use with service members who are having difficulty adjusting to a new place, particularly those who have recently entered military service or are far from home for the first time. It takes a primarily cognitive-behavioral approach of identifying and testing unrealistically negative thoughts about the service member's situation, followed by offering guidance in seeking activities that will improve contentment and quality of life. Follow-up can include reading assignments from the books listed for this issue in Appendix A of *The Veterans and Active Duty Military Psychotherapy Treatment Planner*, and/or video-therapy using films suggested for the topic of "Friends and Support Systems" in *Rent Two Films and Let's Talk in the Morning*, 2nd ed., by John W. Hesley and Jan G. Hesley, also published by John Wiley & Sons, and reporting back to the therapist and treatment group, after 3 to 4 weeks about the results of the actions suggested in this exercise.

MAKING THE BEST OF WHEREVER I AM

Homesickness and loneliness can seem overwhelming the first time we experience them, and this is a challenge for many people in the military. It's true that leaving a familiar place and the people you know there can be highly stressful. However, there are several strategies for adapting to a new place that will help you get through this phase of your move as quickly as possible and save you some heartache.

1. What we tell ourselves about our situations shapes our perception of those situations and our feelings about them. We aren't suggesting that you deny reality or try to live in a fantasy, but often the very same facts can take on totally different meanings depending on how they're expressed. There's an old cartoon that shows a man and a cat shipwrecked on a small island with nothing in sight but the beach and some palm trees.

    The man is thinking, "Nothing but fish to eat, these stupid trees and sand everywhere ... this is horrible!"

    Meanwhile, the cat is thinking, "Fish every day, the biggest litter box in the world, and these great scratching posts ... I'm in heaven!"

    Making the best of a new place means finding ways to think more like the cat and less like the man.

2. Let's start by looking at a few of the thoughts a person can focus on in a new place, both negative and positive. Please read the examples, then write in some of your own:

Negative Thoughts

I'm with a bunch of people I don't know.

I can't do the things I like to do for fun here.

_____

_____

_____

_____

Positive Thoughts

This is a chance to make some new friends.

I can find some new things here that I couldn't do where I was before.

_____

_____

_____

_____

3. A psychologist named Mihaly Csikszentmihalyi researched what makes people happy and described what he learned in the book *Flow*. To boil it down, he found that we are happiest when we're doing things that interest us enough that we lose ourselves in them—when we lose track of time and aren't thinking about anything except the activity while we're engaged in it. The people who are the happiest are those who spend the most time in whatever activities interest them in this way. What are some of your favorite "flow" activities?

    _____

    _____

4. You may not be able to do those things where you are now. So the trick is to figure out what it is about those activities that makes them so enjoyable for you, then look for other activities that share those qualities. Some examples of qualities that make different activities fun for different people could include: physical action (individual or team sports, dancing); deep concentration (games like chess, working difficult puzzles); attention to detail (building models, painting, writing); producing something you're proud of (building computers, working on cars); and so on. The hobbies you like may be individual pursuits or things you do with a group; fast-paced or painstaking; long-lasting or things you can finish quickly. Think of other characteristics that different hobbies may have. What qualities do the activities you like have in common? Once you have some listed, you can look for activities with the same qualities, and the odds are you'll like them, too.

    _____

    _____

5. As for friendships: if you're feeling isolated, it's a good idea to find some new people to spend time with. The information from item 4 is a good place to start, because one of the best ways to find people you may like is to go do things you enjoy and meet other people who are doing the same things for fun. Maybe you can find a group to join, like a running club or a sports team. If you're a musician you might find (or start) a band; if there are classes available in subjects you're interested in, they'll be interesting and a good place to make friends. Sometimes being stationed far from family is an opportunity to put more of our off-duty time into taking classes than we could if we were back at home. What activities might be good sources of new friendships or ways to achieve goals for you?

    _____

    _____

6. If you're in a new place where there are things to see and do that you couldn't do where you were before, it can be rewarding to explore and learn about it. You could get yourself a camera and enjoy some tourism, learn to dive if you're near the ocean, go mountain climbing, or see cities you'd probably never have gotten to see otherwise. What are a few things you can do in this new place that you couldn't do where you were before?

_____

_____

7. There's nothing wrong with staying in touch with friends and family you're temporarily away from, as long as you don't try to rely on those long-distance ties to meet all your needs for interesting things to do. What can you do to stay in regular contact with people that you miss?

_____

_____

Be sure to bring this handout back to your next therapy session, and be prepared to discuss your thoughts and feelings about the exercise.

THIS, TOO, SHALL PASS: TAKING IT ONE DAY AT A TIME

GOALS OF THE EXERCISE

1. Reduce thoughts of home, family, and friends to a level that is not distressing.
2. Increase comfort and contentment with the new environment.
3. Reduce feelings of homesickness/loneliness.
4. Increase social contacts and new friendships.
5. Maintain contact with family and friends back home, while recognizing the importance of limits.

ADDITIONAL PROBLEMS FOR WHICH THIS EXERCISE MAY BE USEFUL

- Adjustment to Military Culture
- Anxiety
- Borderline Personality
- Depression
- Separation and Divorce

SUGGESTIONS FOR PROCESSING THIS EXERCISE WITH SERVICE MEMBERS

The "This, Too, Shall Pass: Taking it One Day at a Time" activity is intended for use with service members who are having difficulty adjusting to a new place and perseverating on how long this situation will last, such as junior service members just beginning their first unaccompanied tours overseas. The strategy of this activity is to address the service member's self-perception as unable to tolerate a situation he or she finds unpleasant for long by guiding him or her in recalling past experiences of unhappy situations that the service member got through, and noting that although at the time it may have also seemed that those experiences would last forever, in retrospect they probably don't seem as long, and the unpleasant feelings they caused are only a memory. Follow-up can include reading assignments from the books listed for this issue in Appendix A of *The Veterans and Active Duty Military Psychotherapy Treatment Planner*, videotherapy using films suggested in *Rent Two Films and Let's Talk in the Morning*, 2nd ed., by John W. Hesley and Jan G. Hesley, also published by John Wiley & Sons, and reporting back to the therapist and treatment group, after 3 to 4 weeks, about the results of actions suggested in this exercise.

THIS, TOO, SHALL PASS: TAKING IT ONE DAY AT A TIME

It can be tough to find ourselves in situations that we dislike and that will last a while. It's natural for our thoughts to focus on how long we'll be in those situations. A person's thoughts can end up getting distorted, exaggerating the long-term nature of the situation along with its unpleasantness and underestimating his or her ability to have a reasonable level of happiness or peace of mind in the meantime. This exercise will help you examine your own thoughts about your situation and make sure you're seeing it realistically and not causing yourself avoidable unhappiness.

1. One of the best examples we can think of is dealing with a physical injury that takes a significant amount of time to heal. Have you ever had a broken arm or leg, for example? If not, perhaps another painful injury or illness on a similar scale. If you're like most people, when you first got hurt, the intense pain captured your attention pretty thoroughly, and you may have had the thought that you couldn't stand it, along with feeling discouraged about how long it would take to heal—to get the cast off, and so on. The same thing can apply with situations that cause emotional pain instead of the physical kind, like the breakup of a relationship or the loss of someone close to you. If you've had an experience like this, with a pain that seemed as if it would last forever, what was it?

_____

_____

Another part of that situation, if you're like most of us, is that when you were past it, it didn't seem as long as it had starting out; also, although you have the memory of the pain, you aren't feeling it anymore. This can be a very helpful way to think about unpleasant situations, remembering those we've overcome when we're in the midst of new ones. What thought(s) have you been having about your situation, and what more balanced thought(s) could you think instead, based on your own experiences and what you've learned about yourself and about your ability to get through tough situations? Use this space to record some examples from your own experiences.

Negative Thoughts	Positive Thoughts
This hurts so much I can't stand it.	This hurts the way (past experience) did, and that was tough, but I got through it.
This is going to take forever to get through!	This is like (past situation) that lasted a long time, but when it was done it didn't seem as long as when it started out.
_____	_____
_____	_____
_____	_____

2. Have you ever heard the old joke about how to eat an elephant? The answer is "one bite at a time." It may not be the funniest one-liner, but it makes a good point. We can handle anything big, whether it's an unaccompanied tour far from home, getting a college degree, or recovering from a serious injury or illness, if we divide it into small, more manageable pieces instead of thinking about the whole task or time ahead. That's why this exercise has the title it does, and if you've ever heard much about Alcoholics Anonymous and other 12-Step recovery programs, you may have heard the slogans "This Too Shall Pass" and "One Day at a Time" as reminders that every situation eventually passes, and that all a person has to do to stay sober is not drink today, whatever day it is. When it's a matter of time until something is over, it can help to break it up into months and/or weeks, keep track of their passage, and give ourselves some kind of small rewards as we put each of those smaller pieces behind us. How can you use this principle in your present situation?

_____

_____

3. It can help to remember another old saying: "a watched pot never boils." The meaning of this, of course, is that even though there's no difference in how long a pot of water takes to boil whether you're looking at it or not, it can seem to take forever if all you're doing is watching it and waiting. It goes much faster if you occupy your attention with other things in the meantime. What are some ways you can keep yourself busy instead of watching the calendar and feeling depressed that it isn't over yet?

   a. First, what familiar hobbies or other recreational activities can you enjoy where you are?

_____

_____

_____

b. Second, what new activities are available where you are that you haven't tried, but think might be fun?

_____

_____

_____

_____

In this exercise, we've looked at things to do when you're stuck for an extended time in a place where you'd rather not be. We've looked at correcting negative distortions in thoughts about it, ways to break the time up into smaller chunks to have more sense of its passing, and finding enjoyable ways to spend as much of it as possible. Keep thinking about these and adding to your lists, and you'll be better equipped for this kind of experience.

Be sure to bring this handout back to your next therapy session, and be prepared to discuss your thoughts and feelings about the exercise.

WHY CAN'T I SLEEP?

GOALS OF THE EXERCISE

1. Practice healthy sleep hygiene behaviors.
2. Use thought-stopping techniques to counter intrusive and disruptive thoughts.
3. Take psychotropic medications as prescribed.
4. Restore restful sleep.

ADDITIONAL PROBLEMS FOR WHICH THIS EXERCISE MAY BE USEFUL

- Anxiety
- Combat Operational Stress Reaction
- Depression
- Mild Traumatic Brain Injury
- Nightmares
- Physiological Stress Response—Acute
- Posttraumatic Stress Disorder (PTSD)
- Shift Work Sleep Disorder

SUGGESTIONS FOR PROCESSING THIS EXERCISE WITH VETERANS/SERVICE MEMBERS

The "Why Can't I Sleep?" activity is designed for use with veterans/service members whose insomnia is having a significant negative effective on their work/duty performance and/or quality of life. Establishing an effective sleep routine is essential to overcoming the sleep disturbances that are so common for many service members and veterans. Help the veteran/service member establish a routine that can be easily and reliably implemented. Keep in mind that this should also be applicable for the service member that is currently deployed. This exercise may also provide further insight into any additional problems that the veteran/service member may be dealing with such as nightmares, anxiety, or depression. Follow-up for this activity can include assignment of the other activity in this section, "Sleep Management"; referral for a sleep study to determine whether the veteran/service member suffers from sleep apnea if this has not been checked; coordination with his/her primary care physician (after obtaining necessary release of information) to ensure that insomnia is being considered in the veteran's/service member's general medical care; and bibliotherapy using books listed in Appendix A of *The Veterans and Active Duty Military Psychotherapy Treatment Planner*.

WHY CAN'T I SLEEP?

Insomnia is a common problem in active duty military personnel and veterans dealing with mental or emotional problems related to military service. Some people believe that they need only four or five hours of sleep each night, when in fact most people need somewhere from seven to nine hours of sleep. Also, some people believe that they do not sleep at all. However, when observed by others they find out that they actually do get some sleep during the night, but it is typically interrupted/fragmented sleep. There are techniques you can use to reduce or eliminate your insomnia to gain more control over your sleep and improve your quality of life. This exercise will provide you with information on a number of techniques you can use.

1. The following strategies to counteract insomnia have worked for many people, and some of them are likely to be useful for you. Please read through this list and put a checkmark next to those that you are willing to use as part of your everyday routine.

    _____ Engage in daily vigorous exercise, finishing no later than six hours before you go to bed.

    _____ If you take prescribed medications, take them exactly as instructed. Tell your doctor you have insomnia so he or she can make sure none of your medications are keeping you awake; your doctor may also prescribe a sleep medication or recommend an over-the-counter medication, supplement, herbal tea, etc. NOTE: IT IS ALSO IMPORTANT TO TALK WITH YOUR DOCTOR ABOUT ANY OVER-THE-COUNTER MEDICATIONS YOU TAKE OR ARE CONSIDERING TAKING, both to make sure they aren't causing your insomnia and to be sure they don't have the potential for negative interactions with prescribed medications. You can also get information on medication interactions from your nearest Poison Control Center.

    _____ Avoid caffeine for at least four hours before bedtime.

    _____ Avoid nicotine for at least one hour before bedtime.

    _____ Avoid large or spicy meals for at least three hours before bedtime.

    _____ Avoid drinking alcohol to get to sleep—it may work for a short time, but once your body has processed the alcohol out of your bloodstream, your brain will become more active than usual in a rebound effect. Daily drinking for effect presents a high risk of alcohol dependence and other health problems anyway.

_____ Avoid emotional conversations with loved ones prior to bedtime. If a loved one brings up a subject that may lead to an emotional conversation, set a time the following day to talk about it. This is a good idea with emotional subjects anyway.

_____ Avoid activities that are mentally stimulating for at least an hour before bed—action films, high-energy music, etc. Reading something that you're interested in but does not cause strong feelings may help you get to sleep, or may make it harder. Try each way and check the results, then keep doing whichever is effective for you.

_____ Take a hot bath/shower 30 minutes before going to bed.

_____ Try wearing socks when you go to bed—this sounds strange, but it works for many people; having warm feet seems to make it easier to fall asleep.

_____ Go to bed and wake up at the same times each day (including weekends). Avoid taking naps during the day, even when you're tired.

_____ Don't watch television or play video games in bed.

_____ Write down disturbing thoughts, thoughts of things you need to do the next day, and any other thoughts that interfere with relaxation. This enables you to put them aside to deal with at an appropriate time. Keep a pen and paper near your bed to write down thoughts of this kind that come to you after you lie down without having to get up.

_____ Practice deep breathing 15 minutes before bedtime.

_____ If possible, make sure your bedroom is dark and quiet when you go to bed. If it helps you get to sleep to have relaxing music playing, make an exception for that.

_____ If you are familiar with the exercise titled "Safe and Peaceful Place Meditation," practice it to get to sleep. If you haven't seen it, your therapist can give you the exercise to learn how it works.

2. If you haven't done so, ask your primary care doctor to help you get to a specialist to check for a condition called sleep apnea. If you have sleep apnea, it disrupts your breathing up to several times per hour while you sleep, and each time this happens you become partly awake until your breathing is back to normal. Even though people with sleep apnea don't usually remember these interruptions and may think they slept through the night, apnea results in not feeling rested even after a full night's sleep. If you do have sleep apnea, there are effective treatments you can discuss with your doctor. Do you know whether you have sleep apnea? _____
If not, when will you talk with your primary care physician about insomnia and possible sleep apnea?_____

3. Keep a journal, and use it to write about any situations that are stressful and interfere with your sleep (don't do this writing during the last two hours before bedtime.) Many people find that putting their thoughts and emotions down on paper helps in letting go of negative emotions and getting rid of tension. As part of your journal, make a point each day of writing about stressful events that day, which methods you know to help you get to sleep, how you slept the night before, and any dreams you remember. This can give you useful information when you want to see how your sleep management program is working over time. Do you already keep a journal? _____ If so, have you been keeping track of sleep, dreams, and/or how rested you feel?_____

If you haven't kept a journal before, when in your daily routine will you take time to write about your day in a journal?_____

Be sure to bring this handout back to your next session with your therapist, and be prepared to discuss your thoughts and feelings about the exercise, including which of these methods you are trying out and which have either worked or failed to work so far.

SLEEP MANAGEMENT

GOALS OF THE EXERCISE

1. Eliminate nighttime sleep interruptions.
2. Eliminate mental and physical side effects caused by sleep deprivation.
3. Verbalize an understanding that poor sleep hygiene habits contribute to insomnia.
4. Take psychotropic medications as prescribed.
5. Restore restful sleep.

ADDITIONAL PROBLEMS FOR WHICH THIS EXERCISE MAY BE USEFUL

- Anxiety
- Combat Operational Stress Reaction
- Depression
- Mild Traumatic Brain Injury
- Nightmares
- Physiological Stress Response–Acute
- Posttraumatic Stress Disorder (PTSD)
- Shift Work Sleep Disorder

SUGGESTIONS FOR PROCESSING THIS EXERCISE WITH VETERANS/SERVICE MEMBERS

The "Sleep Management" activity is designed for use with veterans/service members suffering from insomnia as a follow-up to the other activity in this section, "Why Can't I Sleep?" This activity builds on "Why Can't I Sleep?" which introduced the concept of sleep hygiene and a number of techniques to reduce or eliminate sleep disturbances. This activity will guide the veteran/service member in developing a more comprehensive and proactive sleep management plan. Follow-up for this activity could include a referral for a sleep study to determine whether the veteran/service member suffers from sleep apnea if this has not been checked, coordination with his/her primary care physician (after obtaining necessary release of information) to ensure that insomnia is being considered in the veteran's/service member's general medical care, and bibliotherapy using books listed in Appendix A of *The Veterans and Active Duty Military Psychotherapy Treatment Planner*.

SLEEP MANAGEMENT

Insomnia is frustrating and stressful. It interferes with being able to perform at your best during the day and can weaken your immune system, making you more vulnerable to common illnesses such as colds and influenza. You may have already done the exercise titled "Why Can't I Sleep?" This exercise will guide you in creating a more effective sleep management program for yourself and provide you with information on a number of techniques you can use.

1. Have you worked through the "Why Can't I Sleep?" exercise, and if so, which of the techniques in that exercise are working most effectively for you?

    _____

    _____

    _____

2. If there are still some techniques from "Why Can't I Sleep?" How many are there and when will you try some or all of them?

    _____

    _____

    For some people it works to try each new one for a week, keeping track of the results in a journal it recommends you use for that purpose.

3. The goal of this exercise is to take the strategies that work for you and combine them in a plan to manage your sleep as effectively as you can. Most people don't think about this, but we normally have management plans, even if we don't call them by that name, for other important things in our lives. For example, if you almost always eat three meals each day, at about the same times each day, that's a basic nutrition management plan—more so if you have particular kinds of food at different meals or on different days. In a similar way, we use management plans to pay bills, clean our homes, go to classes, and do homework if we're in school.

4. The easiest way to see these plans can be on a chart or grid that matches actions or other events with the times and places where they happen. Depending on the kind of plan, the chart may cover any time period from a day to several years. For a sleep management plan, we'll use a chart that covers one day, since it works best to follow the same sleep management routine every day, including weekends.

5. Following is a sample sleep management chart filled in with actions that work for some people—please ask your therapist for blank copies to fill in with your own plan. When you've done that, start following it, and keep talking about it with your therapist in your future sessions.

Time	Action or Event	How Long
05:30	Wake up—write notes on how I slept and any dreams I remember	5 min.
05:35	Personal hygiene—brush teeth, shave, etc.	20 min.
05:55	Dress in PT gear	5 min.
06:00	Go running/work out at gym	45 min.
06:45	Shower, get dressed for the day	30 min.
07:15	Breakfast	30 min.
07:45	Go to work—normal work day routine/weekend day activities	4 hrs.
11:45	Go to lunch	1 hr.
12:45	Back to work/weekend day activities—no caffeine from 15:00 on	4 hrs.
16:45	Leave work/break in weekend day—evening meal	1 hr.
17:45	Evening activities—social, recreational, educational, chores, etc. No nicotine from 18:30 on; avoid watching TV or playing video games in bed	3 hrs.
20:45	Prep for sleep—no more mentally/emotionally stimulating activity. Write in journal, personal hygiene, take meds, etc.—possibly try a new sleep management technique I haven't tried before	45 min.
21:30	Lights out—use meditation, visualization, etc. that I've found work for me to get to sleep	8 hrs.

ADAPTING TO A BRAIN INJURY

GOALS OF THE EXERCISE

1. Identify common symptoms of mild traumatic brain injury.
2. Reduce behavioral symptoms of mild traumatic brain injury.
3. Decrease memory, attention, and concentration deficits through adaptive strategies.
4. Reduce the level of daily distress caused by mild traumatic brain injury.

ADDITIONAL PROBLEMS FOR WHICH THIS EXERCISE MAY BE USEFUL

- Anxiety
- Attention and Concentration Deficits
- Chronic Pain after Injury
- Depression
- Financial Difficulties
- Posttraumatic Stress Disorder (PTSD)

SUGGESTIONS FOR PROCESSING THIS EXERCISE
WITH VETERANS/SERVICE MEMBERS

The "Adapting to a Brain Injury" exercise allows the veterans/service members to identify common symptoms resulting from mild traumatic brain injury (MTBI), and then to find ways to compensate for those symptoms for however long they last. This is important, given that many of the symptoms of MTBI are vague and overlap with many psychiatric conditions. In addition to assisting the clinician with treatment recommendations, it can also alleviate much of the veteran's/service member's anxiety and confusion about the diagnosis. This exercise also provides assistance to the veteran/service member in coping with two of the more common and concerning symptoms of MTBI, memory and attention/concentration problems. Follow-up for this exercise could include reporting back to the therapist/therapy group on actions related to this assignment and their outcomes, as well as bibliotherapy using books suggested in Appendix A of *The Veterans and Active Duty Military Psychotherapy Treatment Planner* and/or videotherapy using films on the topic of "Chronic Illness and Disabilities" recommended in *Rent Two Films and Let's Talk in the Morning*, 2nd ed., by John W. Hesley and Jan G. Hesley, also published by John Wiley & Sons.

ADAPTING TO A BRAIN INJURY

Mild traumatic brain injury (MTBI), or what is sometimes called a concussion, is a relatively common occurrence in the general population with slightly higher rates in military personnel. This exercise will help you identify some of the more common symptoms of MTBI. It will also teach you a few strategies on how to lessen the impact of two of the more common symptoms of MTBI, memory and attention/concentration problems. It is important to keep in mind that for most people the symptoms of MTBI generally disappear three to six months after the injury, with very few people having symptoms one year after the injury.

1. Please circle any of these different symptoms of mild traumatic brain injury that you are currently experiencing.

• Fatigue • Headaches • Blurred vision • Memory loss • Poor attention and concentration

• Sleep problems • Dizziness • Lack of coordination • Irritability • Easily angered • Anxiety

• Sadness • Seizures • Nausea • Changes in smells • Slowed thinking • Getting lost or confused

• Sensitivity to light and sounds • Loss of initiative • Work and/or relationship problems

---

2. Using the format below, develop a set of daily to-do lists, one for each day of the week, to help you remember the important things you need to get done on that day.

Day of the week: _____

Activity/Task #1	Time to be completed	Outcome
Activity/Task #2	Time to be completed	Outcome
Activity/Task #3	Time to be completed	Outcome
Activity/Task #4	Time to be completed	Outcome
Activity/Task #5	Time to be completed	Outcome

3. Please list three activities that have become difficult for you since your injury due to lapses in attention and concentration. Once you've done that, break the desired time you wish to spend engaging in these activities into 15-minute segments. For example, if you need to spend an hour reading a book or manual for an upcoming exam, break the reading assignment into four 15-minute segments, and check off each 15-minute segment once you finish it. In between, try switching to different activities or just taking a few minutes to relax; you may need to set a time to return to that activity or another one. It helps to have an inexpensive sports-type wristwatch with an alarm you can set.

#1:

Activity _____

Amount of time to spend in activity

_____ minutes _____ hours

15-minute segments

_____ (15 minutes)   _____ (15 minutes)   _____ (15 minutes)   _____ (15 minutes)

_____ (15 minutes)   _____ (15 minutes)   _____ (15 minutes)   _____ (15 minutes)

#2:

Activity _____

Amount of time to spend in activity

_____ minutes _____ hours

15-minute segments

_____ (15 minutes)   _____ (15 minutes)   _____ (15 minutes)   _____ (15 minutes)

_____ (15 minutes)   _____ (15 minutes)   _____ (15 minutes)   _____ (15 minutes)

#3:

Activity _____

Amount of time to spend in activity

_____ minutes _____ hours

15-minute segments

_____ (15 minutes)   _____ (15 minutes)   _____ (15 minutes)   _____ (15 minutes)

_____ (15 minutes)   _____ (15 minutes)   _____ (15 minutes)   _____ (15 minutes)

Be sure to bring this handout back to each session with your therapist and discuss with him or her about which parts of this exercise have worked the best for you and which parts haven't worked, and also about any other coping methods you've started using to adapt to your injury.

HELPING MY FAMILY AND FRIENDS HELP ME

GOALS OF THE EXERCISE

1. Decrease memory, attention, and concentration deficits through adaptive strategies.
2. Reduce the level of daily distress caused by mild traumatic brain injury.
3. Reduce behavioral symptoms of mild traumatic brain injury.
4. Attend and participate in a family session.

ADDITIONAL PROBLEMS FOR WHICH THIS EXERCISE MAY BE USEFUL

- Anxiety
- Attention and Concentration Deficits
- Chronic Pain after Injury
- Depression
- Financial Difficulties
- Posttraumatic Stress Disorder (PTSD)

SUGGESTIONS FOR PROCESSING THIS EXERCISE WITH VETERANS/SERVICE MEMBERS

The "Helping My Family and Friends Help Me" exercise seeks to enlist the aid of the family and friends of a veteran/service member who has suffered a mild traumatic brain injury (MTBI) in routines designed to help him/her with activities of daily living and any recuperative/therapeutic activities in progress. The first step is brainstorming with the veteran/service member to think of ways that people close to him/her could provide this kind of help. Then plan a family/group counseling session with them to explain the effects of the MTBI and how they can help. Finally, ask them for that help. Alternately, depending on the insight of the veteran/service member about the approach most likely to be effective, this type of conversation can take place with each of the people involved one at a time—either one-on-one with the veteran/service member or jointly with the therapist. Follow-up for this exercise could include reporting back to the therapist/ therapy group on actions related to this assignment and their outcomes, as well as bibliotherapy using books suggested in Appendix A of *The Veterans and Active Duty Military Psychotherapy Treatment Planner* and/or videotherapy using films on the topic of "Chronic Illness and Disabilities" recommended in *Rent Two Films and Let's Talk in the Morning*, 2nd ed., by John W. Hesley and Jan G. Hesley, also published by John Wiley & Sons.

HELPING MY FAMILY AND FRIENDS HELP ME

A mild traumatic brain injury (MTBI), also called a concussion, can cause some problems in general functioning in any of our lives. However, we don't have to try to solve these problems alone. This exercise will guide you in finding ways that other people in your life can help you adapt, and then planning how you can ask them for that help.

It is important to keep in mind that for most people the symptoms of MTBI generally disappear three to six months after the injury with very few people having symptoms one year later. So part of the information to present to family members and friends is that you are unlikely to need whatever assistance you're asking them to give you for very long.

You may be uncomfortable with this idea because you're determined to handle this yourself, or because it's hard for you to ask people for things in general. It's good to have the drive to take charge of your life situation—it will help you along the way—but there's nothing wrong with letting other people give you a hand, either. Think of it this way: If you could help them in a similar way and they needed that help for a while, would you want them to let you know, and would you want to help them out? The answer is probably yes, and they probably feel the same way about you. Think of it as another way to put the Golden Rule into action and treat others in the same way you want them to treat you.

1. If you've already gone through the exercise titled "Adapting to a Brain Injury," you've identified symptoms of your MTBI that you've been experiencing. If you haven't done that exercise, you can make a list now as the first step in this exercise. Please circle any of the following symptoms you're experiencing, and check off the areas where they affect your life:

Symptoms	Relationship/ Family Life	Work/ School	Social Life	Recreation/ Hobbies	General Health
Fatigue					
Headaches					
Blurred vision					

Symptoms	Relationship/ Family Life	Work/ School	Social Life	Recreation/ Hobbies	General Health
Nausea					
Dizziness					
Poor coordination					
Sensitivity to light or sounds					
Changes in smells or tastes					
Sleep problems					
Seizures					
Slowed thinking					
Problems with memory					
Getting lost or confused					
Poor focus and concentration					
Loss of initiative					
Sadness					
Anxiety					
Irritability					
Being easily angered					

2. Now that you've captured that information, please think of the people around you who could help you—maybe by calling you and reminding you of something or giving you some encouragement—in each of the activities or parts of your lives in which you're affected, and how they could help you with the problems affecting you in that part of your life.

Area of Life	People	How They Could Help	How to Ask Them to Help You Out
Relationship/ Family Life			
Work/School			
Social Life			
Recreation/Hobbies			
General Health			

3.   Step three is to carry out this plan and keep talking with your therapist about how it's working. Keep this up for however long it takes for these symptoms to improve to the point where you no longer need these people's assistance.

Be sure to bring this handout back to each session with your therapist and discuss with him or her about how it's working out and any areas you want to change or improve.

WHAT ARE MY DREAMS TELLING ME?
KEEPING A DREAM JOURNAL

GOALS OF THE EXERCISE

1. Create a coherent story to confusing dreams.
2. Immediately process emotional content through writing.
3. Fall back to sleep after distressing and/or strange dreams.

ADDITIONAL PROBLEMS FOR WHICH THIS EXERCISE MAY BE USEFUL

- Anxiety
- Bereavement Due to the Loss of a Comrade
- Depression
- Insomnia
- Panic/Agoraphobia
- Posttraumatic Stress Disorder (PTSD)
- Pre-Deployment Stress
- Sexual Assault by Another Service Member
- Suicidal Ideation
- Survivor's Guilt

SUGGESTIONS FOR PROCESSING THIS EXERCISE
WITH VETERAN/SERVICE MEMBER

The "What Are My Dreams Telling Me?" activity is for veterans/service members experiencing unpleasant or confusing dreams that interfere with their sleep or quality of life. It guides the veteran/service member in keeping a dream journal to bring to therapy sessions. Often the most helpful thing we can do is help identify possible meanings of dreams through Socratic questioning or help the veteran/service member brainstorm possible meanings. Follow-up could include bibliotherapy using books listed in Appendix A of *The Veterans and Active Duty Military Psychotherapy Treatment Planner* and/or videotherapy using films suggested for "Inspiration" in *Rent Two Films and Let's Talk in the Morning*, 2nd ed., by John W. Hesley and Jan G. Hesley, published by John Wiley & Sons.

WHAT ARE MY DREAMS TELLING ME?
KEEPING A DREAM JOURNAL

Dreams can be very confusing. All of us have, at one time or another, sat up in bed wondering what the dreams we just had meant. Dreams can seem illogical, nonsensical, and downright weird. Not only that, our dreams can sometimes become frightening, depressing, horrifying, or otherwise distressing, and can negatively impact our mood and behavior the following day. Sometimes they also leave us unable to get back to sleep due to the emotions and/or strangeness of the content. This exercise will help you make sense of those confusing dreams, help you handle the emotions caused by the dreams, and get back to sleep as soon as possible.

1. Get a notebook to use as a dream journal and keep the notebook and a pen by your bed. When you wake up from a distressing dream, immediately write down as much as you can remember about it. It doesn't matter if the information doesn't make sense or is strange. It's important to do this right away, because after even five minutes some details that might be important will be fading from your memory.

2. Once you've written down what you can remember about the dream, use the feelings below to describe how you feel and write as much as you can about how the dream affected each of these feelings in your dream journal.

    a. Afraid (fearful, scared, panicky)

    b. Sad (tearful, grieving, sorrowful)

    c. Confused (upset, doubtful, perplexed, curious, puzzled)

    d. Helpless (alone, paralyzed, vulnerable)

    e. Angry (enraged, irritated, annoyed)

    f. Ashamed (guilty, embarrassed)

    g. Happy (satisfied, glad, grateful, triumphant)

    h. Peaceful (calm, content)

    i. Other emotions

3. For a dream that didn't have a clear ending, or had an ending that left you feeling bad, think of an ending that would make sense and leave you with positive emotions. Write your ending in your dream journal after you write about the feelings the dream caused.

4. Before you try to get back to sleep, visualize your new ending for the dream—like a movie in your mind's eye. Do this twice before going back to sleep.

5. The next day, read over the entry(ies) in your sleep journal and write down any ideas that come to mind about what the different parts of the dream might stand for. Don't worry if it seems weird or silly, just let your imagination go with this part. It may help to know that some psychologists think that in many dreams everything represents a different part of the life of the person having the dream— his or her options, desires, past actions, impulses, and so on. Your therapist may be able to help you figure this out, although there are no universal rules about what dreams mean. You might see books that say certain things appearing in a dream always have the same meaning, but that's not true. The meaning of anything in your dream depends on the unique mixture of your past life experiences, your personality, your present situation, and your plans, hopes, and worries about the future.

6. If you have a nightmare or unpleasant dream that you keep having over and over, it may be related to an important situation in your life. Sometimes you can find the connection by thinking about any real-life situations that cause you to feel the same emotions as the ones the dream does. There's a two-step process for dealing with this situation:

    a. First, try the "write a new ending" method described above in items 3 and 4. If this works, it solves the problem of this dream.

    b. If this doesn't work, look again at any life situations that make you feel the same way as the dream does, and think about whatever you are doing or plan to do to resolve that situation. Each night before you go to sleep, spend 5 to 10 minutes thinking about this plan and see whether your dreams change. If not, keep thinking about whether the dream is connected to any other situation in your life—past, present, or future.

Be sure to bring this handout and your sleep journal back to your next session with your therapist, and be prepared to discuss your thoughts and feelings about the exercise.

AVOIDING AND COPING WITH NIGHTMARES

GOALS OF THE EXERCISE

1. Eliminate distressing dreams.
2. Eliminate anxiety about falling asleep.
3. Restore consolidated and uninterrupted sleep.

ADDITIONAL PROBLEMS FOR WHICH THIS EXERCISE MAY BE USEFUL

- Anxiety
- Bereavement Due to the Loss of a Comrade
- Depression
- Insomnia
- Panic/Agoraphobia
- Phobia
- Physiological Stress Response—Acute
- Posttraumatic Stress Disorder (PTSD)
- Pre-Deployment Stress
- Separation and Divorce
- Sexual Assault by Another Service Member
- Spiritual and Religious Issues
- Suicidal Ideation
- Survivor's Guilt

SUGGESTIONS FOR PROCESSING THIS EXERCISE WITH VETERANS/SERVICE MEMBERS

The "Avoiding and Coping with Nightmares" activity is an alternative to the "What Are My Dreams Telling Me?" activity. Providing relief from nightmares for the veteran/service member is essential for treating traumatic stress disorders and restoring sleep. Assist the veteran/service member in choosing a nightmare and changing the content of the nightmare to something that is less distressing. The veteran/service member may want to choose the most distressing dream for the first trial, but encourage him/her to choose a nightmare that is more manageable until he/she has some success with the technique. It is also important to review relaxation and breathing techniques with the veteran/service member as this technique can be stressful.

AVOIDING AND COPING WITH NIGHTMARES

Nightmares can be a way for the mind to process and adjust to experiences in the first few days and weeks following a traumatic event. In order to process the negative emotions associated with a trauma the mind replays the event again and again to understand and make sense of it. This process happens when you are awake and when you are asleep. However, when you sleep your thoughts and dreams tend to take on a life of their own. They can develop into an ongoing loop and replay over and over again like a scratched record, and this can make it difficult or impossible for you to get to sleep or get a good night's rest. If this is going on the dreams are no longer useful to you. This exercise will help you break this loop and regain control over your nights.

1. First, make yourself comfortable by using relaxation and breathing exercises:

   a. *Diaphragmatic breathing*—Breathe slowly and deeply from the diaphragm. You can tell when you're doing this correctly because your stomach will rise when you inhale rather than just your chest. Do this for five minutes.

   b. *Progressive muscle relaxation*—Starting with one foot and lower leg, tense the muscles in that part of your body, hold them tensed for about ten seconds, then relax them completely and move on to the next muscle group. If you start with your left foot, the sequence would be: left foot and calf; right foot and calf; left thigh; right thigh; left hand and forearm; right hand and forearm; left upper arm; right upper arm; buttocks and lower torso; mid- and upper torso and shoulders; neck; jaw and face.

   c. *Pleasant visual imagery*—If you've learned the "Safe and Peaceful Place" meditation exercise, this is a good time to use it. If not, just think of the most pleasant, peaceful, and relaxing place you can, and spend five minutes picturing it in your mind's eye.

2. Next, select a nightmare that rates about a "50" on the distress scale below.

   No distress: 0

   Low distress: 25

   Moderate distress: 50

   High distress: 75

   Most extreme distress possible: 100 (panic attacks, crying, etc.)

3. Change the nightmare by "rewriting" it—any way you wish to create an alternate version of the dream that is less disturbing or not disturbing at all. (Don't run the nightmare in its distressing form through your mind while doing this.) Briefly describe the dream you have created here:

_____

_____

_____

_____

4. Rehearse this new dream in your mind twice daily for 20 minutes each time until the original nightmare disappears. Please document the times you rehearse the new dream here:

Monday	Rehearsal #1_____	Rehearsal #2_____
Tuesday	Rehearsal #1_____	Rehearsal #2_____
Wednesday	Rehearsal #1_____	Rehearsal #2_____
Thursday	Rehearsal #1_____	Rehearsal #2_____
Friday	Rehearsal #1_____	Rehearsal #2_____
Saturday	Rehearsal #1_____	Rehearsal #2_____
Sunday	Rehearsal #1_____	Rehearsal #2_____

5. Now repeat this process, except with a more disturbing dream. Again, rewrite it without dwelling on the unpleasant original form, and then document your version here:

_____

_____

_____

_____

6. Again, rehearse this new dream in your mind twice daily for 20 minutes each time until the original nightmare disappears. Please document the times you rehearse the new dream here:

Monday	Rehearsal #1_____	Rehearsal #2_____
Tuesday	Rehearsal #1_____	Rehearsal #2_____
Wednesday	Rehearsal #1_____	Rehearsal #2_____
Thursday	Rehearsal #1_____	Rehearsal #2_____
Friday	Rehearsal #1_____	Rehearsal #2_____
Saturday	Rehearsal #1_____	Rehearsal #2_____
Sunday	Rehearsal #1_____	Rehearsal #2_____

7.   Repeat the process for any other dreams you want to get rid of.

   Be sure to bring this handout back to your next session with your therapist, and be prepared to discuss your thoughts and feelings about the exercise.

NEAR-TERM AND LONG-TERM EFFECTS OF OPIOID DEPENDENCE AND WITHDRAWAL

GOALS OF THE EXERCISE

1. Withdraw from mood-altering substance(s), stabilize physically and emotionally, and then establish a supportive recovery plan.
2. List and discuss the negative emotions that were caused or exacerbated by substance dependence.
3. Establish and maintain total abstinence while increasing knowledge of the disease and the process of recovery.
4. Learn and use coping strategies to manage urges to relapse into chemical use.

ADDITIONAL PROBLEMS FOR WHICH THIS EXERCISE MAY BE USEFUL

*   Amputation, Loss of Mobility, Disfigurement
*   Anxiety
*   Chronic Pain after Injury
*   Depression
*   Substance Abuse/Dependence

SUGGESTIONS FOR PROCESSING THIS EXERCISE WITH VETERANS/SERVICE MEMBERS

The "Near-Term and Long-Term Effects of Opioid Dependence and Withdrawal" activity is intended for use with veterans/service members who have become dependent on opioid drugs and are now newly clean and sober or working to achieve that state. The approach of this activity is primarily psychoeducational, seeking to educate the veteran/service member about the effects of this category of drugs and the typical things people experience while going through withdrawal. Follow-up can include reading assignments from books listed for this issue in Appendix A of *The Veterans and Active Duty Military Psychotherapy Treatment Planner*, and/or videotherapy using films suggested for the topic of "Substance Abuse" in *Rent Two Films and Let's Talk in the Morning*, 2nd ed., by John W. Hesley and Jan G. Hesley, also published by John Wiley & Sons.

NEAR-TERM AND LONG-TERM EFFECTS OF OPIOID DEPENDENCE AND WITHDRAWAL

Being dependent on a drug or experiencing withdrawal is rough physically, mentally, and emotionally. Nothing can change that, but for reducing unpleasantness, knowledge is power. This exercise will give you information that can lower your levels of stress and anxiety by explaining what the normal and common parts of this experience are.

1. We'll start with the effects of the drug dependence itself, both near-term and long-term. With any kind of drug, people use it for the effect it causes. With opioid drugs that effect is relief of pain and discomfort, physically and emotionally. This family of drugs, which includes opium, morphine, heroin, methadone, Demerol, codeine, OxyContin, Hydrocodone, and others, can be swallowed in pill form, smoked, sniffed, absorbed via skin patch, or injected. They can cause drowsiness, constricted "pinpoint" pupils, confusion, and apathy. In overdose, they can cause nausea and vomiting, unconsciousness, convulsions, coma, and death. As a side effect, unrelated to the effects for which users take opioids, they often cause relaxation of the muscles; drying up of the sinuses, mouth, and throat; and constipation. Which of these symptoms, if any, have you experienced after using an opioid drug?

    _____

    _____

2. Two other critical long-term effects of opioids are the development of tolerance and withdrawal. Tolerance means that it takes more of the drug to get the same effect, or that if a person uses the same amount it has less effect with repeated use. This is similar to the experience many people have with other drugs like alcohol or caffeine—the first time they try those substances, the effects are powerful, but over time it may take a six-pack to get the same effect that one beer gave at first or a pot of coffee to match the effects of the first cup. With opioids, the effect is due to the fact that they are chemically similar to natural substances in the brain called endorphins—the word endorphin means "endogenous (made in the body) morphine." Endorphins work a lot like opioids, and the body uses them to cope with severe injury or physical stress—they're the source of the "runner's high" you may hear about from long-distance runners. The problem—and the reason tolerance

happens—is that the body is always trying to keep its chemistry in balance, and the similarity of opioids to endorphins leads the brain to think it has a surplus and should make less. So over time, the levels of endorphins drop drastically. Have you developed some tolerance? Please describe how the effect has changed over time for you:

_____

_____

3. With repeated use of a drug over time, withdrawal develops. When a person whose body chemistry has adapted to the opioid stops using it, the balance the body has achieved with the opioid is thrown off again, like a person leaning into a stiff wind when the wind suddenly stops. And since natural production of endorphins has been lowered, it leaves a person worse off than before he or she first used the drug. Withdrawal symptoms for any drug will usually be a rebound causing effects that are the opposite of the drug's effects. What are the short-term withdrawal symptoms for opioids? Let's take a look:

Opioid Effects	Withdrawal Effects
Relief of physical pain and discomfort	More sensitivity to pain and discomfort
Relaxed or elevated mood	Depression and anxiety
Relaxation of muscles	Stiffness and cramps
Drying of sinuses, mouth, throat	Runny nose
Constipation	Diarrhea

Please describe any withdrawal symptoms you've experienced:

_____

_____

4. Many people who have been dependent on opioids find another aspect of withdrawal hard to deal with. Long after there are no traces of the drug left in their bodies, they are still experiencing some after effects. These can include difficulty concentrating and thinking clearly; problems with memory; increased anxiety, depression, and irritability; mood swings; emotional numbness, or overreaction to things; trouble with sleep; and trouble with physical coordination. This is called Post-Acute Withdrawal (PAW). It can really scare people. Some of these things may still be happening weeks or months after the last use of the drug, and it's natural for a person in this situation to fear PAW will be permanent. If you've been clean long enough that the drug has completely left your system, are you experiencing any of these PAW effects? Which ones?

_____

_____

5.   Again, there's a bright spot—PAW is not permanent. It happens because even after the drug is gone, the body is trying to restore its chemical balance, and that takes time. It can take more than a year for PAW to completely disappear—but it will keep getting better as time passes. The best way to cope is to watch as the symptoms diminish and recognize your progress. You can also increase your comfort level by doing things that cause your brain to release more endorphins. Those activities fall into three main categories. The first is sustained cardiovascular exercise, like running or swimming; the second is engaging in "adrenaline rush" activities like riding roller coasters, skydiving, or rappelling; and the third is laughing hard. So if you know someone who always makes you laugh, spending more time with that person can improve your quality of life. Who would that be for you?

_____

_____

Be sure to bring this handout back to your next therapy session, and be prepared to discuss your thoughts and feelings about the exercise.

SAFE AND HEALTHY ALTERNATIVES: WAYS TO COPE WITH PAIN AND ANXIETY WITHOUT DRUGS

GOALS OF THE EXERCISE

1. Learn and implement pain management techniques as an alternative to coping through opioid use.
2. List and discuss the negative emotions that were caused or exacerbated by substance dependence.
3. Establish and maintain total abstinence while increasing knowledge of the disease and the process of recovery.
4. Learn and implement personal coping strategies to manage urges to lapse back into chemical use.

ADDITIONAL PROBLEMS FOR WHICH THIS EXERCISE MAY BE USEFUL

- Amputation, Loss of Mobility, Disfigurement
- Anxiety
- Chronic Pain after Injury
- Depression
- Substance Abuse/Dependence

SUGGESTIONS FOR PROCESSING THIS EXERCISE WITH VETERANS/SERVICE MEMBERS

The "Safe and Healthy Alternatives: Ways to Cope with Pain and Anxiety Without Drugs" activity is intended for use with veterans/service members who are newly clean and sober and are experiencing the effects of opioid withdrawal (i.e., heightened physical discomfort, anxiety, depression). This activity is primarily cognitive-behavioral, offering the veteran/service member ways to relieve emotional distress without drugs. Follow-up can include reading assignments from books listed for this issue in Appendix A of *The Veterans and Active Duty Military Psychotherapy Treatment Planner*, and/or video-therapy using films suggested for "Emotional and Affective Disorders" and "Chronic Illness and Disabilities" in *Rent Two Films and Let's Talk in the Morning*, 2nd ed., by John W. Hesley and Jan G. Hesley, published by John Wiley & Sons.

SAFE AND HEALTHY ALTERNATIVES: WAYS TO COPE WITH PAIN AND ANXIETY WITHOUT DRUGS

Many people begin using opioid drugs to manage chronic pain, physical or emotional. Sometimes those drugs are prescribed, and in other situations they may be self-medicating with street drugs. Regardless of how and why a person's opioid use started, he or she may need to stop using these drugs but still need to manage physical pain, anxiety, or depression. This situation can feel like a trap, a choice between addiction or suffering. It doesn't have to be that way, though. There are ways to cope with pain and anxiety without drugs. This exercise will introduce you to some methods you may be able to use to manage physical or emotional pain without chemicals.

1. The first step is to look at how the drug works. The opioids—opium, morphine, heroin, methadone, Demerol, codeine, OxyContin, Hydrocodone, and others—have an effect on the brain by imitating natural chemicals called endorphins. The brain uses endorphins to help us cope with physical and emotional pain. If opioids work because they chemically reproduce the effects of endorphins in the brain, doesn't it make sense that raising your endorphin levels could take the place of opioid use? What are some ways you know to increase your endorphin levels? Have you found any ways to relieve your pain without drugs?

    _____

    _____

2. It turns out that there are natural ways to raise endorphin levels. The first is sometimes called a "runner's high"—long-distance runners sometimes feel renewed energy, relief from pain, and a strong sense of well-being, happiness, and pleasure after they've been running for a while. Other forms of sustained cardiovascular exercise, like cycling and swimming, can also cause this. What kinds of cardiovascular exercise could you do to boost your endorphin levels?

    _____

    _____

3. The second way to boost endorphins is to trick the brain into thinking it's facing a life-or-death crisis—such as participating in activities that involve danger (but

managed or simulated danger)—like skydiving, riding high-intensity roller-coasters, or watching horror movies. People often talk about getting an adrenaline rush with experiences like these, and there is a boost of adrenaline, the "get ready for action, fight, or flight" chemical, during the activity itself, but it's followed by a wave of endorphin effects immediately afterward. What are some activities or situations in which you've experienced these feelings, and are these methods you could use again to increase your endorphin levels to cope with pain and anxiety?

_____

_____

4. A third thing that will raise your endorphin levels is laughing really hard. You can take advantage of this by spending more time with people who make you laugh a lot; you can also build a collection of funny movies and watch them to raise your mood. Have you ever experienced a situation where you were in pain and laughing relieved that pain? What was it?

_____

_____

5. There are also some other ways to improve your quality of life and get some relief from physical pain without using addictive pain medications like opioids. Here's a short list:

Soaking in a hot tub or sauna	Therapeutic massage
Stretching	Getting a healthy amount of sleep
Avoiding actions that aggravate the pain	Physical therapy with a trained professional

You can probably think of several more. What do you think might work for you, and when will you give those activities a try?

_____

_____

6. For emotional pain, there are also quite a few ways to cope without drugs. Here are a few:

Psychotherapy	Doing things that are fun or relaxing
Doing things that give you a sense of achievement	Spending time with a pet
Spending time, with a good friend	Creating poetry, music, or other art forms

Again, you can probably think of more. What will you try, and when?

_____

_____

In this activity we've looked at several strategies people can use to cope with physical and emotional pain without drugs, and there's something that will work for just about everyone. The key is to start trying these approaches and find which work best for you. This is a vital topic, because unrelieved pain and anxiety can be strong triggers for relapse into opioid addiction.

Be sure to bring this handout back to your next therapy session, and be prepared to discuss your thoughts and feelings about the exercise.

WORKING WITH FEAR

GOALS OF THE EXERCISE

1. Reduce the frequency, intensity, and duration of panic attacks.
2. Reduce the fear that panic symptoms will recur without the ability to manage them.
3. Implement calming and coping strategies to reduce overall anxiety and to manage panic symptoms.
4. Identify, challenge, and replace biased, fearful self-talk with reality-based, positive self-talk.

ADDITIONAL PROBLEMS FOR WHICH THIS EXERCISE MAY BE USEFUL

- Anxiety
- Borderline Personality
- Brief Reactive Psychotic Episode
- Combat and Operational Stress Reaction
- Depression
- Nightmares
- Phobia
- Physiological Stress Response—Acute
- Posttraumatic Stress Disorder (PTSD)
- Sexual Assault by Another Service Member

SUGGESTIONS FOR PROCESSING THIS EXERCISE
WITH VETERANS/SERVICE MEMBERS

Like the other exercise in this section, "Preventing Panic in Myself and Others," the "Working With Fear" activity is intended for use with veterans/service members whose lives are disrupted by panic or anxiety attacks or other problems related to overwhelming fear, either fear of specific situations or generalized anxiety. The approach of this activity is primarily cognitive-behavioral, aimed at building habits that can reverse the effects of intense fear and reality-testing fearful thoughts. Follow-up can include reading assignments from the books listed for this issue in Appendix A of *The Veterans and Active Duty Military Psychotherapy Treatment Planner*.

WORKING WITH FEAR

Fear is a vital and necessary part of human perception—it's unpleasant, but we need it. It's what lets us know we need to fight, flee, or freeze when we become aware of danger. As M. Scott Peck wrote in *The Road Less Traveled*:

> Most people think that courage is the absence of fear. The absence of fear is not courage; the absence of fear is some kind of brain damage. Courage is the capacity to go ahead in spite of the fear, or in spite of the pain. When you do that, you will find that overcoming that fear will . . . make you stronger . . .

A person who was actually fearless would probably not even survive childhood; he or she would lack the common sense to avoid danger and would wander into traffic, walk off a cliff, or do something else equally deadly. So the goal of a reasonable person can't be to have no fear—it has to be finding a way to live and work with fear. This exercise will introduce you to some methods you may be able to use to tame and manage fear so that it truly is a valuable source of guidance and not a problem that interferes with your life.

1. A big part of fear is the perception of being helpless in the face of a threat. The first step to breaking the grip of that feeling is to find a way to respond when you suddenly feel intense fear. Often, starting to take any effective action breaks the spell of the fear and keeps it from paralyzing you or panicking you into a blind effort to get away. Fear is intensely uncomfortable, and for people struggling with panic or anxiety attacks even the thought of having an attack can trigger one and become a self-fulfilling fear. However, fear can actually be a vital aid to survival, not only by making us cautious but also by helping us cope with danger when we do face threats. How would you say fear is useful in dangerous situations?

   _____

   _____

2. Fear can help us survive because of its physiological and mental effects. When we need to fight or flee, fear can make us stronger, faster, and more decisive—it even sharpens vision and hearing. But to deal successfully with danger, we still need to know how to control and manage fear, or it becomes panic.

Effective responses to fear are broken down into internal and external actions. Internal actions are aimed at maintaining or regaining self-control. They start by focusing on reversing the physical effects of fear. When we're scared, our breathing gets faster and more shallow, and our large muscle groups tense up, so try reversing those effects. The more you practice, the more quickly and easily you'll be able to use this skill:

Practice saying "Breathe" to yourself, and take slow, deep breaths from the belly, through your nose rather than your mouth. Next, focus on relaxing those large muscle groups, using a cue word like "Loose." Being tensed up won't help in a situation that doesn't call for an immediate physical response, and in one that does, you can act faster and with more flexibility if your muscles are relaxed.

You may wonder how to build these habits if you don't have scary situations to practice on regularly. A good method is to think of past situations that were highly stressful, especially if they still bother you; picture them as clearly as you can. You'll probably find your body reacting as we've described here. When that happens, use the "Breathe" and "Loose" steps to reverse those changes. Try this technique and briefly describe the experience here:

_____

_____

3. Once you've gone through "Breathe" and "Loose" and the actions they call for, the next step is also internal. Pause and say to yourself "Think," assuming, again, that this isn't a situation where you're under fire or about to get into a wreck. "Think" is the cue to ask yourself, "What am I afraid is happening?" and to do a reality check. When it comes to fears we all sometimes "catastrophize," which is to think of the worst possible outcome or even one that's worse than anything possible, and react as if it's reality. This leads to panic all too often, and though fear can be valuable, panic is not. Can you think of an example of catastrophizing and panic in reaction to a situation that wasn't really that bad, in yourself or someone you know? If so, briefly describe that initial catastrophizing impression of the situation and what was actually taking place:

_____

_____

4. Once you've made sure you're in control of yourself, it's time to shift to external actions.

These relate to other people and to changing what's going on, especially if you're in a leadership role. Depending on the situation, this may be where drills and practice come into play—or example, immediate action drills for response to ambushes. Obviously, not all frightening situations will be in a combat setting, but you may be able to think of a more general response that you can rehearse yourself and with your team.

If you are a leader, you may find yourself in situations where you must also keep other people from panicking and get them into effective action. It's a good idea to think this through ahead of time. Beyond standard immediate action drills, what might you do to prepare yourself and your people for this? One thing would be to train them to go through the same steps discussed in items 1 and 2—Breathe, Loose, and Think. How could you teach this to others?

_____

_____

In this exercise we've looked at strategies you can use to cope with fear and work through it. Remember, as Peck said, fear is natural, but we can work through it. The more you practice these, the more easily and effectively you'll be able to put them to use when you're facing real fear.

Be sure to bring this handout back to your next therapy session, and be prepared to discuss your thoughts and feelings about the exercise.

PREVENTING PANIC IN MYSELF AND OTHERS

GOALS OF THE EXERCISE

1. Reduce the frequency, intensity, and duration of panic attacks.
2. Reduce the fear that panic symptoms will recur without the ability to manage them.
3. Reduce the fear of triggering panic and eliminate avoidance of activities and environments thought to trigger panic.
4. Increase comfort when in public environments.

ADDITIONAL PROBLEMS FOR WHICH THIS EXERCISE MAY BE USEFUL

*   Anxiety
*   Borderline Personality
*   Brief Reactive Psychotic Episode
*   Combat and Operational Stress Reaction
*   Depression
*   Nightmares
*   Phobia
*   Physiological Stress Response—Acute
*   Posttraumatic Stress Disorder (PTSD)
*   Sexual Assault by Another Service Member

SUGGESTIONS FOR PROCESSING THIS EXERCISE WITH VETERANS/SERVICE MEMBERS

Like, "Working with Fear," the "Preventing Panic in Myself and Others" activity is for veterans/service members whose lives are disrupted by panic, anxiety attacks, or other overwhelming fear, either fear of specific situations or generalized anxiety. Its approach is cognitive-behavioral with the addition of titrated exposure to increasing levels of fear stimuli to desensitize the veteran/service member and extinguish the panic/anxiety attack response. Depending on resources, it may be possible to use virtual reality systems for this purpose. The Department of Defense (DOD) is exploring this method to help service members with posttraumatic stress disorder (PTSD) caused by events such as improvised explosive device (IED) blasts. Follow-up can include reading assignments from books listed for this issue in Appendix A of *The Veterans and Active Duty Military Psychotherapy Treatment Planner.*

PREVENTING PANIC IN MYSELF AND OTHERS

Panic and fear are two different things. Fear is sometimes unavoidable for any sane person, but fear does not equal loss of control. Panic is loss of control, and there are no situations that are improved or handled better by a person experiencing panic. Whether you're on active duty in combat, a veteran dealing with a house fire, or a parent whose child is suffering a medical emergency, it can be a matter of life and death to prevent panic in yourself and in others. This exercise will present you with some tools for avoiding panic, maintaining self-control, improving your ability to think in a crisis, and helping others do the same.

1.   Panic doesn't happen instantaneously—it takes at least a short time to develop, because it's a reaction to what a person is thinking about a situation. For that to happen, he or she has to perceive events, interpret them, assign a meaning to them, and decide at some level that this is a situation he or she cannot handle. If you can short-circuit that process and keep from ever coming to that point, you can avoid panic. The first step is recognizing when fear is starting to build toward panic. If you've experienced a state of panic or seen someone else going through it, can you recall some things that were happening just before you or the other person panicked? If so, briefly describe them here:

     _____

     _____

2.   You may have noticed some physical signs first, similar to those people sometimes feel under other kinds of intense stress. These may include pounding heartbeat, rapid shallow breathing (possibly hyperventilation, which can cause dizziness and fainting), rigid muscles, trembling, the proverbial butterflies in the stomach, and a dry mouth. Some people also experience a roaring or buzzing in their ears and lightheadedness. If these things are happening to you or another person, it's vital to reverse them as quickly as possible. To do this, get as physically relaxed as is practical in the situation—sit down if you can. Make the effort to slow your breathing down and breathe through your nose and not your mouth. If it's hard to get your breathing under control or you're feeling dizzy or lightheaded, take a small paper bag, the size people pack lunches in, and breathe in and out of it. This will help you avoid hyperventilating. Force yourself to pay attention to one part of

your body at a time and relax the muscles there. If you've done the exercise titled "Safe and Peaceful Place Meditation," you can use the meditation you created for that exercise in this situation. Other quick meditation techniques can be equally useful. If you aren't feeling panicky but someone else is, talk them through the steps listed here. Have you ever used methods like these to control panic in yourself or someone else? If so, what worked the best?

_____

_____

3. It can also be helpful to reconnect to the here and now using your senses. To do this, you might try splashing some cool water on your face, rubbing your hands together, stamping your feet, and looking around and noticing the details of your surroundings; for other people, guide them in doing the same. These can help keep you from getting carried away by fear and losing awareness of what's actually going on around you. Try some of these and note here which work best for you:

_____

_____

4. While you act to regain control over your body, turn to your thoughts. It helps to have a fair amount of practice at using techniques to control runaway fearful thoughts. The "Safe and Peaceful Place Meditation," mentioned in item 2, is also effective in restoring your calm and clarity of thought. In addition, it's a good idea to check your thinking for distortions. Identify the thought that's triggering the worst of the fear—usually anticipating the worst possible outcome from the situation, maybe even an outcome so outrageous it makes you laugh when you realize what you're thinking. Once you identify the thought, run through this short list of thinking errors to see whether you're making one or more of these mistakes:

    Catastrophizing: predicting the worst possible outcome when you don't really know what will happen and not giving yourself enough credit for being able to take it if that worst outcome does happen;

    Assuming: not having all the information to understand the situation, but filling in the blanks with negative guesswork;

    Personalizing: interpreting everything as being about you and directed at you;

    Mind-reading: deciding you know what other people are thinking, their motives, and their intentions;

    Overgeneralizing: deciding that because one part of a situation is bad that the rest of it will be the same way;

    Emotional reasoning: thinking that if you have a strong emotional feeling that something is true, it must really be true (usually a negative judgment about yourself, the situation, or the future);

Learned helplessness: a person has been powerless to change or escape painful situations in the past and doesn't see that he or she now has that power.

Which of these do you see in your own thinking? Please give a brief example:

_____

_____

When you catch yourself, or someone else, falling into one or more of these thinking errors that lead to panic, take another look at the situation and come up with a more realistic, more positive replacement thought, and repeat it to yourself or the other person aloud.

In this activity we've looked at strategies to stop and reverse panic in yourself and those around you. Some will take practice to learn to use automatically without checking your notes—that's normal, just keep at it. The more you practice, the easier and more effective it will become.

Be sure to bring this handout back to your next therapy session, and be prepared to discuss your thoughts and feelings about the exercise.

HOW WILL I EXPLAIN THIS DEPLOYMENT TO MY CHILDREN?

GOALS OF THE EXERCISE

1. Resolve guilt issues surrounding leaving the child.
2. Learn proven parenting techniques.
3. Implement proven techniques daily.
4. Obtain a greater sense of adequacy and competency in parenting.

ADDITIONAL PROBLEMS FOR WHICH THIS EXERCISE MAY BE USEFUL

- Adjustment to the Military Culture
- Anxiety
- Borderline Personality
- Pre-Deployment Stress
- Separation and Divorce

SUGGESTIONS FOR PROCESSING THIS EXERCISE WITH SERVICE MEMBERS

The "How Will I Explain this Deployment to My Children?" activity is designed to provide service members who are parents of minor children, and are preparing to deploy away from home for a significant time, with guidance on preparing their children for their absence. Its goal is to help these service members, and their spouses/partners/other adult caregivers who will be taking care of their children, prepare those children for the deployment by answering common questions and concerns to minimize the stress the deployment causes. Follow-up for this exercise could include discussing the completed plan with the therapist, possibly in a couples session, before the deploying service member departs; bibliotherapy using books suggested in Appendix A of *The Veterans and Active Duty Military Psychotherapy Treatment Planner* and/or videotherapy using films on the topics of "Friends and Support Systems" and/or "Parent-Child Relationships" recommended in *Rent Two Films and Let's Talk in the Morning*, 2nd ed., by John W. Hesley and Jan G. Hesley, also published by John Wiley & Sons.

HOW WILL I EXPLAIN THIS DEPLOYMENT TO MY CHILDREN?

Deployments are difficult for both parents and children, but the stress they cause children can vary a lot depending on what they know about where you're going and what you'll be doing. The way you present this information should depend on the children's ages and levels of understanding. This activity will share some pointers that may help you reduce the stress for your children.

1. *Where to start*: A good way to start is to ask your children what they want to know and what they're worried about, and answer those questions first. When will you ask them what questions they have about your deployment? Set aside time to talk for a while.

    _____

    _____

    In general, children want to know about these things:

    a. *Where are you going*? The answer will vary depending on your children's understanding of the world, but maps are helpful for most ages. Beyond place names and points on the map, they'll want to know what the place is like. It's important to ask what they already know, or think they know. Mistaken ideas may cause them a lot of needless stress. What will you tell them about where you're going, matching it to their levels of understanding?

    _____

    _____

    b. *When will you leave and when will you come back*? For older children, straightforward answers in terms of dates and duration are what they're looking for. With younger children, those may not mean much; for them, it may work better if you can compare the length of time to another they're familiar with, along the lines of "as long as it has been since your birthday," "after Halloween," etc. How will you explain this to your children?

    _____

    _____

c. *What will you be doing and what will be happening*? This may be an area where their ages make the most difference in what they can grasp and what is wise to share with them, especially if your mission will involve, or might involve, combat duty. The key is to be as reassuring as possible while still being honest. Give them a chance to express upset feelings if they need to do so and validate their feelings. How you answer this question?

_____

_____

_____

d. *Why*? The younger the child, the more you'll hear this question. Beyond the nature of the mission, the answer depends on the child's level of understanding; positive answers about ways you'll be helping people, and parallels between children where you're going and your children, are good. With young children, expect this question to keep coming up because they often want to go over the same information again and again; it's part of the way children younger than about kindergarten age process information. It may also mean they're anxious and want the answers confirmed for them. It can be stressful for you when they keep asking the same questions, but bear with it and stay patient and positive. It can be a cue to ask them whether that particular question is one they're worried about, too, and give them a chance to express their feelings to you. How will you handle this question?

_____

_____

e. *What will happen to them while you're away*? Children may want reassurance that they'll be taken care of while you're deployed. The best answer has two parts: first, a straightforward explanation of what to expect in their daily lives. "Mom/Dad will be here and will take care of you," "You'll keep going to school the way you do now," and so on. Part two concerns how you'll stay in touch (the activity titled "How Will I Stay in Touch with My Children?" may help). A plan with the children's input for frequent communication will go a long way to ease their worries. How will you answer this?

_____

_____

2. *Age differences*: The answers children can understand vary with age roughly as follows (adjust to your own children's thinking and personalities):

a. *Toddler through kindergarten*: Children in this stage think in very literal, concrete terms, and they don't understand differences in the scale of time and distance well. For example, they may not be able to grasp the difference between two weeks and two months, or between fifty miles and a thousand. Visual aids can help, like a calendar with a box per day for them to color in, say before dinner every day.

b. *Kindergarten through mid-elementary school*: Grasp of scale is improving but can still be hazy. Children in this age range may be more aware of world events on the news and form fears based on things they hear—check for this, along with any misinterpretations.

c. *Upper elementary through middle school*: These children are more aware of world events and are able to grasp the scales of time and distance. They still tend to see issues in simplistic all-or-nothing terms, but are often interested in learning complexities they may not have known about. Take your cue from them as to when they've heard enough to satisfy them.

d. *High school*: Adolescents, somewhere between childhood and adulthood, can often understand concepts at adult levels but have trouble with emotions. They may be the most interested in the complexities of the situation where you're going, and may have a realistic grasp of whatever risks are involved. Be as positive as you can and still be honest.

How will you tailor your explanations to your children's needs?

_____

_____

3. *The hard questions*: These vary with age, the child's personality, and the deployment's nature, but they usually relate to danger to you, whether you'll be fighting or killing people, and maybe any controversy in the news about the situation. It may be best to plan your answers with your therapist, ideally in a joint session with your spouse/partner. Part of your answer may need to be an acknowledgment that the questions don't have comfortable answers.

Be sure to bring this handout back to your next session with your therapist, and be prepared to discuss your thoughts and feelings about the exercise.

HOW WILL I STAY IN TOUCH WITH MY CHILDREN?

GOALS OF THE EXERCISE

1. Resolve guilt issues surrounding leaving the child.
2. Learn proven parenting techniques.
3. Obtain a greater sense of adequacy and competency in parenting.

ADDITIONAL PROBLEMS FOR WHICH THIS EXERCISE MAY BE USEFUL

- Adjustment to the Military Culture
- Anxiety
- Homesickness/Loneliness
- Pre-Deployment Stress
- Separation and Divorce

SUGGESTIONS FOR PROCESSING THIS EXERCISE WITH SERVICE MEMBERS

The "How Will I Stay in Touch with My Children?" exercise is for service members who are parents of minor children and are preparing to deploy for a significant time. Its goal is to help these service members and the spouses/partners/other adult caregivers who will take care of the children, plan ways to maintain relationships with the children while deployed and address everyone's concerns about the separation. It guides the adults in concrete planning in four areas that can be sources of concern or problems: arranging communication between the deployed service member and the caregiver and children at home; agreement between the adults on rules and discipline techniques for the children while the deploying parent is away; sources of practical and emotional support for the caregiver at home, who is temporarily functioning as a single parent; and ways for the service member and children to reconnect after the deployment, including preparation for developmental changes in the children that have taken place while the service member was away. Follow-up can include discussing the plan with the therapist in a couples session before the service member departs, as well as bibliotherapy with books listed in Appendix A of *The Veterans and Active Duty Military Psychotherapy Treatment Planner* and/or videotherapy using films on "Friends and Support Systems" and/or "Parent-Child Relationships" recommended in *Rent Two Films and Let's Talk in the Morning*, 2nd ed., by John W. Hesley and Jan G. Hesley, published by John Wiley & Sons.

HOW WILL I STAY IN TOUCH WITH MY CHILDREN?

Being separated from your children can be one of the most difficult parts of deployment. Particularly with very young children, service members who will be deployed for any significant length of time may worry about their bonds with their children being weakened or even the children forgetting them; as for the children, they may feel abandoned or rejected and react with fear, anger, or depression. The adult staying at home with the children may feel overwhelmed and at risk for depression or burnout, and will be in greater need than usual of a good emotional support system. Finally, as the deployment nears its end, there are questions about ways to reconnect when the service member gets home. This exercise will help you and your spouse or other caregiver plan for each of these concerns so you can minimize the difficulty of your deployment for everyone involved.

1. *Staying in Touch*: There are many ways to stay close to your children while you're away. Your choices will depend on their ages and the length and nature of your deployment and your command may provide resources in this area. Here are some things you can do—circle the ones that you think would be helpful for your family.

    a. *Using maps and globes*: Put a map showing both where the children are and the place(s) you'll be deployed on a wall at home, and use push-pins to mark both places; if you're going to be at sea or otherwise going to a number of places, the adult who is with the children can use a marker to trace your travels so the children can follow your movements. A globe can be used the same way. How will you do this?

    _____

    _____

    b. *Calendars*: Use either a regular calendar or one you create on a computer to show the passing of time from the beginning to the end of the deployment. If your return date is fixed, mark that date on the calendar so the children can see it getting closer. What kind of calendar would work best with your children and what occasions will you put on it?

    _____

    _____

c. *Information about deployment locations*: Find books, magazines, etc. with information and photos so your children can see what things are like where you're going. What information would your children be most interested in, and where will you find it?

_____

_____

d. *Regular communication*: You may have the opportunity to phone and/or email home, or even use a webcam for conversations so you can see and hear each other. Make a communication schedule, especially for occasions like birthdays. Letters are also good because the children can read letters from you over and over, put them on the wall, and so on. They can mail written messages, art from school, and so on, to you. How and when will you communicate?

_____

_____

e. *Talking about feelings*: It's good to have the children tell you their thoughts, concerns, and emotions, and for you to tell them how you feel about them. This is a chance to validate their feelings, and it may turn out that they misunderstand the situation in some way that causes them distress that you can correct. When will you sit down with them for this talk?

_____

2. *Rules and Discipline*: It's important for you and the at-home adult to agree before you depart. It's best to change things as little as possible from the norms when you're home, and for you to sit down with the children and present this as a united front. The adult who is home should keep you informed while deployed; let the children know that you are still a team. Avoid the "wait until your father comes home" scenario—you don't want the children to fear your return! Every chance you get, praise the children for following rules and being helpful. It can help to give them more responsibilities and let them know you're depending on them. When will you plan for rules and discipline, and when will you have this talk with the children?

_____

3. *Support for the Parent/Other Caregiver at Home:* Beyond your expression of support during your communications, your command may make arrangements for spouses to meet to provide mutual emotional support and practical assistance (e.g., taking turns babysitting so they can have a chance to spend some time going to a movie) and to decompress and de-stress. This may be a good time, if work and school allow, for the adult home with the children to take them on a trip to visit relatives. What are your plans for this kind of emotional and practical support for the adult not deploying?

_____

_____

4. *Preparation for Homecoming and Reconnecting:* As your return approaches, be sure the at-home caregiver keeps you up-to-date on the children's development—the younger they are, the more they'll change. Prepare the children for any changes that will happen when you get home. The ideal is no surprises for anyone (other than gifts, of course). The caregiver at home may have gotten used to being the sole adult and this can lead to friction; this is normal, and communication will help you work through it. Also, don't be surprised if the children resist your authority at first or try to play you off against each other—it doesn't mean there is anything wrong with them; just don't let them succeed. It's good to spend a lot of unstructured, low-stress time getting used to each other again—a relaxed family vacation may be in order. Also, though this exercise is mainly about the children, you and your partner will want time alone. Relatives may be able to watch the children for a few days so you can have that. What are your plans for activities when you return?

    _____

    _____

    _____

    _____

Be sure to bring this handout back to your next session with your therapist, and be prepared to discuss your thoughts and feelings about the exercise.

NEAR-TERM AND LONG-TERM EFFECTS OF STIMULANT DEPENDENCE AND WITHDRAWAL

GOALS OF THE EXERCISE

1. Refrain from use of all over-the-counter and illegally obtained performance-enhancing supplements.
2. Verbalize an understanding of the negative health consequences that performance-enhancing supplements can cause.
3. Dispose of all performance-enhancing supplements.
4. Establish and maintain total abstinence while increasing knowledge of the disease and the process of recovery.
5. Learn and use coping strategies to manage urges to relapse into chemical use.

ADDITIONAL PROBLEMS FOR WHICH THIS EXERCISE MAY BE USEFUL

- Anger Management and Domestic Violence
- Antisocial Behavior in the Military
- Brief Reactive Psychotic Episode
- Conflict with Comrades
- Depression
- Insomnia
- Substance Abuse/Dependence

SUGGESTIONS FOR PROCESSING THIS EXERCISE WITH VETERANS/SERVICE MEMBERS

The "Near-Term and Long-Term Effects of Stimulant Dependence and Withdrawal" activity is for veterans/service members who have become dependent on stimulant drugs and are newly clean and sober or working to achieve that state. This activity is psychoeducational, educating the veteran/service member about effects of this category of drugs and typical things people experience while going through withdrawal. Follow-up can include reading assignments from books listed in Appendix A of *The Veterans and Active Duty Military Psychotherapy Treatment Planner* and/or videotherapy with films suggested for "Substance Abuse" in *Rent Two Films and Let's Talk in the Morning*, 2nd ed., by John W. Hesley and Jan G. Hesley, published by John Wiley & Sons.

NEAR-TERM AND LONG-TERM EFFECTS
OF STIMULANT DEPENDENCE AND WITHDRAWAL

Being dependent on any drug, or experiencing withdrawal, is stressful physically, mentally, and emotionally. Each type of drug has its own characteristics and its own dangers—here we are looking at stimulants (i.e., cocaine, amphetamines), and their variants. This will arm you with information to help you have a clear picture of the risks that go with stimulants and lower your levels of stress and anxiety by explaining what are normal and common parts of this experience.

1. We'll start with the effects of the drug, near-term and long-term. With any drug, people use it for its effects. This class of drugs, which includes cocaine, amphetamines (Adderall, Benzedrine, Dexedrine), methamphetamine, MDMA/Ecstasy, and others, can be swallowed in pill form, smoked, sniffed, or injected. Stimulants cause increased energy, concentration, and motivation; suppressed appetite; and increased confidence. Specifically for these effects, they have been used by military forces in wartime, by athletes, and by people doing tiring and tedious jobs. But there are also dangerous side effects, including higher blood pressure and risk of heart attack or stroke, poorer judgment and impulse control, increased irritability, aggressiveness, paranoia, and hallucinations and delusions due to going too long without sleep. Another side effect is sometimes called "meth mouth." The drug causes a dry mouth, making teeth vulnerable to decay, since saliva helps protect the teeth from bacteria. Of course, cocaine and its derivatives such as Novocaine, procaine, xylocaine, and so forth, are also used as local short-term anesthetics for dental work and minor surgery.

    Also, when a person stops use after any period of use lasting more than a day or so, he or she will usually experience exhaustion and may sleep for much longer than usual. Which of these symptoms have you experienced while using a stimulant, or seen someone else experience?

    _____

    _____

2. As with other addictive drugs, there are two other critical long-term effects of stimulants—the development of tolerance and withdrawal. Tolerance means that it takes more of the drug to get the same effect, or that if a person uses the same

amount it has less effect with repeated use. This is similar to the experience many people have with other drugs like caffeine (a weaker stimulant in its own right)— the first time they try them the effects are powerful, but over time it may take a pot of coffee to match the effects of the first cup. With stimulants, the effect is mainly due to their triggering release of greater amounts of the brain chemical called dopamine, which leads to the effects described above. The reason tolerance happens is that the body is always trying to keep its chemistry in balance, and this flood of dopamine leads the brain to think it has a surplus and should make less. So over time, the levels of dopamine and/or the number of dopamine receptor cells drop drastically. Have you experienced the development of tolerance? Please describe how the effect has changed over time for you:

_____

_____

A final note on tolerance: Some of the effect, the partial burnout of the brain's dopamine system, can be permanent with prolonged heavy use. Even after quitting, a user may be less able to feel pleasure and more prone to depression and anxiety for the rest of his or her life.

3. We also said that with repeated use over time, withdrawal develops. When a person whose body has adapted to the presence of the stimulant stops using it, the balance the body has achieved with the stimulant as part of the mix is thrown off again—and since the natural production of dopamine and number of receptor cells has been lowered, it leaves a person worse off than before he or she first used the drug. The withdrawal symptoms for any drug will typically be the opposite of the drug's effects. So for stimulants, what would be the normal short-term withdrawal symptoms? Typical withdrawal effects in stimulant dependence are exhaustion, prolonged sleep, inattention, anxiety, depression that can sometimes include suicidal thoughts, and intense irritability. (Oddly, some effects, such as agitation, increased irritability, paranoia, and temporary psychosis, are common to both extended use and withdrawal.) Please describe any withdrawal symptoms you've experienced:

_____

_____

A positive note: Even though it's miserable, it's only temporary, and withdrawal from a stimulant is not physically dangerous, unlike some other drugs such as depressants.

4. Many people find another aspect of withdrawal difficult. Long after there is no trace of the drug left in their bodies, they still experience after effects. These can include difficulty concentrating and thinking clearly; problems with memory; anxiety, depression, and irritability; mood swings; emotional numbness or overreaction; trouble with sleep; and trouble with physical coordination. This is

called Post-Acute Withdrawal (PAW). It scares people because symptoms may last for weeks or months after the last use of the drug, leading to the fear that the problems will be permanent. If you've been clean long enough that the drugs have left your system, are you experiencing any of these effects? If so, which ones?

_____

_____

Thankfully, PAW is not permanent. It takes time for the body to restore its chemical balance, but it will keep getting better as time passes. The best way to cope is to watch as the symptoms diminish and recognize your progress.

In this exercise we've gone over the effects of stimulants in use and withdrawal, so you can understand things you've experienced and make informed decisions. You may know someone else who would benefit from this information; if so, please pass it on.

Be sure to bring this handout back to your next therapy session, and be prepared to discuss your thoughts and feelings about the exercise.

NEAR-TERM AND LONG-TERM EFFECTS OF ANABOLIC STEROID DEPENDENCE AND WITHDRAWAL

GOALS OF THE EXERCISE

1. Refrain from use of all performance-enhancing supplements.
2. Verbalize an understanding of the negative health consequences that performance-enhancing supplements can cause.
3. Dispose of all performance-enhancing supplements.
4. Establish and maintain total abstinence while increasing knowledge of the disease and the process of recovery.
5. Learn and use coping strategies to manage urges to relapse into chemical use.

ADDITIONAL PROBLEMS FOR WHICH THIS EXERCISE MAY BE USEFUL

- Anger Management and Domestic Violence
- Antisocial Behavior in the Military
- Brief Reactive Psychotic Episode
- Conflict with Comrades
- Depression
- Insomnia
- Substance Abuse/Dependence

SUGGESTIONS FOR PROCESSING THIS EXERCISE WITH VETERANS/SERVICE MEMBERS

The "Near-Term and Long-Term Effects of Anabolic Steroid Dependence and Withdrawal" activity is for veterans/service members who have become dependent on anabolic steroids and are newly clean and sober or working to achieve that state. This activity is psychoeducational, educating the veteran/service member about this category of drugs and typical things people experience while going through withdrawal. Follow-up can include reading assignments from books listed in Appendix A of *The Veterans and Active Duty Military Psychotherapy Treatment Planner*, and/or videotherapy using films listed for "Substance Abuse" in *Rent Two Films and Let's Talk in the Morning*, 2nd ed., by John W. Hesley and Jan G. Hesley, published by John Wiley & Sons.

NEAR-TERM AND LONG-TERM EFFECTS OF ANABOLIC STEROID DEPENDENCE AND WITHDRAWAL

Being dependent on any drug or experiencing withdrawal, can be very rough physically, mentally, and emotionally. Each type of drug has its own characteristics, including its own dangers—in this exercise we are looking at anabolic steroids. This will arm you for this struggle, with information that can help you have a clear picture of the risks that go with steroid use as well as lowering your levels of stress and anxiety by explaining what are normal and common parts of this experience.

1. We'll start with the effects of anabolic steroids, near-term and long-term. The reason people use any drug is for its effects. This class of drugs, which mimic the action of the male sex hormones testosterone and dihydrotestosterone, can be swallowed in pill form, absorbed via skin patch, or injected. It's important not to confuse anabolic steroids with other steroids sometimes used to treat allergies and autoimmune disorders, like cortisone and prednisone. The effects of anabolic steroids in the body are many and can be dramatic. They increase muscle mass and body and beard hair, make the voice deeper, and increase libido. They are sometimes used medically to treat patients (typically boys) suffering from impaired testosterone production.

   Which of these symptoms have you experienced while using an anabolic steroid, if any, or seen someone else experience?

   _____

   _____

2. There are also serious negative effects. In women, anabolic steroids also increase body hair, deepen the voice, masculinize the musculoskeletal structure of the body, disrupt the menstrual cycle, and can cause the clitoris to grow. In adult men, they lower sperm production and can cause the testicles to shrink. In both genders, they tend to lower production of natural sex hormones (leading to deficiencies when use is stopped), cause acne, and increase balding on the scalp. In adolescents, they may prematurely stop the growth of the body's long bones, permanently stunting growth. Even more dangerous, anabolic steroids can increase blood pressure and

cholesterol levels, raise the risk of stroke; cause heart disease; and raise the risk of several kinds of life-threatening cancers.

In higher doses they can have negative psychological and emotional effects. Anabolic steroids can cause increased aggressiveness and irritability (the pattern informally called "roid rage"), psychosis, and symptoms that can resemble bipolar disorder, both mania and depression, that can become suicidal. Research is ongoing, but it seems that some of these effects can be permanent. Anabolic steroids sometimes seem to be "gateway drugs"—once people start using them, they're more likely to also use other mind-altering substances.

Another common risk factor that is due to the method of use rather than the drug itself, is the danger of transmitting diseases including hepatitis and HIV/AIDS between steroid users who share needles or share multidose vials of the drug.

Scientists are also still researching the risk of physical addiction, with the development of tolerance and withdrawal, but at this point it appears that this risk is minor with these steroids compared to narcotics, stimulants, or depressants. Because of this, withdrawal's effects are also more psychological than strictly physical, most commonly an increase in irritability and depression. Which of these symptoms have you experienced while using an anabolic steroid, if any, or seen someone else experience?

_____

_____

3. The best estimate of the researchers studying anabolic steroid use is that about 1% of the U.S. population uses them. Users are most likely to be middle-class men in their mid-20s who use the steroids to look better or to improve their performance as amateur athletes; they also estimate that between 2% and 3% of American high school students use anabolic steroids for the same reasons. Steroid users are more likely than average to suffer from a psychological disorder that causes them to see their muscular development as inadequate even when it is average or better, somewhat like the way people with anorexia see themselves as heavier than they are. Steroid users also tend to be in denial about the negative effects and risks and to believe that the researchers reporting the information in this exercise are exaggerating, although the facts here are accurate. Of the effects described in this exercise, which would be the most important to you in the categories of benefits and of dangers or drawbacks?

_____

_____

Something worth thinking about would be ways you can achieve the benefits you've listed without exposing yourself to the risks. What activities come to mind, if any?

_____

_____

In this exercise, we've gone over the effects of anabolic steroids, both positive and negative, to help you understand things you may have experienced and make informed decisions. You may know someone else who would benefit from this information; if so, please pass it on.

Be sure to bring this handout back to your next therapy session, and be prepared to discuss your thoughts and feelings about the exercise.

USEFUL AND USELESS FEAR

GOALS OF THE EXERCISE

1. Identify, challenge, and replace biased, fearful self-talk with positive, realistic, and empowering self-talk.
2. Verbalize the costs and benefits of remaining fearful and avoidant.
3. Commit self to not allowing phobic fear to take control of your life and lead to avoidance of normal responsibilities and activities.

ADDITIONAL PROBLEMS FOR WHICH THIS EXERCISE MAY BE USEFUL

- Anxiety
- Borderline Personality
- Combat and Operational Stress Reaction
- Nightmares
- Panic/Agoraphobia
- Physiological Stress Response–Acute
- Posttraumatic Stress Disorder (PTSD)
- Sexual Assault by Another Service Member

SUGGESTIONS FOR PROCESSING THIS EXERCISE WITH VETERANS/SERVICE MEMBERS

The "Useful and Useless Fear" activity is for veterans/service members who suffer from phobias of any kind. This activity is primarily preparation for Activity XXV.B, "Understanding and Overcoming Phobias." This activity guides the veteran/service member in seeing which fears are valid and which really are phobic (i.e., interfering with life instead of making him/her safer), then seeing the impact unrealistic fears are having on his or her life, activities, ability to perform tasks, and so on. Follow-up can start with Activity XXV.B and can also include reading assignments from books listed in Appendix A of *The Veterans and Active Duty Military Psychotherapy Treatment Planner*, and/or videotherapy using *What About Bob?* or films suggested for the topic of "Emotional and Affective Disorders" in *Rent Two Films and Let's Talk in the Morning*, 2nd ed., by John W. Hesley and Jan G. Hesley, also published by John Wiley & Sons.

USEFUL AND USELESS FEAR

Fear is not bad in and of itself. It doesn't feel good, but when it's valid it can save our lives—it can alert us to dangers, then trigger changes in our bodies that temporarily increase our ability to defeat or escape the threat. That kind of fear is useful, and we wouldn't survive long without it.

You may be concerned that if you feel fear, it means you lack courage, but the truth is just the opposite. Courageous people may be scared, but they find ways to do what needs to be done despite the fear. If a person felt no fear, he or she couldn't have courage and wouldn't need it, but probably wouldn't survive long.

However, some fear is useless. Fear is useless when it focuses on something that isn't really a threat that we need to react to, or is exaggerated in a way that leads to panic and makes us unable to cope with whatever situation, person, or thing we're afraid of. This exercise will help you learn to respond to fear by figuring out which kind it is, useful or useless, and to prepare you for "Understanding and Overcoming Phobias," which will help you regain the freedom to react in a way that makes sense rather than a way forced on you by useless fear.

1. First, let's look at useful fear. What kinds of situations, people, and things do you think it's wise and reasonable to be afraid of?

    _____

    _____

    _____

2. How has fear benefited you, or others, in dealing with the kinds of things you listed in your answer to question 1? Can you think of a situation where fear saved you or someone you know from being badly hurt or killed?

    _____

    _____

    _____

3. Now to move on to useless fear that benefits no one: Everyone has useless fear to some degree and about something. People fear all kinds of things from harmless bugs to elevators to having to speak in front of a group of people. This kind of useless fear, which is called a phobia, can either be fear of something that is really harmless, like the one about public speaking, or of something that actually would

be bad but is very unlikely to happen, like people who travel by car due to a fear of plane crashes, in spite of the fact that it's actually more dangerous to drive. That's one that leads people to act in a way that's actually more dangerous. These fears cause problems when they keep us from doing things we want or need to do. There's an exercise we mentioned earlier titled "Understanding and Overcoming Phobias" that your therapist may give you—it goes into more depth explaining how phobias form and how to overcome them in general. This assignment is simply aimed at helping you take the first step and test your fears to see whether they're helping or getting in your way. You may already know that some fears are useless and keep you from doing things you need or want to do. If you can see that a fear in your life is useless, what is it and what does it stop you from doing?

_____

_____

4. To test a fear and see whether it's keeping you safer from a real threat or is just an obstacle wasting your time and energy, go through these steps when you find yourself struggling with fear. First, get a clear picture of what you're afraid will happen. Think about a situation that scares you and ask yourself, "What is the worst thing I'm afraid will happen?" and then write that answer here:

_____

5. Now ask yourself, "How likely is that to happen?" and rate its chances of really coming true, from 0% to 100%. If you don't have solid information about this, where can you find it?

_____

6. Now ask yourself whether you have other fears about the same situation—other things you're afraid might happen. If so, what are they? Please identify them and rate their chances of really happening, rating each from 0% to 100% on the likeliness they will take place:

_____

_____

7. Now, for each of the feared events you listed for questions 5 and 6, ask yourself, "Could I cope with that if it did happen?" and think about how it would affect your life—would it kill or injure you, get you in serious trouble or damage an important relationship, cost you a lot of money, embarrass you, or lead to some other painful outcome? Please write the answers here:

_____

_____

8. Finally, for each action the fear(s) keep you from taking, ask yourself, "How is not being able to do this (or feeling this fear while I have to do it) interfering with my

life?" and "What goal is it keeping me from achieving, or what is the fear leading me to do that's more likely to cause me more harm or trouble than the thing I'm afraid of?" Write the answers here:

_____

_____

_____

In this exercise, we've gone over a method to test fears that stop you from doing things you want or need to do, or cause you to do things that could be worse for you than the action you're afraid to take—in other words, to identify useless fears that aren't protecting you. The next exercise, "Understanding and Overcoming Phobias," will show you how to conquer them.

Be sure to bring this handout back to your next therapy session, and be prepared to discuss your thoughts and feelings about the exercise.

UNDERSTANDING AND OVERCOMING PHOBIAS

GOALS OF THE EXERCISE

1. Reduce fear of the specific stimulus object or situation that previously provoked phobic anxiety.
2. Reduce phobic avoidance of the specific object or situation, leading to comfort and independence in moving around in the environment.
3. Learn and use skills and strategies to reduce and manage anxiety symptoms.
4. Identify, challenge, and replace biased, fearful self-talk with positive, realistic, and empowering self-talk.

ADDITIONAL PROBLEMS FOR WHICH THIS EXERCISE MAY BE USEFUL

- Anxiety
- Borderline Personality
- Combat and Operational Stress Reaction
- Nightmares
- Panic/Agoraphobia
- Physiological Stress Response—Acute
- Posttraumatic Stress Disorder (PTSD)
- Sexual Assault by Another Service Member

SUGGESTIONS FOR PROCESSING THIS EXERCISE WITH VETERANS/SERVICE MEMBERS

The "Understanding and Overcoming Phobias" activity is for veterans/service members who suffer from phobias. This is a follow-up for Exercise XXV.A, "Useful and Useless Fear." It takes a cognitive-behavioral approach to this problem by guiding the veteran/service member to correct cognitive distortions that feed into the phobia, then engage in progressively more direct exposures to the situation or object of the phobia. Follow-up can include reading assignments from books listed in Appendix A of *The Veterans and Active Duty Military Psychotherapy Treatment Planner*, and/or videotherapy with films listed for "Emotional and Affective Disorders" in *Rent Two Films and Let's Talk in the Morning*, 2nd ed., by John W. Hesley and Jan G. Hesley, published by John Wiley & Sons.

UNDERSTANDING AND OVERCOMING PHOBIAS

If you've completed the exercise titled "Useful and Useless Fear," you will have some information written down about one or more fears that don't serve your interests, the kind of useless fears called phobias. This exercise will help you learn and use skills to understand where your phobia comes from and then to reduce or eliminate it and free yourself to do things you need or want to do, reacting in a way that makes sense rather than a way forced on you by useless fear.

1. First, let's make sure that what we're dealing with is a phobia. What is it about the fear that you believe is distorted, exaggerated, or inaccurate?

    _____

    _____

2. What is the impact of this fear in your life—how does it limit your actions? What does it keep you from doing? What is its effect on your stress level? Describe its impact:

    _____

    _____

3. Next we need to look at the fear's beginnings. Is this a fear you've always had, as far as you can remember, or did the fear develop more recently, and if so, when and where?

    _____

    _____

4. Sometimes we have phobias because someone taught them to us, maybe when we were children. Thinking of this fear, is it something someone else taught you? If so, who was that and when did this happen? Do you believe they were right or were mistaken?

    _____

    _____

5. Another way phobias can develop is when something bad does happen to us, even though it is a rare event, and we become afraid it will happen again. Is that

something that has happened with this phobia and if so, what happened, when, and how?

_____

_____

6. A third way phobias take root is when we have reasonable fears of specific things or events, then start fearing others with any resemblance. For example, a person who is bitten by one dog may start fearing all dogs. If something like this happened to you, please describe it:

_____

_____

7. There are some phobias whose source is a mystery; we just know we have always been afraid of something without knowing why. If this fits, describe what that fear is for you:

_____

8. Now to start overcoming this fear you need to think of a way you can approach the feared activity, thing, or person one step at a time. To use our example of fear of dogs again, you could start by just thinking about it and picturing yourself petting a dog and scratching behind its ears. From there, you might look at pictures of dogs, and after that, watching films or TV programs featuring dogs. The next step might be to observe some dogs from a safe distance, and then gradually get closer. After that, you would take the step of getting close to a dog—a friendly one, of course—and touching it, stroking its fur, and so on. You might even go on to taking a dog for a walk on a leash, then start having contact with more dogs. When you think about this, what is your reaction, and is this an approach you think might work for your own phobia(s)? Of course, different situations call for different activities. For example, soldiers who have been traumatized by improvised explosive devices (IEDs) have found that virtual reality computer programs with increasingly realistic simulations of situations involving IEDs helped them get back to a normal and appropriate level of caution instead of being too terrified to carry out their duties. If you are having a hard time thinking of a step-by-step approach for your own fear, try brainstorming with your therapist to come up with ideas. If you have some ideas, please describe them here:

_____

_____

_____

9. Another method is to write about the situation or thing you fear, describing the event you fear in as much detail as you can. Include a lot of sensory details in your written description to make sure you're picturing it as clearly as possible. Also, please include your thoughts and emotions. The next step is to read it to yourself

silently, and then to read it aloud to yourself, and then to read it to your therapist and/or a close friend or family member. Once you've done this, wait a week, and then write about it a second time, making this second account even more detailed, especially about your thoughts and feelings and the meaning of the event to you, as you can. Repeat the steps of reading it to yourself and then to someone else; afterward, compare your reactions to those you felt when you started this process and see whether your distress level is reduced. What change in yourself do you see as a result of doing this?

_____

_____

Talk with your therapist about the results, and about any other strategies you and he or she think might help make you comfortable enough with your feared situation to do all the things you need to do in your daily life without it taking too high an emotional toll on you. The goal is to help you retake as much control of your mental and emotional life and your ability to do what you need or want to do as possible.

Be sure to bring this handout and the accounts you've written to your future therapy sessions, and be prepared to discuss your thoughts and feelings about the exercise.

QUICK STRATEGIES FOR COPING WITH INTENSE STRESS RESPONSE

GOALS OF THE EXERCISE

1. Decrease hypervigilance and hyperarousal to levels that are manageable.
2. Prevent development of posttraumatic stress disorder.
3. Verbalize an understanding of typical reactions to a traumatic stressor.
4. Verbalize an understanding that cognitions contribute to the maintenance of fear, hypervigilance, and hyperarousal.

ADDITIONAL PROBLEMS FOR WHICH THIS EXERCISE MAY BE USEFUL

- Anxiety
- Borderline Personality
- Combat and Operational Stress Reaction
- Nightmares
- Panic/Agoraphobia
- Posttraumatic Stress Disorder (PTSD)

SUGGESTIONS FOR PROCESSING THIS EXERCISE WITH VETERANS/SERVICE MEMBERS

The "Quick Strategies for Coping with Intense Stress Response" activity is intended for use with veterans/service members who experience intense hypervigilance and hyperarousal in response to trigger events, either internal (cognitions) or external (events in the immediate environment). It takes the psychoeducational and solution-focused approach of teaching the veteran/service member to identify this process as early as possible and self-intervene using cognitive and behavioral strategies to maintain or regain physical and emotional equilibrium. Follow-up could include reporting back to the therapist/therapy group on outcomes of the strategies from this exercise and reading assignments from the books listed for this issue in Appendix A of *The Veterans and Active Duty Military Psychotherapy Treatment Planner*.

QUICK STRATEGIES FOR COPING WITH INTENSE STRESS RESPONSE

The human mind and nervous system respond to emergencies with rapid changes from everyday levels of arousal to escalated alertness, physical readiness for combat or escape, and accelerated thinking and decision-making. This can save our lives, but this state is too intense to spend much time in without heavy wear and tear, physical and mental. Unfortunately, we can get stuck in a mode where that crisis response is on a hair-trigger and can be easily set off. It may end up getting triggered so often that this defense against trauma becomes a source of trauma itself and takes a heavy toll on our quality of life and even our health. This exercise will show you some ways to catch this process as early as possible and, when it isn't necessary, reverse it quickly and regain a state of calm.

1. First, let's see what changes occur when we go from a normal state to emergency mode. Mentally, we normally divide thoughts and attention between tracking and responding to the immediate situation on one hand, and inner thoughts on the other. You may be driving home from work, listening to a song on the radio, thinking about your plans for the weekend, and deciding whether to stop at a store. If the trip home is routine, the chances are good that you won't even remember a lot of the drive—you could say that part of your mind was on autopilot. It's a different story if you encounter a situation your brain interprets as a crisis—such as the driver in front of you slamming on his brakes. Instantly, you are no longer aware of the radio, and your thoughts about the weekend and the grocery store are gone—your full attention is on avoiding a wreck, and you will definitely remember this when you get home. Thinking and decision-making speeds up, sometimes so much that it seems to us the world has gone into slow motion. What are some other situations where you've experienced this instant high alert?

   _____

   _____

2. The body goes through similar changes. At rest, our breathing, pulse, and blood pressure are in economy mode, just keeping the body working smoothly. Most muscles are relaxed and a lot of the body's energy and oxygen supply is going to routine functions like digesting lunch. But when the brain sends the crisis signal,

the change happens in a heartbeat. The adrenal glands dump adrenalin, the body's own stimulant, into the bloodstream. The blood supply and the oxygen it delivers shift instantly to the large muscles needed for fight or flight, switching off non-crisis functions like digestion. That's why we get the feeling called "butterflies in the stomach." Pulse, breathing, and blood pressure spike; vision and hearing even get sharper. This change can be so intense it feels like an electric shock. The body is ready to do anything it takes to survive. When have you experienced this, and what did it feel like?

_____

_____

3. In a tenth of a second we've gone from relaxation to readiness for maximum focus and effort. It might seem that it would be an advantage to just stay in that ready-for-anything condition all the time. But it's very hard on the mind and body. If we spend a lot of time in that state it causes severe wear and tear—it ages us rapidly and it can make us sick. Also, if this happens a lot, the brain decides that we must be in a very high-risk environment and keeps getting more and more sensitive to alarms, until our emergency mode is in hair-trigger mode and is often set off in situations that aren't really crises, like a too-sensitive car alarm. If you've experienced any physical fallout from frequent intense stress responses, describe it here:

_____

_____

4. To avoid getting sick and worn-out, we need to find ways to reverse this mental and physical change quickly when we see that we aren't really facing a crisis. Just as that switch is both mental and physical, so is the reversing process. Notice the wording in question 2 about what sets it off: "a situation *your brain interprets* as a crisis." The word "interprets" is important. When the mind develops that hair-trigger oversensitivity, we get false alarms, but the body gets its orders from the brain and doesn't know that. As the brain realizes it's not facing a threat after all, we need to take the body back to normal mode, which involves both rethinking the situation and direct physical action. Note: it's better not to use alcohol or other drugs for this purpose. They suppress the symptoms more than relieve them, and that stress response may come back when the chemical wears off.

    Resetting the brain to normal mode has two parts. First, ask yourself, "What's the threat?" If it's already past—you stopped without hitting the car ahead—or if it was something your brain misinterpreted for some reason, it's safe to mentally thank the brain/body emergency system for doing its job and focus your thought on the new situation. You might say to yourself something like "Crisis over, no current threats," and switch to directing the body's shifting gears. For the body, try concentrating first on taking deep, slow breaths from the belly, then on paying attention to each part of the body in turn, tensing the muscles for a few seconds and then relaxing them, paying close attention to how it feels. You can follow up with a relaxing thought or visualization like the one in the activity titled "Safe and Peaceful Place Meditation." With practice you can use that method to become completely calm in a few seconds. If you've found ways to get back to a relaxed state quickly after being triggered, what works best for you?

_____

6. Finally, let's come back to the important fact that this response is based not on the situation, but on how the brain interprets it. If you're experiencing a lot of false alarms, you can work on reprogramming that part of your brain so it's not on such a light hair-trigger. Individual and group therapy can help a lot, and any well-stocked bookstore has a whole section of books on subjects related to this. How will you explore your options for making your mind less prone to interpret non-crisis situations as emergencies?

_____

_____

Be sure to bring this handout back to your next therapy session, and be prepared to discuss your thoughts and feelings about the exercise.

SAFE AND PEACEFUL PLACE MEDITATION

GOALS OF THE EXERCISE

1. Decrease hypervigilance and hyperarousal to manageable levels.
2. Eliminate agitation, irritability, and sleep disturbances.
3. Reduce or eliminate negative physical effects of prolonged/severe hyperarousal.

ADDITIONAL PROBLEMS FOR WHICH THIS EXERCISE MAY BE USEFUL

*   Anger Management and Domestic Violence
*   Anxiety
*   Borderline Personality
*   Chronic Pain
*   Combat and Operational Stress Reaction
*   Insomnia
*   Nightmares
*   Panic/Agoraphobia
*   Posttraumatic Stress Disorder (PTSD)

SUGGESTIONS FOR PROCESSING THIS EXERCISE WITH VETERANS/SERVICE MEMBERS

The "Safe and Peaceful Place Meditation" activity is useful for managing stress and anxiety, particularly if these are chronic. It is also useful for pain management and coping with insomnia. This exercise guides the veteran/service member in a personalized multisensory imagery exercise in which he/she creates a mental construct of a safe and peaceful place and practices temporarily withdrawing from engagement with stressors. With practice, this exercise is an effective way to achieve quick relaxation. It can be used in individual or group therapy and as an opening for groups. Follow-up can include practice at home and reporting on outcomes. Often, teaching the exercise to others is a very effective way to master it. Some veterans/service members may benefit from biblio-therapy using the book *We're All Doing Time* by Bo Lozoff or other books listed in Appendix A of *The Veterans and Active Duty Military Psychotherapy Treatment Planner*.

SAFE AND PEACEFUL PLACE MEDITATION

Do you sometimes wish you could just get away from whatever situation you're in, or from whatever you're thinking and feeling? This is a normal and healthy wish. It may not be practical to actually leave a situation right away, though, and sometimes it's hard to leave our own thoughts and feelings behind even when we do physically go somewhere else.

This exercise will teach you how to get away even when you can't go anywhere. It will guide you through a process of creating a mental picture of a safe and peaceful place where you can temporarily relax, so that you can come back to your situation calm and refreshed. Practice is important. The more you practice this, the better you'll get at it and the better it will work for you. With enough repetition, people have used this to achieve calm and inner peace very quickly, often in a few seconds, even in the midst of great pain, anger, and/or anxiety.

For many people, it works best to do this with their eyes closed, so you may want to have someone you trust and feel safe with read this to you while you follow the instructions, or record it in your own voice to play back and listen to.

1. *Image.* What is a place that makes you feel calm, peaceful, and safe to think about? Please think of the place that best fits this description for you and form a mental picture of it. It may be a real place you've been—anything from a favorite beach to your grandparents' kitchen; a place you've heard about and would like to go; or an imaginary place. Whatever is relaxing for you is right for you. Briefly describe this safe and peaceful place.

   _____

   _____

   _____

2. *Emotions and sensations.* Focus on this image or mental picture. What emotions do you feel? What pleasant physical sensations do you feel, and where are they located in your body?

   _____

   _____

   _____

3. *Enhancement.* Please explore this imagery in more detail. Take a few moments to savor it with all your senses and enjoy the idea of being in this safe and peaceful place. When you look around this place in your mind's eye, what do you see happening? What do you hear? Is it warm or cool? What does the air feel like against your face? Is there a distinctive aroma? Please describe these sensory details.

_____

_____

_____

_____

_____

_____

4. *Cue or key word.* Please think of a single word to represent this picture, and keep this word in mind while you once again bring up the mental picture—the sights, the sounds, and all the sensations of peace and safety and pleasure in this place you've created for yourself. Focus on whatever pleasant things come to each of your senses in turn, keeping this key word in mind. Now let your mind dwell on those pleasant sensations and repeat the key word to yourself over and over. Try blanking out the pleasant place you have been thinking of, then thinking of the key word, and see how the image comes back to you quickly and vividly. Notice how your body is feeling relaxed.

5. *Coping with mild stress.* Let's test this as a way for you to relax and overcome negative feelings. Blank out your safe and peaceful place again. Now think of a minor annoyance, a situation or person that isn't a big problem but gets on your nerves. What kinds of negative physical sensations are coming to you when you think of this annoyance? Where are they located in your body?

_____

_____

_____

Now think of your key word. Again, think of the safe and peaceful place in your mind's eye that goes with the key word. Think of the visual image, the scenery, the sounds, and the pleasant physical sensations. As you think of this, how does your body feel? What is happening to the negative sensations you felt in your body?

_____

_____

6. *Practice.* For the next two weeks, practice this at least twice a day, and use it when you find yourself getting irritated or anxious. You can also use it when you are feeling physical pain or discomfort, or if you have trouble sleeping. As you practice, keep noticing anything about the mental image of your peaceful and safe place that

makes it more vivid and more relaxing for you, and keep those details in mind for future times when you do this exercise. As an added help to learning to use it, try teaching it to someone else and see how it works for them.

Use this space to record anything you noticed or learned while doing this meditation exercise.

_____

_____

_____

_____

_____

_____

Be sure to bring this handout back to your next therapy session, and be prepared to discuss your thoughts and feelings about the exercise.

WHY AM I HAVING TROUBLE NOW?

GOALS OF THE EXERCISE

1. Reestablish and strengthen connections with significant other and children.
2. Acclimate to the return to home, friends, family, and community from deployment.
3. Return to previous level of social and occupational functioning prior to deployment.

ADDITIONAL PROBLEMS FOR WHICH THIS EXERCISE MAY BE USEFUL

- Anger Management and Domestic Violence
- Depression
- Insomnia
- Nightmares
- Panic/Agoraphobia
- Parenting Problems Related to Deployment
- Posttraumatic Stress Disorder (PTSD)
- Survivor's Guilt

SUGGESTIONS FOR PROCESSING THIS EXERCISE WITH VETERANS/SERVICE MEMBERS

The "Why Am I Having Trouble Now?" activity is for veterans/service members ambivalent about being home after combat or other overseas duty. Service members are often conflicted about being home, for reasons that can range from not wanting to deal with relationship infidelity to guilt about leaving comrades in the war zone to having unrealistically idealized life at home. Service members are trained to systematically analyze and solve problems. This exercise calls on that skill, guiding the veteran/service member via Socratic open-ended questioning to find the source of ambivalence and generate solutions. The veteran/service member will probably be familiar with the Military Problem Solving Process, the focal point of the exercise. You may need to encourage introspection in this exercise, as denial is common. Follow-up can include reporting back to the therapist/therapy group on actions from this assignment and outcomes as well as bibliotherapy with books from Appendix A of *The Veterans and Active Duty Military Psychotherapy Treatment Planner*.

WHY AM I HAVING TROUBLE NOW?

Although it may not seem to make sense, sometimes veterans or service members are conflicted about being back home. This conflict can cause a variety of feelings including sadness, guilt, and disappointment. It's important to understand that these feelings are normal and will lessen with time. Although a veteran or service member might feel this way for a number of reasons, the most common cause is uncertainty about what life will be like once back home. Many things change over a 6-, 7-, or 12-month deployment. In this exercise you will identify what is causing this conflict for you and use a modified version of the Military Problem Solving Process to fix things.

1. Please place a check by the reason or reasons you are feeling conflicted about being back home. Please note that there is a place to add reasons that aren't listed. This is your time to be your own "shrink" so look down deep and give this question some thought.

_____	Financial Difficulties	_____	Relationship Difficulties
_____	Career Uncertainty	_____	Fear of Being in Public
_____	Lack of Friends	_____	Problems with Children
_____	Legal Problems	_____	Concern about Your Anger
_____	Alcohol/Drug Problems	_____	Guilt for Leaving Comrades
_____	Increased Responsibility	_____	Being Back under the "Flagpole"
_____	Too-High Expectations before Return	_____	Missing the Intensity

    Others:

    _____   _____

    _____   _____

    _____   _____

2. Using this modified version of the Military Problem Solving Process, generate solutions to the issues causing the conflict. The good news is that you have already

completed Step 1 above. Still, it helps to put your thoughts down on paper so please do that here:

a. *Identify the Problem* (Who, what, where, when, and why)

_____

_____

_____

b. *Gather Information* (Identify facts, assumptions, and interests)

_____

_____

_____

c. *Develop Criteria* (Are facts, assumptions, and interests valid? If so, why? If not, why?)

_____

_____

_____

d. *Generate Possible Solutions*

_____

_____

_____

e. *Analyze Possible Solutions*

_____

_____

_____

f. *Determine the Best Solution*

_____

_____

_____

g. *Make and Implement the Decision*

_____

_____

_____

_____

h. *Analyze Results* (if unsatisfactory, adjust solution as necessary and repeat steps d–h)

_____

_____

_____

_____

Be sure to bring this handout back to your next session with your therapist, and be prepared to discuss your thoughts and feelings about the exercise.

WHAT'S DIFFERENT AND HOW WILL I ADAPT?

GOALS OF THE EXERCISE

1. Minimize adjustment difficulties upon return home.
2. Determine priorities related to family, work, and social obligations.
3. Set boundaries with family and friends.
4. Return to level of family and social functioning prior to deployment.

ADDITIONAL PROBLEMS FOR WHICH THIS EXERCISE MAY BE USEFUL

- Anxiety
- Depression
- Insomnia
- Posttraumatic Stress Disorder (PTSD)
- Separation and Divorce
- Social Discomfort

SUGGESTIONS FOR PROCESSING THIS EXERCISE SWITH VETERANS/SERVICE MEMBERS

The "What's Different and How Will I Adapt?" activity is for veterans/service members who have returned from deployments and are becoming overwhelmed by responsibilities and requests for social interactions. The service member may have unrealistic expectations, or feel obligated to agree to all requests and neglect his or her need to take things slowly for the first several weeks. This exercise aims to help the veteran/service member prioritize household, family, and social responsibilities, and to help the service member see that it is okay to say "No" and set boundaries with family and friends. The service member may need reassurance that most friends and family members will understand his/her need for space in the early days back home. You may also need to challenge feelings of guilt or shame, using techniques such as Socratic questioning or the Gestalt "empty chair" to help the veteran/service member realistically assess demands and expectations. Follow-up can include reporting back to the therapist/therapy group on actions related to this assignment and their outcomes, as well as bibliotherapy with books from Appendix A of *The Veterans and Active Duty Military Psychotherapy Treatment Planner*.

WHAT'S DIFFERENT AND HOW WILL I ADAPT?

Within a few days of being back home you may feel the pressure (either from others or from your own expectations of yourself) to take over all your old responsibilities such as paying the bills or doing the yard work. You may have friends and family wanting to spend time with you to an extent which may be creating strain between you and your spouse and children. Although getting back into your old routines and spending quality time with loved ones is important, if you take on more than you have time and energy for you can become overwhelmed. If this happens, the time it takes you to adjust to being back will be greater and your quality of life and your most important relationships will suffer. In this exercise, you will prioritize things you want or need to do, separating those responsibilities that can't wait from those that can. Then you can develop a "script" that you can use to tell family and friends that you need time to decompress and reconnect with your family.

1. *Prioritizing Responsibilities*

    a. Please list up to eight tasks or functions of everyday life for which you are expected (by yourself or by others) to take over responsibility (e.g., paying the bills), and rate them from 1 to 8 with the rating of 1 being the responsibility most in need of being taken over as soon as possible and 8 being the least critical.

        Task/Function   **Rating**

        _____   _____

        _____   _____

        _____   _____

        _____   _____

        _____   _____

        _____   _____

        _____   _____

        _____   _____

    b. After filling out the list above, talk with your significant other about your results and ask for his/her input. After this discussion, re-rank your responsibilities if they have changed.

Task/Function	Rating
_____	_____
_____	_____
_____	_____
_____	_____
_____	_____
_____	_____
_____	_____

2. With the help of your significant other, develop a "script," or a ready answer, that you can rehearse and use each time someone asks you for your time or energy in a way that would interfere with the priorities you established in item 1.b. above or with taking care of yourself and getting enough rest and time with your significant other and children. Here's an example: you can use all or part of this one or create one of your own.

    It's great to hear/see you and it's great to be back from deployment. I am really looking forward to spending time with you. However, our unit Chaplain/Commander told us about the importance of taking things slow and reconnecting with our wives/husbands and children during the first several weeks. It's a way to help us decompress after being gone for so long. But, don't worry. We will be spending time with each other again real soon. We have a lot to catch up on. Thanks again for thinking of me.

    _____

    _____

    _____

    _____

3. Once you've got your script, practice it. Your significant other can help by role-playing as part of your rehearsal—playing the part of someone asking for your time and attention and perhaps being pushy about it. Do you find yourself using the script? How effective do you think it is?

    _____

Be sure to bring this handout back to your next session with your therapist, and be prepared to discuss your thoughts and feelings about the exercise.

I AM A SURVIVOR, NOT A VICTIM—PTSD AS LIFE SAVING ADAPTATION

GOALS OF THE EXERCISE

1. Eliminate or reduce the negative impact trauma-related symptoms have on social, occupational, and family functioning.
2. Return to the pretrauma level of psychological functioning.
3. Regain confidence in abilities as an effective Soldier, Sailor, Airman, Marine, or Coast Guardsman.

ADDITIONAL PROBLEMS FOR WHICH THIS EXERCISE MAY BE USEFUL

- Adjustment to Killing
- Anxiety
- Borderline Personality
- Combat and Operational Stress Reaction
- Insomnia
- Nightmares
- Panic/Agoraphobia
- Physiological Stress Response—Acute

SUGGESTIONS FOR PROCESSING THIS EXERCISE WITH VETERANS/SERVICE MEMBERS

The "I Am a Survivor, Not a Victim—PTSD as Lifesaving Adaptation" activity is for veterans/service members whose quality of life and ability to function in one or more domains are markedly reduced by PTSD symptoms. It uses a psychoeducational and cognitive-behavioral approach, reframing PTSD symptoms as functional adaptations to danger that are simply no longer useful, that having adapted to a deadly situation, the veteran/service member has a proven ability to adapt and can do so again, and that adapting to a more benign situation may be hard, but not as hard as adapting to combat. Follow-up can include the exercise "Identifying and Avoiding or Coping with PTSD Triggers," and can also include reading assignments from books listed in Appendix A of *The Veterans and Active Duty Military Psychotherapy Treatment Planner*.

I AM A SURVIVOR, NOT A VICTIM—PTSD AS LIFESAVING ADAPTATION

If you've been told you have posttraumatic stress disorder (PTSD), you may feel some confusion or mixed emotions for various reasons. The terminology can be complicated; the entertainment industry portrays people with PTSD in ways you don't identify with; and in the military and in popular culture, you may have learned to think of people with PTSD as weak, malingering, or too messed up to ever have a decent life. Those are views of PTSD no one would like. On the other hand, it can be reassuring when someone confirms that you had a terrible experience and aren't just feeling sorry for yourself. This exercise will give you a clearer picture of PTSD and a more positive way to look at it. Another exercise that's useful as a follow-up to this one is titled "Identifying and Avoiding or Coping with PTSD Triggers"; it will give you some practical skills for living with PTSD.

1. Let's start with a plain-language definition of PTSD. As defined by the American Psychiatric Association, there are five categories of criteria. The first is just that a person has experienced a traumatic event that involved the actual or potential death or serious injury of that person or someone else, and that he or she felt intense fear, helplessness, or horror. This is often a combat experience, but it could be a violent crime, car crash, work accident, natural disaster, life-threatening illness, or other life-threatening situation. Does this fit for you? What was the situation, and what about it caused your feelings of fear, helplessness, or horror?

    _____

    _____

    a. If you've had such an experience, there are three groups of symptoms that determine whether you have PTSD. The first group pertains to intrusive recall of the event—they are ways in which the traumatic experience comes to mind when you don't want it to and interferes with your life. This can take the form of memories, visual images, flashbacks, nightmares, or feeling intensely upset if something reminds you of the event. How does this fit your experience?

        _____

        _____

b. The next symptom group relates to persistently avoiding reminders of the trauma event and being emotionally numb and distant from others. There are seven different symptoms in this group, and it takes three to diagnose PTSD. Again, how does this fit for you?

_____

_____

c. The last set of symptoms are signs of hyperarousal, or being jumpier and edgier than before the trauma. There are five, from insomnia to irritability to hypervigilance (inability to relax and stop watching your surroundings). A PTSD diagnosis looks for two or more.

_____

_____

    The final criteria have to do with how long these things have been happening and with how disruptive they are to important parts of your life.

2. Looking over this information you may notice that it doesn't sound as extreme as the portrayals of PTSD we see all too often on TV and in films. It isn't. In fact, in some ways PTSD serves a positive purpose in the right time and place in a person's life—it's a survival adaptation, a proof of the mind's ability to adjust to a very hostile environment and make the changes needed to survive. In the situations that cause PTSD, many of its symptoms improve a person's chance of survival _under those conditions_. Look back at the symptoms listed: The first group relates to intrusive memories and intense reactions to reminders of the trauma. We need to think about memory's role in self-preservation. It's important to remember dangerous or painful things so we'll be on guard if we face them again. The worse the experience, the more vividly we remember it—did you ever touch a hot stove burner? As for the intense physical and emotional reactions, if we did find ourselves in similar situations, those intense reactions might give us the edge it would take to survive, and having it happen instantly would be a good thing. Has this pattern helped you take care of yourself in a dangerous environment?

_____

3. The same is true for the avoidance and numbing—avoiding things that hurt us is basic survival, and the emotional numbing is there to help people get through situations without breaking down, like the temporary numbness we sometimes get with physical injuries. Finally, the last group, forms of hypervigilance, is clearly pro-survival in a dangerous environment. So the symptoms of PTSD are adaptations that may have saved your life in the environment where they developed. Does looking at it this way change the emotions you feel when you think about PTSD? If so, describe your before-and-after feelings about it:

_____

_____

4. No matter how valuable some of these symptoms were in the right circumstances, they aren't making your quality of life better now. But here is a positive but realistic way to think about that: To develop PTSD, you had to make a fast adaptation to a deadly environment possibly without a lot of guidance or support from other people. You did, and you got through some experiences that some other people couldn't. You are a survivor because you proved your ability to adapt. Now, you need to adapt again, but there are three differences:

    a. You aren't facing the kind of danger you were before, so you can take more time;

    b. You don't have to figure it out on your own—there are a lot of resources available; and

    c. You have the benefit of the wisdom and life experience you've gained since then.

    This isn't to say it's easy, but it won't be as rough as that first time you had to adapt. As long as you don't give up, you can overcome a lot of the effects of PTSD, as many other veterans/service members have done before you and are doing right now.

Be sure to bring this handout back to your next therapy session, and be prepared to discuss your thoughts and feelings about the exercise.

IDENTIFYING AND AVOIDING OR COPING WITH PTSD TRIGGERS

GOALS OF THE EXERCISE

1. Eliminate or reduce the negative impact trauma-related symptoms have on social, occupational, and family functioning.
2. Learn and use relaxation and calming strategies.
3. Return to the pretrauma level of psychological functioning.
4. Regain confidence in abilities as an effective Soldier, Sailor, Airman, Marine, or Coast Guardsman.
5. Learn relapse prevention strategies to manage future PTSD symptoms.

ADDITIONAL PROBLEMS FOR WHICH THIS EXERCISE MAY BE USEFUL

- Amputation, Loss of Mobility, Disfigurement
- Anxiety
- Borderline Personality
- Combat and Operational Stress Reaction
- Insomnia
- Nightmares
- Panic/Agoraphobia
- Physiological Stress Response–Acute

SUGGESTIONS FOR PROCESSING THIS EXERCISE WITH VETERANS/SERVICE MEMBERS

The "Identifying and Avoiding or Coping with PTSD Triggers" activity is for veterans/ service members with PTSD whose quality of life and ability to function in one or more domains are markedly reduced by reactive PTSD symptoms being triggered in their lives. The activity uses a cognitive-behavioral approach like recovering addicts use in regard to potential relapse triggers, guiding the veteran/service member in planning to avoid being surprised by these triggers, to avoid them when practical, and to use proven coping techniques when they are unavoidable. This activity is a follow-up to "I Am a Survivor, Not a Victim—PTSD as Lifesaving Adaptation," and can itself be followed up with reading from books listed in Appendix A of *The Veterans and Active Duty Military Psychotherapy Treatment Planner*.

IDENTIFYING AND AVOIDING OR COPING WITH PTSD TRIGGERS

One of the goals of treatment for PTSD is to enable us to live as unrestricted a life as we can by not having to hide from possible triggers for PTSD symptoms. Still, it's smart to plan ahead and avoid triggers if we don't need to expose ourselves to them, as well as planning how to minimize our emotional discomfort when we meet triggers we can't avoid or predict. This activity will guide you in some simple planning that can improve your quality of life.

1. First, it's important to get a clear picture of the kinds of situations, events, and objects that trigger your PTSD symptoms. This will depend largely on the nature of your traumatic experience(s), but if you've been dealing with this for a while, you have a good idea of the general kind of situation that makes it hard for you to stay calm and positive. Please use this space to jot down some information about common patterns in your particular PTSD triggers:

    _____

    _____

    _____

2. Looking over this information and reflecting on experience, identify some places and situations that are likely to trigger your symptoms. For example, some people get uneasy in crowds, while certain sights, sounds, or smells trigger memories and emotions for others. Please list some situations you have to deal with in the next month that may be upsetting for you in this way. Once you've done this, divide them into categories. One group will be situations you can avoid without any problems as a result; next will be situations you can't avoid, or ones where avoidance would cause more stress in your life than the symptoms that may be triggered; the third type are situations you may encounter, but can't predict when or where.

Can Avoid	Can't Avoid	Can't Predict
_____	_____	_____
_____	_____	_____
_____	_____	_____
_____	_____	_____
_____	_____	_____

3. For the situations you can easily avoid, the plan is simple—unless you need to go there, don't. This is a reasonable strategy. A goal of PTSD treatment is to stop being ruled by avoidant behavior, but there's no point in going out of your way to be uncomfortable. If anyone asks about a change in your habits, please describe how you will explain it to them—a simple explanation like "I don't really like crowds," or something similar, is fine.

_____

_____

4. Next come trigger situations that are impractical to avoid—maybe they are part of your job, or they are important family occasions. For predictable stressful situations, there are some simple and basic things to do that will make the experiences more pleasant for you. We will present them here, and ask you to fill in the details that will fit your own situations.

   a. *Support from family and friends*: Spend time before the event doing something relaxing with someone whose company you enjoy; if it's somebody that makes you laugh, even better. Let them know the upcoming situation may be stressful for you and get their encouragement. If they will also be there, plan to touch bases now and then during the event; you may also want to plan to go for coffee or something like that afterward so you can relax again.

   b. *Take breaks*: Find a way to step away from the event for a couple of minutes every so often, and when you do make a point of doing some slow, deep breathing and loosening up of any muscles you realize you've been tensing up.

   c. *Departure plan*: Have your departure planned in advance and discuss it with anyone who's going with you so they will know when you plan to arrive and to leave. To avoid inconveniencing anyone, have your own transportation. If this is a party or other gathering of family and friends, you can quietly explain to your hosts in advance why you'll be doing this so they don't think it's about them.

   d. *Avoid alcohol:* If the situation is already testing you, adding alcohol will only make it more stressful and undermine your self-control—stick to coffee, tea, and sodas.

   Those are just some starters—you may think of other things that will help you relax and have a more pleasant time. What are some strategies that you will use?

_____

_____

5. Third, we have the "can't predict" situations. For these, the best approach is to have some simple "immediate action" strategies you've thought through. These might include:

a. Breathing and muscle relaxation routines;

b. People you can call (make sure to have a cell phone and their numbers with you, and have enough names that if some aren't available, you'll be able to get hold of someone else); and

c. Activities to re-calm yourself afterward if you're agitated.

What can you do to stay calm when a high-stress situation takes you by surprise?

_____

_____

6. If these strategies aren't enough and you find yourself triggered and agitated, focus on physical sensations and your immediate surroundings. Try rubbing your hands together, finding a restroom and splashing cool water on your face, humming, eating or drinking something and focusing on the taste and texture, and paying close attention to the non-triggering things you see and hear around you. Reconnecting with the here and now helps us avoid getting focused on the past and traumatic memories. How can you stay in touch with the here and now?

_____

_____

Be sure to bring this handout back to your next therapy session, and be prepared to discuss your thoughts and feelings about the exercise.

AM I READY FOR DEPLOYMENT?

GOALS OF THE EXERCISE

1. Acknowledge that fear and anxiety are normal and expected reactions prior to deployment.
2. Identify and discuss the nature of the anxiety related to the actual deployment.
3. Discuss expectations and realities regarding communication while deployed.
4. Develop a plan of how to recognize birthdays, anniversaries, and graduations for loved ones.

ADDITIONAL PROBLEMS FOR WHICH THIS EXERCISE MAY BE USEFUL

- Adjustment to the Military Culture
- Anxiety
- Insomnia
- Parenting Problems Related to Deployment
- Separation and Divorce

SUGGESTIONS FOR PROCESSING THIS EXERCISE WITH SERVICE MEMBERS

The "Am I Ready for Deployment?" activity is a companion unit to "Helping My Family Prepare for My Deployment." Where that activity focuses strictly on practical preparation such as making financial and legal arrangements, this one is written with the goal of helping the service member and his or her family prepare on an intra- and interpersonal level. It can also be considered a unit to be used in conjunction with the two activities listed for *Parenting Problems Related to Deployment*. Follow-up could include reviewing the list with the service member, possibly in a joint session including his/her significant other, as well as bibliotherapy using books listed in Appendix A of *The Veterans and Active Duty Military Psychotherapy Treatment Planner*.

AM I READY FOR DEPLOYMENT?

There are many things to do and think about when you're getting ready to be deployed and it can be easy for the strictly practical matters, like finances and household operations, to take up all your time and energy. Those are vital, but it's also critical for you to prepare emotionally and have a plan addressing how you'll stay in communication with your significant other and with your children, if you have children. You may also want to go through the exercises titled "How Will I Explain this Deployment to My Children?" and "How Will I Stay in Touch with My Children?" They offer a number of useful ideas and questions to ask and answer with your family before you deploy. This exercise will touch on those matters, but will also focus on preparing yourself, since you are the person who is going to be deployed.

1. What are the things that cause you the most anxiety when you think about your upcoming deployment? Please check off up to five of the items listed here:

    _____ Significant other's health

    _____ Child(ren)'s health

    _____ My health

    _____ Other family member's health

    _____ Worry about safety of family while I'm deployed

    _____ Danger of being killed or wounded in combat

    _____ Communication with significant other

    _____ Communication with child(ren)

    _____ Impact of separation on marriage/primary relationship

    _____ Stress of "temporary single parent" role for significant other

    _____ Emotional effect of separation on children

    _____ Children having behavior and discipline problems while I'm deployed

    _____ Children having problems at school while I'm deployed

    _____ Financial problems while I'm deployed

    _____ Missing important occasions while I'm deployed—specify: _____

Other:

_____

_____

_____

_____

2. Please look at the items you checked as causing you the most anxiety, and rank them in order from 1 to 5, with 1 being the item that worries you the most. What item did you rank as #1?

_____

3. For your item #1, please use this modified version of the Military Problem Solving Process to generate solutions. The good news is that you have already completed Step 1 above. Still, it helps to put your thoughts down on paper so please do that here:

    a. *Identify the Problem* (Who, what, where, when, and why)

    _____

    _____

    _____

    b. *Gather Information* (Identify facts, assumptions, and interests)

    _____

    _____

    _____

    c. *Develop Criteria* (Are facts, assumptions, and interests valid? If so, why? If not, why?)

    _____

    _____

    _____

    d. *Generate Possible Solutions*

    _____

    _____

    _____

    e. *Analyze Possible Solutions*

    _____

    _____

    _____

f. *Determine the Best Solution*

_____

_____

_____

g. *Make and Implement the Decision*

_____

_____

_____

_____

h. *Analyze Results* (if unsatisfactory, adjust solution as necessary and repeat steps d–h)

_____

_____

_____

4. Now repeat this process for each of the other items you selected as your top five concerns. For example, if you chose items related to communication with your significant other and children, you would want to complete a plan, created with their help, to ensure regular and meaningful communication and to avoid their being unnecessarily worried if events keep you from being able to communicate with them at all times. A key aspect of analyzing any concern is to include, in question 3.c (*Develop Criteria*), a realistic estimate of how likely or unlikely the item or event is to happen, and how serious a problem it will be if it does. For question 3.f. (*Determine the Best Solution*), don't forget to draw on your past successes at similar challenges.

Be sure to bring this handout back to your next session with your therapist, and be prepared to discuss your thoughts and feelings about the exercise.

HELPING MY FAMILY PREPARE
FOR MY DEPLOYMENT

GOALS OF THE EXERCISE

1. Feel comfortable about level of pre-deployment preparation reached.
2. Feel confident with financial plan in place prior to deployment.
3. Identify community and family supports that can assist the family while the service member is deployed.
4. Identify and locate all important documents that may be needed by the service member or family members during the deployment.

ADDITIONAL PROBLEMS FOR WHICH THIS EXERCISE MAY BE USEFUL

- Adjustment to the Military Culture
- Anxiety

SUGGESTIONS FOR PROCESSING THIS EXERCISE WITH SERVICE MEMBERS

The "Helping My Family Prepare for My Deployment" activity is written as an aid for service members who are feeling anxious about pending deployments and the question of whether they've made adequate administrative, financial, and logistical preparations to enable their families, in particular their significant others, to keep the household running while the service members are deployed. The extensive and necessary preparations can seem overwhelming for the most organized service member, particularly if this is his/her first deployment. This exercise will help service members get their affairs in order before leaving, increase their sense of control, and decrease their levels of anxiety by ensuring that preparations are as thorough as possible. It will also make things easier for the significant others that are left at home and reduce stress and anxiety for them. It's important to remind the service member that the list in this exercise is not all encompassing and that he/she and his/her significant other should spend adequate time discussing pre-deployment preparation issues and brainstorming other preparations that might need to be taken care of. Follow-up could include reviewing the list with the service member, possibly in a joint session including his/her significant other, as well as bibliotherapy using books listed in Appendix A of *The Veterans and Active Duty Military Psychotherapy Treatment Planner*.

HELPING MY FAMILY PREPARE FOR MY DEPLOYMENT

Getting prepared for deployment is a huge undertaking. Whether you are leaving for 3 months or 15 months, it's imperative to have your affairs in order. This will reduce your anxiety and that of your family before you deploy and make life more manageable for them while you're away. This exercise provides a checklist of common items to take care of before deployment and is designed as a tool to help you and your significant other prepare. Please keep in mind that every situation is unique and you may have additional items to prepare that aren't on this list—don't assume it's complete for your situation. As you go through this list together, check off each item as you complete it and plan your time to enable you to complete all the items that apply in your situation before you deploy. This list is long, so make sure you set aside at least three hours to review all the items.

PAY-RELATED MATTERS

Paychecks and Financial Readiness

☐ Have you and your spouse discussed and prepared a budget?

☐ Have arrangements been made for your spouse to have access to adequate funds during deployment?

☐ Is Direct Deposit in effect?

☐ Does spouse know expected pay dates?

☐ Does spouse know how much of each paycheck is available to him/her?

☐ Is spouse aware of upcoming pay changes due to advancement, gain or loss of government housing, longevity?

☐ What are the effective dates of pay changes?

☐ What is the amount of change and the reason?

Banking and Investments

☐ Does spouse have information about checking account(s): account number(s) and bank's address and phone number?

☐ Does spouse have information about savings account(s): account number(s) and bank's address and phone number?

☐ Does spouse have access to, and know how to use, all accounts?

☐ Does spouse know how to balance accounts when statements are received?

☐ Does spouse know about investments that must be managed: Money market funds, mutual funds, savings certificates, etc.?

☐ Does spouse know what payment(s) should be made to IRA(s)?

☐ Does spouse know where financial documents are kept?

☐ Does spouse have a list of actions on investments needed during deployment?

☐ Does spouse have account numbers, company names, addresses, and phone numbers of companies with which investments are placed?

☐ Does spouse have information on all credit accounts, especially bankcards, including: name of creditor, account number, phone number, address, and latest statement with account balance due?

☐ Does spouse know about any safety deposit boxes? Where it/they are located? Location of key(s)?

Taxes

☐ Does spouse know how to prepare taxes or what preparer to go to for tax preparation?

☐ Does spouse know how to acquire necessary tax information and forms for federal, state, and county taxes, as applicable?

☐ Does spouse have adequate funds to cover the cost of tax preparation, if necessary?

☐ Have service member and spouse talked thoroughly about using extensions to ease the preparation of taxes?

☐ Do estimated state/federal income taxes need to be paid?

Emergency Financial Resources

☐ Does spouse know what emergency financial assistance is available through Navy/Marine Corps Relief Society, Army Emergency Relief, Red Cross, etc.?

☐ Does spouse know contact information for agencies which provide emergency assistance?

☐ Does spouse know that budget counseling and referrals are available on base/post?

INSURANCE MATTERS

Life Insurance

☐ Does spouse know location of policy(ies)?

☐ Are beneficiaries up-to-date on policy(ies)?

☐ Are annual, semi-annual, or quarterly premiums due during deployment? If yes, when?

☐ Does spouse understand benefits from policy(ies)?

☐ Will renewal or changes be necessary during deployment? If yes, what should be done and when?

☐ Does spouse know name, address, phone number, and account numbers for carrier(s)?

Medical Insurance

☐ Does spouse know location of policy(ies)?

☐ Are names of eligible family members up-to-date on policy(ies)?

☐ Are annual, semi-annual, or quarterly premiums due during deployment? If yes, when?

☐ Does spouse understand payment method on policy(ies)?

☐ Does spouse understand coverage included in policy(ies)?

☐ Will renewal or changes be necessary during deployment? If yes, what should be done and when?

☐ Does spouse know the name, address, phone number, and account numbers of carrier(s)?

Homeowners/Renters Insurance

☐ Does spouse know location of policy(ies)?

☐ Are coverage amounts up-to-date and adequate on all policies?

☐ Are annual, semi-annual, or quarterly premiums due during deployment? If yes, when?

☐ Does spouse understand payment method on policy(ies)?

☐ Does spouse understand all coverage included in policy(ies)?

☐ Is the deductible set where you want it?

☐ Does spouse understand what the deductible is and are adequate funds available to cover it?

☐ Will renewal or changes be necessary during deployment? If yes, what should be done and when?

☐ Does spouse know the name, address, phone number, and account number for carrier(s)?

Automobile Insurance

☐ Does spouse know location of policy(ies)?

☐ Is coverage up-to-date and adequate on policy(ies)?

☐ Is deductible set where you want it?

☐ Does spouse understand what the deductible is and are there adequate funds available to cover it?

☐ Are annual, semi-annual, or quarterly premiums due during deployment? If yes, when?

☐ Does spouse understand payment method on policy(ies)?

☐ Will renewal or changes be necessary during deployment? If yes, what should be done and when?

☐ Does spouse know the company name, address, phone number, and account number for policy(ies)?

☐ Does policy have a towing clause? If not, does spouse have adequate funds to cover this expense?

☐ Does policy have a rent-a-car clause? If not, does spouse have adequate funds to cover this expense?

☐ Does spouse know what information to gather and what to do in the event of an accident with another vehicle?

TRANSPORTATION

Inspect the Condition of:

☐ Radiator and heater hoses

☐ Engine vacuum lines

☐ Fuel lines

☐ Brake linings, discs, pads, brake lines

☐ Engine drive belts, fan, alternator

☐ Air filters

☐ Oil filters

General

☐ Do you both have current driver's licenses?

☐ Who will help with transportation in an emergency?

☐ Does spouse know how to drive? If not, can he/she learn and receive a license before deployment?

☐ Do you have adequate transportation available? If not, how will spouse get groceries, get to the doctor's office, get to work, etc.?

Does Spouse Know:

☐ Location of spare bulbs/fuses?

☐ How to check oil and other fluid levels in the car?

☐ How to check tire pressure?

☐ How to change a tire?

☐ How to draw up a preventive maintenance checklist for your vehicle(s): cars, trucks, motorcycles?

☐ Whether your vehicles are under warranty? If yes, what the warranties do and don't cover?

☐ Maintenance requirements to maintain effectiveness/validity of the warranties?

☐ When the next tune-up is due on your vehicle?

☐ Where to take the vehicle to have it worked on?

☐ What kind of gasoline is used in each vehicle?

☐ Who to call if the vehicle won't start?

☐ If you belong to an auto club? If yes, does spouse know:

- What the membership name/number is?
- What services will the club provide?
- Any additional costs above the membership fees for those services?

☐ If the tires are in good shape? If they must be replaced during deployment, what brand and size to buy?

☐ Has the radiator been checked for coolant/antifreeze?

☐ Has the air conditioning system been charged recently?

☐ When is the next scheduled maintenance due? Where should the spouse get the work done?

☐ What other maintenance is coming due during the deployment? If yes, where should it be done?

☐ What to do in the case of an accident or breakdown?

Vehicle(s) Registration and Other Documents

☐ Location of papers: (registration, title, insurance)?

☐ Do you have the title? Where is it located?

☐ Who holds the lien if there is one?

☐ Will vehicle registration(s) need renewing during deployment?

☐ Will vehicle safety inspection(s) need renewing during deployment?

☐ Does spouse know where to go for these, how much they cost, what paperwork is needed, etc.?

☐ Does spouse have a specific Power of Attorney from service member that covers registering cars, etc.?

☐ Does the base/post registration of the vehicle(s) expire during deployment? If yes, can service member renew before deployment? If unable to renew prior to deployment, does spouse know where to go and how to apply for base/post registration?

☐ Is (are) the current insurance ID card in the appropriate vehicle(s)? If so, where? If not, place them there as required by law.

☐ Does spouse know where to go for financial assistance in case of unexpected vehicle repair costs?

☐ Does spouse have an extra set of keys for vehicle(s) and know where the extra keys are?

PERSONAL READINESS AND SUPPORT

☐ Have children been included in the discussions on where the service member is going, when he/she is expected home, and why he/she is going?

☐ Does spouse know service member's social security number?

☐ Does spouse know service member's complete official mailing address while deployed?

☐ Does spouse know the name of the chaplain and how to reach him/her?

☐ If an emergency arises, does your spouse know who to contact to get the word to the service member?

☐ Have you made arrangements for the care of your children in the event that something should happen to your spouse while you are deployed?

☐ Does spouse know how to get ID cards replaced if lost or stolen?

☐ Has service member made note of all birthdays, anniversaries, holidays, etc. that will be celebrated during deployment and is service member prepared to send gifts, cards, etc.?

☐ Is the service member's family photo album updated and ready to take along, as a reminder of the family?

☐ Has spouse made plans for a baby-sitter once in awhile during deployment to get out and "de-stress?"

☐ Have you made plans to get a baby-sitter (if needed) to spend some special time together before deployment?

HOUSING

Government Housing

☐ Are you on the waiting list for quarters? If yes, what is your latest status?

☐ Does the Housing Office know how to contact the spouse while service member is deployed?

☐ Does spouse know how to arrange the move into quarters if they become available during deployment?

☐ Does spouse have a Specific Power of Attorney to cover acceptance of quarters?

☐ If in government quarters, does spouse know how and when to contact the housing maintenance office for repairs?

☐ Does spouse have a Housing Handbook?

Renters

☐ Does spouse know the name of, and how to contact, the landlord?

☐ Does spouse know when to contact the landlord for repairs?

☐ Does lease or rental agreement expire during deployment?

☐ Does spouse have Power of Attorney to renew lease or rental agreement, if necessary?

Homeowners

☐ Does spouse know what is required for maintenance?

☐ Does spouse know who to call for electrical, plumbing, roofing, carpentry, and painting needs?

☐ Does spouse know the details of your real estate taxes: how much, when due?

☐ Does spouse know where mortgage papers and other important documents are kept?

☐ Does spouse know requirements for renewing homestead exemption declaration, if necessary?

Miscellaneous

☐ Do all doors and windows have good locks?

☐ Does spouse have extra house keys and know where they are?

☐ Does your home have a security system (this may earn you a decrease in insurance costs that will help pay for it, and some systems include smoke and carbon monoxide detection)?

☐ Are smoke detectors and fire extinguishers working?

☐ Does spouse know how to check and use them?

☐ Do you have an escape plan in case of fire (everyone knows how to get out and where to meet after leaving the house)?

☐ Have you had a recent fire safety inspection?

☐ Does spouse know where the electrical circuit breaker box is located? Is it labeled? Does spouse know how to use the main circuit breaker?

☐ Does spouse know where the valve for the water main is, and how to operate it?

☐ Does spouse know how and where the gas line is turned off?

☐ Are all major appliances in good working order?

☐ Who will spouse call if an appliance needs repair?

☐ Do you have appliance maintenance agreements or warranties, and does spouse understand them? Where are they located?

☐ Where are the flashlights and candles? Are there fresh batteries?

☐ Where are basic hand tools (hammer, pliers, screw drivers, etc.) kept?

☐ Where do you keep important papers concerning the home?

☐ Do you have a plan for the yard work (mowing, tree trimming, etc.)?

☐ Are yard tools (lawn mower, edger, string trimmer, etc.) in good working order?

☐ Does spouse know how to operate the yard tools safely?

MEDICAL PREPARATION

- ☐ Are all family members enrolled in DEERS?
- ☐ Are any dependent family members eligible for medical care but not enrolled in DEERS?
- ☐ Does the spouse know where the family's medical records are held?
- ☐ Are the family's immunizations and check-ups up-to-date?
- ☐ Have you and your family made a selection about which CHAMPUS/TRICARE program you will participate in?
- ☐ Have you arranged for CHAMPUS/TRICARE fees to be paid by payroll allotment?
- ☐ Is spouse familiar with your CHAMPUS/TRICARE program, how it functions, and where to get information?
- ☐ Where are your TRICARE cards located?
- ☐ If you are pregnant, who will care for your children while you deliver?
- ☐ Does anyone else have or need a Medical Power of Attorney for your children?

SCHOOLS

- ☐ If your child(ren) are in school, do you know where he/she attends?
- ☐ Who is your child's teacher?
- ☐ Have you told your child's teacher about the upcoming deployment?
- ☐ Do you know how, where, and when to register children for school?

LEGAL READINESS

- ☐ Do you and your spouse have up-to-date wills?
- ☐ Are wills kept in a secure and convenient place?
- ☐ Does spouse know where the wills are kept and how to get them?
- ☐ Has service member given spouse adequate Power(s) of Attorney for all anticipated needs?
- ☐ Does the spouse know the location of Power(s) of Attorney?
- ☐ Are there other legal matters to which the spouse must attend during the deployment?

MILITARY MATTERS

- ☐ Is service member due for orders during deployment?
- ☐ If yes, does spouse know how to arrange the move (household goods, vehicle shipment, etc.)?
- ☐ Does spouse have Power of Attorney to enable him/her to arrange the move?

Communication Readiness

- ☐ Does spouse know the various ways to communicate with service member?
- ☐ Does spouse know the full and correct address for deployed service member?
- ☐ Does spouse know where to turn for help in sending communications to service member?

EMERGENCY PLANS

- ☐ Have you and your spouse discussed the following possible emergencies that the family may face while service member is deployed? What are some possible solutions?

_____

_____

_____

- ☐ Automobile breakdown
- ☐ Automobile accident
- ☐ Appliance breakdown
- ☐ Loss of heat, power, water
- ☐ Flooding in the home
- ☐ Critical illness or death in the family
- ☐ Obscene/harassing phone calls

CHECKLIST OF IMPORTANT PAPERS

Be sure you know the location of, and how to use, the following papers:

- ☐ Saving account passbooks and loan payment coupons
- ☐ Insurance policies
- ☐ Automobile lien papers
- ☐ Wills
- ☐ Birth certificates
- ☐ Divorce decree(s)
- ☐ Adoption papers
- ☐ Tax documents
- ☐ Payment receipts
- ☐ Warranties
- ☐ Checkbook/investment documents
- ☐ Automobile title(s)
- ☐ Automobile registration(s)

☐ Power(s) of Attorney

☐ Marriage certificate

☐ Custody papers

☐ Credit agreements

☐ Immunization records

☐ Canceled checks

☐ Mortgage/lease agreement

Note: It is a wise precaution to get a small fireproof document safe and keep all important documents in it. Office supply stores sell them in sizes that will hold all of a typical household's important documents, usually for less than $200.00. This offers these advantages:

- It keeps all these documents together in one place where they won't be misfiled, misplaced, or damaged (if a document is lost and you have to take even one day off work to get it replaced, that might cost more in lost pay than the price of the safe).
- In case of fire, flood, tornado, and so forth, the safe will protect its contents.
- In the event you need to evacuate suddenly due to a natural disaster or other reason, it's easier to just put the document safe in your vehicle than to dig through a filing cabinet or other places your documents might be kept.

Be sure to bring this handout back to your next session with your therapist, and be prepared to discuss your thoughts and feelings about the exercise.

GETTING THROUGH THE LOSS
OF A RELATIONSHIP

GOALS OF THE EXERCISE

1. Evaluate the possibility of resolving the differences and review the pros and cons of remaining married.
2. Consistently uphold "the best interests of the children" as paramount and act accordingly, regardless of the final fate of the marriage.
3. Resolve the initial confusion and turmoil of separation.
4. Mourn the end of the relationship and reach a fair divorce agreement.

ADDITIONAL PROBLEMS FOR WHICH THIS EXERCISE MAY BE USEFUL

*   Anger Management and Domestic Violence
*   Anxiety
*   Borderline Personality
*   Depression
*   Homesickness/Loneliness
*   Parenting Problems Related to Deployment
*   Post-Deployment Reintegration Problems

SUGGESTIONS FOR PROCESSING THIS EXERCISE
WITH VETERANS/SERVICE MEMBERS

The "Getting Through the Loss of a Relationship" activity is for veterans/service members who are either experiencing relationship problems that may lead to loss of the relationship, or are currently or recently ending a relationship. Its approach is cognitive-behavioral, guiding the veteran/service member in identifying and correcting depressive distortions in his or her thinking, as well as replacing negatively distorted self-talk with positive and realistic self-talk. Follow-up can be the exercise "Avoiding Rebounds, Replays, and Resentments: Identifying and Changing Patterns That Aren't Working," reading assignments from books listed in Appendix A of *The Veterans and Active Duty Military Psychotherapy Treatment Planner*, and videotherapy with films suggested for "Adoption and Custody" and "Divorce" in *Rent Two Films and Let's Talk in the Morning*, 2nd ed., by John W. Hesley and Jan G. Hesley, published by John Wiley & Sons.

GETTING THROUGH THE LOSS
OF A RELATIONSHIP

There is no easy or painless way to get through a divorce or the breakup of another committed long-term relationship, at least not for anyone who had his or her heart in it in the first place. Loss of a primary relationship is one of the most stressful experiences a person can have. In some ways it's a lot like the death of a loved one. There are things we can do to cope with this situation as well as possible, especially in terms of the emotional pain involved and of not letting our feelings of anger, hurt, and loss lead us to actions we would regret in years to come. This exercise will give you the benefit of the experience of others who've traveled the same road.

1. The first and possibly most important thing in this situation: Don't be hasty or reckless. When a relationship has been difficult or we've suffered a major betrayal, the urge to end it can be powerfully fueled by strong emotions, and the uncertainty of leaving things unsettled can seem like torture. Ending the relationship may be the best thing to do—but be sure. Ending a marriage or other long-term committed relationship may be the second biggest decision of a lifetime, second only to entering the relationship in the first place. If children are involved, it may be the biggest. It's important to your future peace of mind to know you've sincerely weighed all less drastic alternatives. If your partner is firmly intent on ending it, you may have no say in the matter. But if you do, unless the relationship is abusive or otherwise dangerous, the best and wisest course may be to try to solve the problems together before giving up on each other. If you succeed, you may emerge with a relationship stronger and warmer than ever. How have you and your partner tried to work through the problems that are now bringing you to the point of contemplating divorce/permanent separation?

   _____

   _____

   _____

2. The next vital consideration is to make sure that no matter how angry, hurt, or devastated you are, you behave in ways you won't regret when those feelings have faded, and they will. It's almost certain that if you are a fundamentally decent

person but do things that are needlessly hurtful to your partner, and even more so to your children if you have them, you will someday wish you had been kinder. It's important to remember three things. First, this is someone you once were so much in love with that you decided to spend the rest of your life with him or her. Second, this was not how either of you planned or wanted things to turn out—you both entered the relationship with loving intentions. Third, all of the hurt you cause each other, your children will feel equally sharply, and how you behave will affect your relationships with them from now on. This is a time when the perspective of a good and wise person who isn't emotionally involved can save you from impulsive words or acts that may echo for decades. Who can you turn to for this kind of feedback?_____

3. A bit more about the children: It's normal for children to blame themselves when bad things happen around them, and they often think it's their fault if their parents split up—"If I'd been a better kid, Mom and Dad wouldn't have been so stressed out . . ." and so on. Please sit down with them, you and your partner together if possible, and make sure they know that this is not about them, and that you both love them as much as ever. Beyond that, the three worst things parents do to their children in these situations are (1) ask them to take sides, (2) use them as go-betweens instead of shielding them as much as possible, and (3) worst of all, use the children as weapons to hurt each other. These things can leave the children feeling guilty for the rest of their lives. They need you to be the adults and let them be children. If you have children, how have you and your partner agreed to cooperate to look out for their best interests?

    _____

    _____

4. Now that we've dealt with responsibilities to others, it's time to look at taking care of yourself. The first three items were intentionally put ahead of this, because those are obligations to others that cannot ethically take a backseat to meeting one's own needs. With that said, though, we do also have the right and duty to look after our own well-being during this process. One way to look at it is that it's a time to treat yourself the way you would treat a sibling or close friend in the same situation. That starts with how you talk to yourself. We all talk to ourselves all day long, sometimes silently, sometimes aloud. It's important to pay attention to what we say to ourselves about ourselves. Even in normal times it's usually much more negative than positive. We call ourselves names and trash our own abilities, intelligence, and actions in ways very different from how we would ever talk to a friend. This is where being your own friend comes in. When you catch yourself in ugly self-talk, stop and correct it (kindly—don't beat yourself up for beating yourself up)! What negative things do you tell yourself most often?

_____

_____

_____

5. Another area that calls for mental monitoring is distorted thinking. It's normal to get depressed during a breakup, and when we get depressed our thinking gets negatively distorted. Distorted thinking is a big enough topic to more than take up this whole handout—we won't try to cover it here; please talk with your therapist and tackle it with him or her. For now, we'll just note that we have an especially strong tendency toward negative distortion in how we see ourselves, our situations, and our futures. Take a couple of minutes and look at how you're seeing those three areas; note anything you suspect may be more negative than realistic.

_____

_____

_____

A closing note: During this process you will be under extreme stress, and you won't be at the top of your game physically, mentally, or emotionally. It's wise to lower your expectations of yourself while you're going through this and for a while afterward. Again, be a friend to yourself.

Be sure to bring this handout back to your next therapy session, and be prepared to discuss your thoughts and feelings about the exercise.

AVOIDING REBOUNDS, REPLAYS, AND RESENTMENTS: IDENTIFYING AND CHANGING PATTERNS THAT AREN'T WORKING

GOALS OF THE EXERCISE

1. Evaluate the possibility of resolving the differences and review the pros and cons of remaining married.
2. Consistently uphold "the best interests of the children" as paramount and act accordingly, regardless of the final fate of the marriage.
3. Resolve the initial confusion and turmoil of separation.
4. Learn to cope with the varied losses that separation entails.

ADDITIONAL PROBLEMS FOR WHICH THIS EXERCISE MAY BE USEFUL

- Anger Management and Domestic Violence
- Borderline Personality
- Depression
- Homesickness/Loneliness
- Social Discomfort

SUGGESTIONS FOR PROCESSING THIS EXERCISE WITH VETERANS/SERVICE MEMBERS

The "Avoiding Rebounds, Replays, and Resentments" activity is for veterans/service members who are ending a relationship or have recently done so. Its approach is cognitive-behavioral, guiding the veteran/service member to examine patterns in his/her thinking that may have contributed to the relationship's failure. Follow-up could include reading assignments from books listed in Appendix A of *The Veterans and Active Duty Military Psychotherapy Treatment Planner*, and/or videotherapy with films suggested for "Adoption and Custody" and "Divorce" in *Rent Two Films and Let's Talk in the Morning*, 2nd ed., by John W. Hesley and Jan G. Hesley, published by John Wiley & Sons.

AVOIDING REBOUNDS, REPLAYS, AND RESENTMENTS: IDENTIFYING AND CHANGING PATTERNS THAT AREN'T WORKING

One of the most common and painful mistakes many of us make under the stress of a divorce or loss of an equivalent relationship is to rebound quickly into a new relationship. It's easy to understand. Losing a relationship can leave a person sad and lonely; it may be a long time since he or she lacked a partner. At the same time, it's a hard blow to the self-esteem, a combination of failure—in front of family and friends, at that—with the most devastating rejection most of us will ever experience. Also, a person going through a divorce or long-term relationship breakup may be substantially older than the last time he or she was single, and we live in the most youth-oriented society imaginable. Finally, beyond the factors feeding a need for reassurance—that he or she is desirable, attractive, and not a loser doomed to grow old alone—there's often at least a bit of excitement about the possibility of finding a great new partner. With all those things working on us, it would be mystifying if a lot of people *didn't* jump into rebound relationships. Unless a newly single person does some work on himself or herself first, though, it usually doesn't end well. The purpose of this exercise is to offer suggestions for doing that work.

1. When we lose relationships we need to go through a grieving process, just as when someone close to us has died, and that takes time. When we seek to start new relationships too quickly it tends to be more because we feel we need to be with someone than because we want to be with that particular person. Rebounds are driven by fear and need; but to be fair to our future partner, we have to be emotionally whole rather than not yet healed. Trying to start a new relationship while a heart is still wounded is like trying to run a marathon on crutches. So we need to be honest with ourselves about how ready we are. What do you think some signs would be that you were recovered enough to have a fair chance of success in a new relationship?

    _____

    _____

    _____

2. The next thing to look at is what you find attractive and exciting. Do you have a friend who keeps getting into relationships with partners who are similar types, and those relationships all turn out the same way? There's a good chance your friend's smart and has a lot going for him or her. Why can't he or she see this obvious pattern? Well, we don't tend to analyze what attracts us—we just go after it. We all have mental profiles of attractive partners. When we meet new people, we look for matches to our templates and focus on those who seem to fit. But there are two problems with this approach: First, we're in a hurry, so we test the depth of the water by jumping in headfirst when we don't really know what's beneath the surface; and second, what attracts us may not be so good for us anyway. Given a choice between somebody stable and dependable, and someone whose first name is Chaos and middle name is Drama, we often go for the "exciting" one. That's why, as many men lament, women seem drawn to the bad boys. But that cuts both ways, as a lot of women know. What about your ideal? Please list key qualities you want in a partner:

_____

_____

Now list several shared qualities you (or your friends) see in your last two or three partners:

_____

_____

Is there a disconnect between what you say you want and what you choose? It pays to work on yourself in this area before you start a new relationship or it's likely to be an instant replay.

3. We've talked about rebounds and replays. What about resentments? Why do you think that's included in this exercise?

_____

_____

There are two reasons. First, check your feelings about your ex-partner. Is there a lot of resentment there? If so, please list the most important things that anger you about him or her:

_____

_____

A lot of resentment toward your former partner is a sign of a couple of things that can wreck any new relationship. One is that if you have a lot of feeling left, even negative feeling, you aren't over that person yet. We don't get agitated about people we aren't interested in. The other is that a lot of resentment means you're seeing your ex as responsible for the relationship's failure, and you're feeling like the victim. If so, you're not looking for changes to make in yourself and you're likely to approach a new relationship the same way you did the one that just ended. Most of the time when a marriage or other long-term relationship ends, both partners share the responsibility and the mistakes. If we want better results we need to become better people. Looking at the resentments you listed, do you think your ex-partner might have similar resentments toward you? _____ How do you know yours are more valid than his or hers?

_____

True story: A man we know asked an older woman he considered wise why he couldn't find a good woman who wanted to be with him. He told her about all he had to offer and how women didn't appreciate him. She asked if he would write a one-page description of the character and personality of his ideal partner. He worked hard on it until he felt he had captured a perfect word portrait of the soul and essence of his ideal partner, then went back and handed the sheet to the woman. She handed it back unread and said, "Become this person, and she'll show up." There's a lot of truth to the saying that we tend to attract, and be attracted to, people who are as healthy as we are at that moment. To find the best possible partner, one needs to be the best possible partner.

Be sure to bring this handout back to your next therapy session, and be prepared to discuss your thoughts and feelings about the exercise.

TAKING CARE OF MYSELF PHYSICALLY AND EMOTIONALLY AFTER A SEXUAL ASSAULT

GOALS OF THE EXERCISE

1. Obtain medical care for injuries suffered during the assault, including testing for sexually transmitted diseases (STDs).
2. Regain a sense of trust for fellow service members, unit, and military.
3. Regain a sense of power and control over life.

ADDITIONAL PROBLEMS FOR WHICH THIS EXERCISE MAY BE USEFUL

- Depression
- Insomnia
- Nightmares
- Panic/Agoraphobia
- Phobia
- Physiological Stress Response—Acute
- Posttraumatic Stress Disorder (PTSD)

SUGGESTIONS FOR PROCESSING THIS EXERCISE WITH VETERANS/SERVICE MEMBERS

The "Taking Care of Myself Physically and Emotionally After a Sexual Assault" activity is for veterans/service members who have recently been sexually assaulted, and is intended to help them take active steps to begin the healing and recovery process. Its approach is solution-focused and cognitive-behavioral, helping the veteran/service member obtain medical treatment, draw support from close friends and family, and regain and reinforce an internal locus of control and sense of efficacy and avert social withdrawal and isolation. Keep in mind that the service member may need prompting to stay or become socially involved while facing issues of trust and fear but refusing to be controlled by them. Follow-up can include reporting back to the therapist/therapy group on actions from this assignment and their outcomes, as well as bibliotherapy with books listed in Appendix A of *The Veterans and Active Duty Military Psychotherapy Treatment Planner* and/or videotherapy with films on the topic of "Friends and Support Systems" recommended in *Rent Two Films and Let's Talk in the Morning*, 2nd ed., by John W. Hesley and Jan G. Hesley, published by John Wiley & Sons.

TAKING CARE OF MYSELF PHYSICALLY AND EMOTIONALLY AFTER A SEXUAL ASSAULT

Being sexually assaulted, especially by someone who's supposed to be on your "team," is a tremendous violation that can leave you with a confusing range of intense and painful emotions, and make you feel like withdrawing from people and neglecting the things you do to take care of yourself. This makes it harder to practice basic self-care and stay connected to the family members and close friends that are your best source of emotional support, just when you need that support most. In this exercise, you'll identify steps to begin your recovery.

1. Although it can be an ordeal, it's important to assess any injuries you received as soon as you can. Getting prompt treatment promotes the best and fastest recovery. Have you seen a doctor and been thoroughly checked for injuries and tested for STDs? If you have, what did the doctor tell you, and what is your next step? If not, when will you do this?

    _____

    _____

2. What instructions did the doctor(s) give you about your physical treatment plan?

    _____

    _____

3. Emotional self-care is equally important and takes more time and energy. The physical aspects of recovery rely on the medical professionals; it's different with your emotional support network. There's a role for professionals here (i.e., your therapist and possibly others), but you'll probably get more benefit from the family members and friends with whom you're closest. It can be hard to turn to them sometimes. You may feel like staying away from people, but that makes your chances of falling into a serious depression greater than letting the people who know you best and care about you most be there for you. If someone you love has been sexually assaulted, remember your feelings then, wanting to help them recover from it—if not, think of how you would feel. Let the people you trust be there for you.

4. With that in mind, please list some people you can count on for support:

Friends

_____

_____

_____

_____

_____

Military Peers

_____

_____

_____

_____

_____

Family

_____

_____

_____

_____

_____

Military Leadership

_____

_____

_____

_____

_____

5. For the individuals you named above, list the ways they can best support you. For example, your First Sergeant can help you navigate any legal issues you may have.

Friends

_____

_____

_____

_____

Military Peers

_____

_____

_____

_____

_____

Family

_____

_____

_____

_____

Military Leadership

_____

_____

_____

_____

_____

6. Please list some other resources that you can rely on for support:

Church/Religious Organizations

_____

_____

_____

Local and Online Support Groups

_____

_____

_____

Books/Movies   **Military Support Agencies**

_____   _____

_____   _____

_____   _____

Be sure to bring this handout back to your next session with your therapist, and be prepared to discuss your thoughts and feelings about the exercise.

HEALING AND CLAIMING MY IDENTITY AS A SURVIVOR

GOALS OF THE EXERCISE

1. Emotionally and cognitively resolve the issue of being sexually assaulted.
2. Regain a sense of trust for fellow service members, unit, and military.
3. Express feelings about the perpetrator including the possibility of forgiveness.
4. Regain a sense of power and control over life.

ADDITIONAL PROBLEMS FOR WHICH THIS EXERCISE MAY BE USEFUL

- Anxiety
- Depression
- Insomnia
- Nightmares
- Panic/Agoraphobia
- Physiological Stress Response—Acute
- Posttraumatic Stress Disorder (PTSD)

SUGGESTIONS FOR PROCESSING THIS EXERCISE WITH VETERANS/SERVICE MEMBERS

The "Healing and Claiming My Identity as a Survivor" activity is for veterans/service members who have progressed in their recovery and can think about and discuss the event without being so overwhelmed as to interfere with reflection on its impact on self-image and their perceptions and feelings about the perpetrator(s). The exercise focuses on two key steps in recovery. First, the service member is guided in affirming that he/she was in no way responsible for the actions of the perpetrator and renouncing any shame or responsibility. Second, the service member is presented with the concept that maintaining intense anger or hatred is not in his/her own interests and that forgiveness in due time will benefit the survivor. Forgiveness must not be addressed too early, and it's critical to make it clear that it does not excuse the crime or change the perpetrator's guilt or the appropriateness of legal consequences. It is also important to recognize the unique betrayal of assault by a comrade. Follow-up can include reporting back to the therapist/therapy group on thoughts and feelings about this assignment and biblio-therapy using books from Appendix A of *The Veterans and Active Duty Military Psychotherapy Treatment Planner*.

HEALING AND CLAIMING MY IDENTITY AS A SURVIVOR

Once your healing reaches a point where you can do so, it will help your recovery to start sorting out your feelings about the assault, the fact that its perpetrator was a person you trusted and relied on, and how the assault has impacted your views on the military and your fellow comrades. It's important to resist the tendency, often seen in crimes like this, for the survivor to feel partially responsible for the assault. At a suitable point in the recovery process it helps to begin thinking about the concept of forgiveness as a healthy step that can help you release bitterness and anger, emotions that are natural but interfere with your own quality of life if they become permanent. This exercise is designed to help you think through the assignment of full responsibility to the person who attacked you, and then at the appropriate stage of recovery, the nature of forgiveness—which in no way lessens his/her guilt, the severity of the crime, or the hurt this has caused you—as a step in further regaining inner peace and a sense of control over your own life.

1. *Impact Letter:* Write an impact letter to the service member who assaulted you. What you do with this letter after writing it is your choice; there is no right or wrong choice in that action, only consideration of what is in the best interest of your continued healing. The purpose and benefit of taking this step is to affirm that the service member who assaulted you bears full responsibility for that act and the pain it has caused you. Consider the following ideas in writing your impact letter:

   - The inexcusable nature of his/her assault on you.
   - His/her sole responsibility for the assault and rejection of any effort that may have been made to say or imply that you somehow share that responsibility.
   - How the sexual assault made you feel at the time it occurred and now.
   - How the sexual assault makes it difficult to trust other service members.
   - How your feelings of being safe in the military have changed.
   - How you felt toward him/her before, during, and immediately after the sexual assault.
   - How you feel toward the perpetrator now.

_____
_____
_____
_____
_____
_____
_____
_____
_____
_____
_____
_____
_____
_____
_____
_____

2. *The Meaning of Forgiveness and the Forgiveness Letter:* The word "forgiveness" often evokes strong feelings of anger and bitterness if it is interpreted as meaning in some way that the perpetrator's actions were acceptable or that you will not hold him/her fully accountable. In this sense, consider forgiveness as more like letting go of the urge to get even—in the same way we speak of forgiving a debt if we let go of the idea of continuing to try to collect on it. Survivors of crimes can forgive those who wronged them *without changing their determination to hold them accountable* and without any lessening of the wrongness or severity of what they did. Forgiveness is something survivors do for their own good, not for the benefit of the perpetrators—it is a way to say that you are not willing to make your identity that of "victim," that you are rising above this event and proving that you are a survivor too strong to be broken by the perpetrator's actions. As one survivor of sexual assault put it, "I decided that I was only going to let him control one day of my life, not the rest of it."

- If you are willing at this point to write a letter stating that kind of forgiveness, it will be for the benefits to you as a positive step in your recovery, not for the person who assaulted you. What to do with it will again be your choice. In writing the letter, consider the following:

- The fact that he/she is solely responsible for the sexual assault.

- Why you are attempting to forgive him/her.

- Forgiveness does not mean that his/her assault was excusable.

- Forgiveness is a process that may take a long time and you are only beginning it now.

- What you expect from him/her now and in the future.

_____
_____
_____
_____
_____
_____
_____
_____
_____
_____
_____
_____
_____
_____
_____
_____

Be sure to bring this handout back to your next session with your therapist, and be prepared to discuss your thoughts and feelings about the exercise.

ALTERNATIVE SLEEP SCHEDULING

GOALS OF THE EXERCISE

1. Develop a sleep schedule to promote adequate sleep quantity and quality.
2. Develop a consistent sleep schedule that applies to work and non-work days.
3. Address cognitive, emotional, and physical symptoms of sleep deprivation.

ADDITIONAL PROBLEMS FOR WHICH THIS EXERCISE MAY BE USEFUL

- Attention and Concentration Deficits
- Depression
- Insomnia
- Post-Deployment Reintegration Problems

SUGGESTIONS FOR PROCESSING THIS EXERCISE WITH VETERANS/SERVICE MEMBERS

The "Alternative Sleep Scheduling" activity addresses the challenge of alternating shift work, a common occurrence in both military and civilian settings. Frequent changes in work schedules can cause symptoms such as fatigue, sleepiness, and attention/concentration deficits, which can increase the risk of accidents and damage moods, relationships, and quality of life. In this activity, the veteran/service member identifies behavioral techniques he/she can use to minimize the effects of shift work, plan healthy sleep hygiene and induction behaviors, and prepare for changes in work schedule. In processing this activity, it helps to emphasize the degree to which sleep problems can contribute to many problems in life. It is also necessary to recognize that for many veterans/service members, it may be more difficult to request changes in schedule due to their military specialty or civilian job title, operational tempo, and rank/seniority. Follow-up can include reporting back to the therapist on actions from this assignment and their outcomes, as well as bibliotherapy using books from Appendix A of *The Veterans and Active Duty Military Psychotherapy Treatment Planner*.

ALTERNATIVE SLEEP SCHEDULING

Frequent work schedule changes are often times a necessary part of one's job. If careful and thoughtful attention is not paid to the potential detrimental effects of work shift changes, the consequences can be dramatic and dire. In the following exercise, you will identify those behaviors that you can commit to engaging in that will minimize sleep disturbances related to schedule changes. You will then identify useful sleep hygiene behaviors and induction techniques that promote falling to sleep and learn how to prepare in advance for upcoming shift work schedule changes.

1. Please place a check by each behavioral technique that you will commit to using on a regular basis to minimize effects of shift work. For each technique you check, make a few notes on how you will accomplish the technique.

    a. _____ Talk with your supervisor about reducing frequency of alternating shift schedules.

    _____

    _____

    b. _____ Minimize exposure to light on the way home from work.

    _____

    _____

    c. _____ Follow bedtime rituals.

    _____

    _____

    d. _____ Go to bed as soon as possible after work.

    _____

    _____

    e. _____ Maintain consistent sleep/wake schedule on days off.

    _____

    _____

f. _____ Set consistent times to take care of errands and responsibilities (e.g., pay bills, shop for groceries).

_____

_____

g. _____ Use modest amounts of caffeine at work to prevent drowsiness and sleep.

_____

_____

2. Check the sleep induction techniques you are most likely to use when it is time to sleep.

a. _____ Avoid caffeine at least four hours prior to bedtime.

b. _____ Avoid nicotine at least one hour before bedtime.

c. _____ Avoid spicy or large meals prior to going to bed.

d. _____ Avoid emotional conversations with loved ones prior to bedtime.

e. _____ Take a hot bath/shower 30 minutes prior to bed.

f. _____ Don't watch television or play video games in bed.

g. _____ Write down disturbing thoughts to get them out of your mind.

h. _____ Practice deep breathing 15 minutes before bedtime.

     i.   _____ Close your eyes and imagine peaceful and relaxing images.

_____

_____

3.   Prepare for upcoming shift schedule change by shifting your sleep/wake schedule back one hour each day for the five days preceding the change.

Normal sleep schedule:

Sleep Time   _____   Wake Time   _____

Day 5 before starting new schedule:

Sleep Time   _____   Wake Time   _____

Day 4 before starting new schedule:

Sleep Time   _____   Wake Time   _____

Day 3 before starting new schedule:

Sleep Time   _____   Wake Time   _____

Day 2 before starting new schedule:

Sleep Time   _____   Wake Time   _____

Day 1 before starting new schedule:

Sleep Time   _____   Wake Time   _____

Be sure to bring this handout back to your next session with your therapist, and be prepared to discuss your thoughts and feelings about the exercise.

ESTABLISHING A SHIFT WORK SLEEP ENVIRONMENT

GOALS OF THE EXERCISE

1. Practice healthy sleep hygiene behaviors.
2. Implement appropriate stimulus control techniques.
3. Create sleeping environment that is devoid of light.
4. Create a noise/disturbance-free sleeping environment

ADDITIONAL PROBLEMS FOR WHICH THIS EXERCISE MAY BE USEFUL

- Attention and Concentration Deficits
- Combat and Operational Stress Reaction
- Depression
- Insomnia
- Post-Deployment Reintegration Problems

SUGGESTIONS FOR PROCESSING THIS EXERCISE
WITH VETERANS/SERVICE MEMBERS

The "Establishing a Shift Work Sleep Environment" activity, like "Alternative Sleep Scheduling," is designed for veterans/service members whose work hours mean that they must sleep during the day. In general, people tend to underestimate the impact a noisy, bright, and uncomfortable bedroom can have on sleep. In this activity, you will help the veteran/service member create a sleeping environment that is conducive to receiving good quality and an appropriate quantity of sleep. You will help the veteran/service member identify those techniques he/she can engage in that will make his/her bedroom less noisy and bright and more comfortable. It is important for you to also emphasize the concept that creating and sticking to a regular bedtime routine allows greater opportunity to receive restful and restorative sleep. Follow-up for this exercise could include reporting back to the therapist on actions related to this assignment and their outcomes, as well as bibliotherapy using books suggested in Appendix A of *The Veterans and Active Duty Military Psychotherapy Treatment Planner*.

ESTABLISHING A SHIFT WORK SLEEP ENVIRONMENT

Creating a noise, stress, and light free sleeping environment is a crucial step in battling the negative effects of alternating work schedules. In a sense, you have to "trick" your internal biological clock to make your body and mind believe it is nighttime. In this exercise, you will identify those techniques you will engage in that will make your sleeping environment as sleep friendly as possible.

1. Please place a check by each technique you can use to make your sleeping environment as free of light as possible:

    _____ Cover windows with dark material

    _____ Stuff towels in crack of door

    _____ Paint walls a dark, non-reflective color

    _____ Cover windows in adjacent rooms

    _____ Wear eye mask while sleeping

    _____ Sleep in a room with least amount of sunlight

    _____ Sleep under the covers

    _____ Cover lights of the alarm clock

2. Please place a check by each technique you can use to make your sleeping environment as free from noise as possible:

    _____ Ask family members to wear headphones when listening to music or watching television.

    _____ Ask family members to avoid vacuuming or washing dishes while you sleep.

    _____ Put a "Do Not Disturb" sign on your front door so that friends or delivery people won't wake you up.

    _____ Turn off the ringer to your phone or put it on low.

    _____ Turn off pager or cell phone if you are not on-call.

    _____ Sleep in a room of the house that has the greatest distance from the street and neighbors.

    _____ Turn on a low and consistent source of noise that filters out background noise (e.g., ceiling fan).

    _____ Wear soft and comfortable earplugs.

3. Please place a check by each technique you can use to make your sleeping environment as comfortable and relaxing as possible:

    _____ Make sure temperature in the room is not too hot or too cold.

    _____ Experiment with different levels of firmness for your mattress and pillows.

    _____ Invest in a sound/sleep machine.

    _____ Wash/change bed linen weekly.

    _____ Use scented fabric softeners that you find soothing.

    _____ Sleep in comfortable and unrestrictive clothes.

    _____ Turn off the television/radio before falling asleep.

Be sure to bring this handout back to your next session with your therapist, and be prepared to discuss your thoughts and feelings about the exercise.

GETTING MORE COMFORTABLE IN SOCIAL SITUATIONS

GOALS OF THE EXERCISE

1. Interact socially without undue fear or anxiety.
2. Identify and replace biased, fearful self-talk with reality-based positive self-talk.
3. Learn and use social skills to reduce anxiety and build confidence.
4. Explore past experiences that may be sources of low self-esteem and social anxiety.

ADDITIONAL PROBLEMS FOR WHICH THIS EXERCISE MAY BE USEFUL

- Adjustment to the Military Culture
- Anxiety
- Borderline Personality
- Depression
- Homesickness/Loneliness
- Panic/Agoraphobia
- Phobia
- Post-Deployment Reintegration Problems
- Posttraumatic Stress Disorder (PTSD)

SUGGESTIONS FOR PROCESSING THIS EXERCISE WITH VETERANS/SERVICE MEMBERS

The "Getting More Comfortable in Social Situations" activity uses a cognitive therapy approach. It guides the veteran/service member to identify negative automatic thoughts that fuel social discomfort, then to identify experiences that contribute to the negative cognitions. Finally, the veteran/service member is asked to do a reality check on each negative belief, choose the three that detract most from his/her quality of life, and replace them with more balanced, realistic, and positive thoughts. It may help to review the examples in item 1 of distorted automatic thoughts that feed fear and add any that fit the situation. The veteran/service member may initially need help to develop positive, realistic statements to build confidence and counteract fear. Follow-up can include reporting back to the therapist/therapy group on thoughts and feelings about this assignment, as well as bibliotherapy with books listed in Appendix A of *The Veterans and Active Duty Military Psychotherapy Treatment Planner*.

GETTING MORE COMFORTABLE IN SOCIAL SITUATIONS

Anxiety about social situations is usually caused by distorted thoughts about ourselves and others. These distorted thoughts lead to negative emotions. We react to imaginary future events as if they have already come true, even if they're not really likely to happen. These thoughts can lead to social withdrawal and isolation. This exercise will help you identify distorted thoughts, see how they might have formed, and replace them with more realistic and positive thoughts.

1. These distorted thoughts may lead to social withdrawal. Please check any you experience:

    _____ I never know what to say.

    _____ I'll make a fool of myself if I speak up.

    _____ I will get yelled at by my superior.

    _____ These people are much smarter than I am.

    _____ This person doesn't like me.

    _____ I'm going to freak out or have a panic attack.

    _____ I'm boring and have nothing to say unless I have a few drinks.

    _____ I can tell by the way he/she is looking at me that he/she doesn't like me.

    _____ Every time I go to a party or social gathering, people ignore me.

    _____ My superior thinks I'm a poor soldier/sailor/airman/Marine.

    _____ I'm not as good as the others in my unit.

2. If other negative thoughts go through your mind about social encounters, what are they?

    _____

    _____

3. What's your greatest fear about social interactions—the possible situation you dread most?

    _____

4. Have you had unpleasant experiences in social situations that taught you to expect future situations to be unpleasant, too, or to lack confidence in your ability to function in them? If so, what were those experiences and when did they happen? This includes childhood experiences of criticism or rejection from your parents, siblings, other relatives, teachers, or peers.

_____

_____

_____

5. Please describe any experiences in the military that increase your anxiety around people:

_____

_____

_____

6. Please review your responses on questions 1 and 2. For each, what evidence tells you they're accurate about yourself, other people, and situations, and what shows they aren't accurate? If you had to bet your next paycheck one way or the other, which would you bet? Note your thoughts about those items and the evidence you considered:

_____

_____

_____

7. Look back at question 3. How likely is that event or situation to actually happen? If it did, could you handle it? Is avoiding that risk worth giving up the enjoyment you've missed to avoid it?

_____

8. Please rate the strength of your desire to overcome your social fears:

   1 = No Desire   2   3   4   5 = Strong Desire

9. Recall a time when you felt good about and enjoyed a social situation. What was different in that situation? What enabled you to overcome your anxiety?

_____

_____

10. How could you apply the coping skills you used then to new social encounters, or find new situations with the same factors that helped you feel comfortable?

_____

_____

11. Please review your answers to the first three questions again, and pick out the three items that seem most drastic—the ones that would bother or embarrass you the most if they became facts. Now write a replacement statement for each that is more realistic and positive. Write these three positive statements on a 3×5 index card, keep them in your pocket, and read them five times a day (when you get up, at each meal, and when you go to bed may be convenient times). As you read each one, picture in your mind's eye an example of that positive statement being true about you in the situation(s) where it applies. Do this daily for a month, then check your original answers to this exercise and see whether your thinking and behavior have changed.

Positive statement a:

_____

Positive statement b:

_____

Positive statement c:

_____

Be sure to bring this handout back to your next session with your therapist, and be prepared to discuss your thoughts and feelings about the exercise.

FINDING A SOCIAL NICHE AND FRIENDSHIPS

GOALS OF THE EXERCISE

1. Interact socially without undue fear or anxiety.
2. Develop the essential social skills that will enhance the quality of relationship life.
3. Learn and use social skills to reduce anxiety and build confidence.
4. Participate in social performance requirements without undue fear or anxiety.

ADDITIONAL PROBLEMS FOR WHICH THIS EXERCISE MAY BE USEFUL

- Adjustment to the Military Culture
- Anxiety
- Borderline Personality
- Depression
- Homesickness/Loneliness
- Panic/Agoraphobia
- Phobia
- Post-Deployment Reintegration Problems

SUGGESTIONS FOR PROCESSING THIS EXERCISE WITH VETERANS/SERVICE MEMBERS

The "Finding a Social Niche and Friendships" activity is designed to help the veteran/ service member reduce loneliness and isolation and find a comfortable peer group based on his/her existing interests. It guides the veteran/service member to identify activities he/she finds rewarding, analyze them to identify the qualities that make them enjoyable, look for new activities that exemplify those qualities, and seek out chances to engage in activities he/she already enjoys and any new activities that are available. The rationale is twofold. First, engaging in those activities is a good way to meet peers who share the same interests. Second, whether new friendships come out of these activities or not, spending more time in activities the veteran/service member enjoys will improve his/her quality of life and reduce distress related to loneliness. Follow-up can include reporting back to the therapist/therapy group on thoughts and feelings about this assignment, as well as bibliotherapy using books listed in Appendix A of *The Veterans and Active Duty Military Psychotherapy Treatment Planner*.

FINDING A SOCIAL NICHE AND FRIENDSHIPS

One of the difficult parts of relocating is being in a new place where you may not know anyone and feeling lonely as a result. If you tend to be shy it can be hard to meet new friends and find a social circle where you fit in comfortably. This exercise will guide you through a strategy that has been useful for many people in this situation.

1. Happiness is a basic goal for all of us. Many of the things we do, we do because we hope or believe they'll make us happy. People try to find happiness in many ways with varied degrees of success. What are some ways you've tried to achieve happiness, and how did they work?

    _____

    _____

    _____

2. A psychologist named Mihaly Csikszentmihalyi decided to find out how happiness works and did extensive research on it. He learned that the thing that makes people happiest is spending time in activities they enjoy so much that they get absorbed in them and forget everything else when they're engaged in those activities. He also found that the people who spend the most time in those activities are the people who have the highest overall levels of happiness and satisfaction with life. Does this match your own experience with recreational or work activities that are the most interesting to you?

    _____

3. A good place to start looking for friendships and a social group where you fit in is to find people who enjoy the same activities as you—and the best way to find them is to go and participate in those activities yourself. However, sometimes the hobbies, sports, or other activities you've enjoyed most in the past aren't available where you live now. Is that part of your situation now?

    _____

4. If so, there's still a way to use this strategy. Look at the activities that are available to you now but that you've never tried and figure out which ones you would like. The first step is to think about the things you have enjoyed doing and figure out what it was that made them fun and satisfying for you. Please list several things you know you like to do:

_____

_____

5. Now we need to look at what makes those particular things more satisfying for you than other activities. A good way to do that is to look for patterns. Here's a list of qualities various activities can have. Please check off those you see as patterns in the things that are the most fun for you:

_____ Fast-paced	_____ Physically intense	_____ Competitive
_____ Outdoors	_____ Can be indoors	_____ Mentally demanding
_____ Requires precision	_____ Cooperative	_____ Doesn't require being athletic
_____ Long-term projects	_____ Quickly completed	_____ Takes a long time to play
_____ Attention to detail	_____ Quickly learned	_____ Takes a long time to master
_____ Played as team	_____ Played one-on-one	_____ Results in something to keep
_____ Requires use of tools	_____ Requires imagination	_____ Different every time
_____ Large groups	_____ Rehearsed technique	_____ Fun to either watch or play
_____ Small groups	_____ Can be fully mastered	_____ Always more to learn
_____ Related to work	_____ Luck plays a role	_____ Determined by skill only

6. Now you have a short list of the qualities that make an activity a source of pleasure for you. The next thing to do is to identify as many hobbies, sports, and other things to do that are available to you now and have most or all of the qualities you enjoy most. Some good places to find this information could be in the phone book, in local newspapers, at recreational facilities on base, on local TV and radio programming, at stores that sell equipment for activities you know you like, and via an Internet search. Looking around at recreational and educational opportunities in your area, which ones seem likely to be fun for you?

_____

_____

7. If you go explore these activities, you're likely to find people participating in them who like to do the same kinds of things you like. The process of checking these activities out, and asking the people you find there questions about how to try them out, will give you an easy, natural way to meet some potential new friends. Which activities will you investigate first, and when will you do this?

_____

There's another benefit, too. Remember what we learned about quality of life— that the people who spend the most time doing things that fascinate them and give them satisfaction are the people who are happiest and most satisfied with their lives overall? That makes it likely that the very act of getting into some new hobbies or other interesting activities will help you improve your level of happiness, whether it leads to new friendships or not. Also, when you do this, it helps you feel more of a sense of control over your life, because you're actively choosing how things go instead of having them just happen to you.

Be sure to bring this handout with you to your next therapy session, and be prepared to discuss your thoughts and feelings about the exercise.

UNDERSTANDING SPIRITUALITY

GOALS OF THE EXERCISE

1. Develop a connection with a higher power that provides satisfaction and fulfillment.
2. Learn the difference between religion and spirituality.
3. Overcome resistance to 12-Step programs based on antipathy toward religion.
4. Develop connections and supports with others that share the same spiritual/religious beliefs.

ADDITIONAL PROBLEMS FOR WHICH THIS EXERCISE MAY BE USEFUL

- Grief/Loss Unresolved
- Substance Abuse/Dependence

SUGGESTIONS FOR PROCESSING THIS EXERCISE WITH VETERANS/SERVICE MEMBERS

The "Understanding Spirituality" activity is written for veterans/service members whose therapeutic progress is impeded by antipathy toward spirituality as a resource for recovery, based on antipathy toward organized religion or perceived conflicts with personal values. Follow-up could include bibliotherapy including books such as *Where in the World Is God* by Robert Brizee or books included in Appendix A of *The Veterans and Active Duty Military Psychotherapy Treatment Planner*.

UNDERSTANDING SPIRITUALITY

This assignment will help you begin working through an issue that troubles many people. This is a big subject, and there's no way that one handout can cover it all, but it can offer some pointers to help you get started.

Why work on spirituality? If you've identified this as an issue, your reasons are your own. You may be one of the many people that have been frustrated in seeking a religious community that feels right to them. You may have felt the need for some system of values, of right and wrong, in ways that didn't seem important earlier in your life. If you're participating in a recovery program, having a spiritual connection can make the difference between success or failure in recovery, and therefore possibly the difference between life or death. It's the key to effective use of Alcoholics Anonymous (AA), Narcotics Anonymous (NA), and other 12-Step programs.

Many people have good reasons to feel skeptical about religion. They may have had bad experiences with religious people or institutions. Perhaps they just feel that God has not been there in their lives. When they attend meetings of 12-Step programs and hear a lot of talk about God, it may look like a barrier making these programs useless to them, but it doesn't have to be. Many people who find that they feel uncomfortable in any of the religious communities they've experienced, who may not believe in God or believe that no one could know whether God exists, can still find that they can come to an understanding of spirituality that will fill a need in their lives, one that can help them cope with life's struggles and connect with other people whose outlooks are like their own. The key is understanding the difference between *spirituality* and *religion*.

1. Write down your description of *religion*. What do you think of when you hear the word?

   _____

   _____

2. Now think about the word *spirituality*, and write your definition for this word.

   _____

   _____

3. Are there differences in the meanings of *religion* and *spirituality* for you? If so, what is the biggest difference you see?

A definition of religion could be: A religion is a specific system of practices and rituals, based on a belief in a specific divine or superhuman power, usually practiced through membership in a specific human organization, such as a church, temple, mosque, or synagogue.

A similar definition for spirituality, on the other hand, might sound like this: Spirituality is a focus on the moral aspects of life, on doing what is right on what matters most, and on being the best people we are capable of being.

So we could put it this way: A religion is a system people create to try to achieve spirituality. We could think of spirituality as water and religion as a bottle, a container to hold water—but other containers can hold water, and some bottles contain other things instead of water.

4. Does this idea make sense to you? _____ What other containers for spirituality can you think of (i.e., other ways to help yourself focus on what is right in life)?

_____

_____

5. At this point, you may be thinking, "Doesn't this definition of religion also describe a 12-Step program? It seems to be a specific system of practices and rituals, and it is practiced through membership in a specific organization!" If you've had the thought that AA, NA, or some other 12-Step program seemed to resemble a religion, what similarities do you see?

_____

_____

6. What differences do you see between 12-Step groups and religions?

_____

_____

Here are three key differences between 12-Step groups and religions:

i. *Definitions of God.* A religion offers specific ways to understand God, and may insist no other way is correct. A 12-Step program asks you to think in terms of a power greater than yourself, and leaves it to you to decide what that power is and how it works.

ii. *Authority.* While a religion almost always has a hierarchy and people in charge, in a 12-Step group there's no one in charge, no chain of command. Decisions are voted on by the group through a process called a "group conscience."

iii. *Membership Requirements.* Religions may restrict their memberships in many ways—by birth, heritage, or obedience to various rules. By contrast, in a 12-Step program, the 3rd Tradition says that the only membership requirement is a desire to solve the problem the group exists to overcome. Anyone who wants to be a member can, and no one can be excluded.

7. Going back to our definition of spirituality, how could paying attention to the moral aspects of life and what is right help you solve the problems facing you with alcohol, drugs, or other addictive behaviors?

    _____

    _____

    If you see that a focus on these parts of your life could be useful, that's all it takes to begin including spirituality in your recovery work.

Be sure to bring this handout back to your next therapy session, and be prepared to discuss your thoughts and feelings about the exercise.

WHAT DO I BELIEVE IN?

GOALS OF THE EXERCISE

1. Resolve conflicts between military service and spiritual/religious beliefs.
2. Develop connections and supports with others that share the same spiritual/religious beliefs.
3. Describe in detail the nature of spiritual/religious issues.
4. Describe current spiritual belief system.

ADDITIONAL PROBLEMS FOR WHICH THIS EXERCISE MAY BE USEFUL

- Adjustment to Military Culture
- Depression
- Homesickness/Loneliness
- Separation and Divorce

SUGGESTIONS FOR PROCESSING THIS EXERCISE WITH VETERANS/SERVICE MEMBERS

The "What Do I Believe In?" activity is designed for work with veterans/service members who are struggling to resolve conflicts between military service and spiritual or religious beliefs or searching for meaning in their lives. Follow-up could include bibliotherapy including books such as *Where in the World Is God* by Robert Brizee or books included in Appendix A of *The Veterans and Active Duty Military Psychotherapy Treatment Planner.*

WHAT DO I BELIEVE IN?

Many of us haven't thought hard about what we really believe in for a long time, perhaps our whole lives. And yet we do all have beliefs and values, and if our actions don't fit them we feel uneasy and may not know why. An important part of peace of mind is what people sometimes call "being comfortable in our own skin." We can't feel that way without the self-respect that comes with being true to what we believe. This exercise will help you explore your own beliefs and values and plan ways to live that are true to them.

1. First, please look at this list of personal qualities. Note that all of these are choices—qualities we can develop or learn—rather than things we don't control. Circle the six that are most important to you in doing what's right.

    1. Honest
    2. Kind
    3. Courageous
    4. Hard-working
    5. Strong
    6. Spiritual
    7. Religious
    8. Good provider
    9. Patient
    10. Positive
    11. Good parent
    12. Good partner
    13. Practical
    14. Respectful
    15. Dignified
    16. Good son/daughter
    17. Dependable
    18. Resilient
    19. Good communicator
    20. Humble
    21. Generous
    22. Self-reliant
    23. Self-confident
    24. Gentle
    25. Loyal
    26. Playful
    27. Understanding
    28. Decisive
    29. Tactful
    30. Enthusiastic
    31. Knowledgeable

2. Why are these things the most important to you? How did you come to value them?

    _____

    _____

3. Now review your life in each of the following areas, and make some notes about how your actions either match up with the qualities you chose or conflict with them:

    Military service and/or job: _____

    _____

    Marriage/partnership: _____

    _____

Parenting: _____

_____

Friendships: _____

_____

Other important parts of your life:

_____

_____

4. Many people have struggled with understanding what is right in religious, spiritual, and moral terms in all of these areas, but most of all in relation to military service. If there were simple or easy ways to settle such conflicts, they would have been settled long ago—each of us has to find our own answers. Still, it may help to think about some key points that have helped other people answer the same questions for themselves.

    a. Do you feel that violence against other people is ever justified (e.g., in defense of self or others)? If so, when is it right and when is it wrong? _____

    _____

    _____

    b. Is it better, worse, or no different in your eyes to actively hurt someone or to let them be hurt by failing to prevent it?

    _____

    c. You may have found yourself in a situation in which someone was going to be hurt or killed no matter what you did or didn't do. If that has happened, briefly describe that situation, what you did, and whether you believe you made the right choice:

    _____

    _____

    d. You may be dealing with a common human mistake, that of judging yourself and your actions more harshly than you would judge anyone else. If you have found yourself in situations in which you did things that clashed with your sense of right and wrong, please think about these points: how clearly you understood the situation at the time you acted; what stresses you were under; and how much time you had to decide what to do. With those factors in mind, would you judge someone else in that situation the same way you may have judged yourself? If not, why should you be held to a different standard than other people? _____

5. Where could you find help in thinking about these questions and deciding how to live in the future and how to decide about things like whether to stay in the military when your current term of service ends, if you are still in? _____

_____

6. Name one thing you will do in each area during the next year to make your actions more consistent with the values you believe are right.

Military service and/or job: _____

Marriage/partnership: _____

Parenting: _____

Friendships: _____

Other important parts of your life: _____

Be sure to bring this handout with you to your next therapy session, and be prepared to discuss your thoughts and feelings about this exercise.

WHAT DOES ADDICTION MEAN TO ME?

GOALS OF THE EXERCISE

1. Identify and accept the need for substance abuse treatment.
2. Accept the unmanageability of use of mood-altering substances, and participate in a recovery program.
3. Verbalize a commitment to abstain from the use of mood-altering drugs.
4. Establish a sustained recovery, free from use of all mood-altering substances other than prescribed medications used exactly as directed by a physician who is aware of the patient's substance use history.

ADDITIONAL PROBLEMS FOR WHICH THIS EXERCISE MAY BE USEFUL

- Antisocial Behavior in the Military
- Financial Difficulties
- Opioid Dependence
- Performance-Enhancing Supplement Use
- Tobacco Use

SUGGESTIONS FOR PROCESSING THIS EXERCISE WITH VETERANS/SERVICE MEMBERS

The "What Does Addiction Mean to Me?" activity is for veterans/service members who resist accepting a diagnosis of substance dependence or abuse due to mistaken ideas about what the terms mean. It explains the *DSM-IV-TR* criteria and analyzes how they fit the veteran/service member's life situation, including non–substance-using addictive behavior. Follow-up can include bibliotherapy on alcoholism and addiction; keeping a journal about lessons learned, conclusions, and plans made; and discussion with the therapist/therapy group of all of the above. Follow-up can also include bibliotherapy using books listed in Appendix A of *The Veterans and Active Duty Military Psychotherapy Treatment Planner* and/or videotherapy using *My Name Is Bill W.* or other films listed for "Substance Abuse" in *Rent Two Films and Let's Talk in the Morning*, 2nd ed., by John W. Hesley and Jan G. Hesley, published by John Wiley & Sons.

WHAT DOES ADDICTION MEAN TO ME?

You may be doubtful about whether you are an alcoholic or addict, no matter what anyone else says. To answer this question for yourself, you need to be able to identify patterns of addictive or abusive use of alcohol, other drugs, or compulsive behavior, and to see whether your life fits these patterns. This exercise explains what these terms mean in plain English to help you decide.

1. For each of the following patterns, please write about whether this has happened in your life, and if it has, please think of at least one example.

    a. *Tolerance.* This is when you need to use more of a chemical or do more of a behavior (or doing it to a greater extreme) to get the same effect, or feeling less effect if you use or do the same amount.

    _____

    _____

    b. *Withdrawal.* This means either feeling ill or uncomfortable after stopping use of the chemical or the behavior, or using the chemical or practicing the behavior to relieve or avoid feeling ill or uncomfortable.

    _____

    _____

    c. *Loss of control.* This means you use, drink, or practice an addictive behavior for longer or in greater quantity than you intended.

    _____

    _____

    d. *Attempts to control.* This fits if you have had a persistent desire to cut down or stop, or have made efforts to control or cut down your using/drinking/addictive actions, including making rules or bargains with yourself to limit it.

    _____

    _____

    e. *Time spent.* This refers to spending a significant amount of time thinking about using, drinking, or practicing the addictive behavior; planning or preparing for it; using/drinking/practicing; and dealing with the consequences (such as being hung over or coming down, or being broke until payday).

_____

_____

f.   *Sacrifices made.* This includes giving up or reducing social, work, family, or recreational activities that were important to you because they conflicted with your addictive behaviors—for example, drifting away from friendships with people who won't drink or use with you.

_____

_____

g.   *Continued use despite known suffering.* This means continuing to use, drink, or practice another addiction in spite of knowing that you have had major physical, psychological, legal, financial, or relationship problems that were caused or made worse by that behavior.

_____

_____

2.   Looking back over these symptoms, what do they tell you about your use of substances or other addictive behaviors?

_____

_____

3.   For each of the following stages of addiction, please note whether you have experienced this, and if you have, please think of an example of how your life fits the description.

a.   *First stage.* The first experience—when you begin using a chemical or engaging in a behavior and discover that you like the way it makes you feel.

_____

b.   *Second stage.* Tolerance and withdrawal appear, and you find that you can use the chemical or behavior to cope with situations or feelings that are difficult or uncomfortable.

_____

c.   *Third stage.* You begin deliberately and routinely using the chemical or behavior to cope with stress or other problems. You may feel uneasy about it, and may try to cut down or control use; your normal life is disrupted and others may start thinking that you have a problem.

_____

d.   *Fourth stage.* You come to feel that you can't cope with your life's stresses without the chemical or behavior. You feel that you must pay whatever price comes with continued use; you feel trapped; your life seems to be falling apart; and/or relationships with others are damaged or lost.

_____

4. Looking over these four phases in the development of an addiction, what have you learned about your own pattern of use?

    _____

    _____

Be sure to bring this handout back to your next therapy session, and be prepared to discuss your thoughts and feelings about the exercise.

PROBLEM IDENTIFICATION

GOALS OF THE EXERCISE

1. List and discuss negative consequences resulting from, or exacerbated by, substance dependence.
2. List and discuss reasons to work on a plan for recovery from addiction.
3. Identify and accept the need for substance abuse treatment.
4. Accept the unmanageability of use of mood-altering substances, and participate in a recovery program.
5. Verbalize a commitment to abstain from the use of mood-altering drugs except for using prescribed medications exactly as instructed by a physician who is aware of the patient's substance use history.

ADDITIONAL PROBLEMS FOR WHICH THIS EXERCISE MAY BE USEFUL

*   Antisocial Behavior in the Military
*   Financial Difficulties
*   Opioid Dependence
*   Performance-Enhancing Supplement Use
*   Tobacco Use

SUGGESTIONS FOR PROCESSING THIS EXERCISE WITH VETERANS/SERVICE MEMBERS

The "Problem Identification" activity is suited for individual or group use. This activity walks veterans/service members through systematically listing, at one time and in one place, negative things that have happened in their lives as the result of substance abuse—in a way, conducting a self-intervention. Follow-up might include writing about reflections afterward; sharing responses with the therapist, treatment group, and program sponsor; and the "Personal Recovery Planning" activity. Other follow-up activities could include bibliotherapy using books listed in Appendix A of *The Veterans and Active Duty Military Psychotherapy Treatment Planner* or videotherapy using "My Name is Bill W." or other films listed for "Substance Abuse" in *Rent Two Films and Let's Talk in the Morning*, 2nd ed., by John W. Hesley and Jan G. Hesley, published by John Wiley & Sons.

PROBLEM IDENTIFICATION

People don't usually get treatment or help until they find themselves in some kind of crisis. Crises are good motivators, but they don't usually last as long as the underlying problems. To stay motivated and stay in recovery, we need to look at our addictive behaviors over the long term, beyond the crises that get us to act. If you wonder whether you have a problem with alcohol, another drug, or another addictive behavior, or how serious your problem is, compare the events in your life with each of these categories.

1. Below is a brief, partial list of common experiences that cause people who are practicing addictive lifestyles to decide that they should change these patterns, that their addictions are causing them problems, and that they want help. Please check all those that apply to you.

    ### Loss of Important Relationships Because of Addictions

_____ Divorce or equivalent	_____ Children, parents, siblings alienated
_____ Loss of close friendships	_____ Loss of respect from coworkers

    ### Practical Difficulties Resulting from Addictions

_____ Unpayable debts	_____ Loss of employment
_____ Loss of a vehicle	_____ Loss of a home
_____ Loss of professional status	_____ Bankruptcy

    _____ Legal problems (e.g., arrest, jail, probation, loss of driver's license)

    ### Dangerous/Harmful Situations Resulting from Addictions

_____ Health problems	_____ Recreational accidents
_____ DUIs, DWIs, or car wrecks	_____ Work injuries, falls, or other accidents
_____ Fights while under the influence or coming down	_____ Harm to others as a result of one's own actions under the influence
_____ Suicidal ideation, attempts	_____ Self-injury
_____ Violence	

Things We Once Thought We Would Never Do

_____ Letting down friends	_____ Repeatedly breaking promises
_____ Lying to partners/families	_____ Stealing from partners/families/work
_____ Letting down employers	_____ Abusing family members
_____ Selling drugs	_____ Committing crimes to support addiction
_____ Exchanging sex for alcohol or other drugs	_____ Endangering others, especially children

2. When you think about your life without alcohol, other drugs, or the other addictive behavior, what emotions do you feel?

    _____

    _____

3. Do you see any other evidence that your use of alcohol, other drugs, or other addictive behavior is causing problems in your life? If you do, what is it?

    _____

    _____

4. On a scale of 1 to 10 (1 = not at all and 10 = extremely important), how important is it for you to make changes to your use of alcohol, other drugs, or other addictive behavior at this time?

    _____

5. On a scale of 1 to 10 (1 = not at all and 10 = extremely confident), how confident are you that you could begin to make changes to your alcohol, other drug, or other addictive behavior if you wanted to?

    _____

Be sure to bring this handout back to your next therapy session, and be prepared to discuss your thoughts and feelings about the exercise.

PERSONAL RECOVERY PLANNING

GOALS OF THE EXERCISE

1. List and discuss negative consequences caused, or exacerbated by, addiction.
2. List and discuss reasons to work on a plan for recovery from addiction.
3. Identify and accept the need for substance abuse treatment.
4. Accept the unmanageability of use of mood-altering substances, and participate in a recovery program.
5. Verbalize a commitment to abstain from the use of mood-altering drugs, except for prescribed medications used exactly as instructed by a physician who is aware of the patient's substance use history.

ADDITIONAL PROBLEMS FOR WHICH THIS EXERCISE MAY BE USEFUL

*   Antisocial Behavior in the Military
*   Financial Difficulties
*   Opioid Dependence
*   Performance-Enhancing Supplement Use
*   Tobacco Use

SUGGESTIONS FOR PROCESSING THIS EXERCISE WITH VETERANS/SERVICE MEMBERS

The "Personal Recovery Planning" activity is for veterans/service members who are at least somewhat motivated for recovery and need structure and direction. It guides veterans/service members in identifying goals for recovery to frame planning and strengthen motivation, then walks them through several domains of life functioning and prompts them to identify supportive resources and relationships and commit to a plan to use them. Follow-up can include keeping a journal; reporting back to the therapist, therapy group, and sponsor on the outcomes of activities in the personal recovery plan; or bibliotherapy using the books listed in Appendix A of *The Veterans and Active Duty Military Psychotherapy Treatment Planner*.

PERSONAL RECOVERY PLANNING

There are many ways to maintain a healthy lifestyle, free of self-defeating addictive behavior. Your recovery plan will be your own creation, not exactly like anyone else's. It won't be a finished product when you're done, but it will give you a guide to fall back on when things get difficult and confusing. You may have tried on one or more occasion to cut back or abstain from addictive behavior and discovered that some things work and some things do not. Please draw on that experience as you work through this exercise.

1. When you think about recovery, what do you want to accomplish? Beyond abstinence, some goals may include self-respect and dignity, peace of mind, healthy relationships, improved health, career progress, avoiding legal problems, and improved finances. Please list the three things most important to you.

   a. _____

   b. _____

   c. _____

2. For each goal, how would a return to your addiction affect your chances of success?

   a. _____

   b. _____

   c. _____

3. For each goal, what successful result will show that you've achieved that desired outcome?

   a. _____

   b. _____

   c. _____

4. For each goal, what specific warning signs will tell you if you're getting off track?

   a. _____

   b. _____

   c. _____

5. Success in recovery has positive and negative parts: finding *things to do* that help you remain abstinent and finding *things not to do* because they may lead to relapse. Drawing on all you have learned and the experiences of others, please fill out the following.

    a. Recovery activities

        (1) What treatment sessions will I attend each week? When and where?

        _____

        (2) What support group meeting(s) will I attend during the week? When and where?

        _____

        _____

        (3) When, where, and for how long will I meet with my sponsor each week?

        _____

    b. Creating a daily structure and routine

        (1) What things will I do as part of my routine each day, and when will I do them?

        _____

        _____

        (2) Each week?

        _____

        _____

        (3) Each month?

        _____

        _____

    c. *Basic self-care.* Living compulsively, we often neglect the basics (e.g., proper nutrition, health care, adequate rest, and exercise). Building these into your life will help you cope with stress. What can you do in each of these areas to take care of yourself?

        (1) Proper nutrition:

        _____

        _____

        (2) Medical care:

        _____

        _____

        (3) Rest:

        _____

        _____

(4) Exercise/physical activity:

_____

_____

d. *Relationships and support systems.* Relationships with loved ones and friends can have a tremendous effect on recovery, either by helping or hurting. You'll need to analyze past and current relationships and keep some, end some, and develop some new ones.

    (1) *Old relationships.* What relationships are likely to support your recovery, and what will you do to strengthen them?

_____

_____

    What relationships will probably undermine your efforts, and how will you end or distance them?

_____

_____

    (2) *New relationships.* Where can you meet people to start some new, healthy, supportive relationships, and how will you go about finding them?

_____

_____

    (3) *How you can get support from relationships.* Please list some people with whom you can talk when you feel troubled, confused, or discouraged, and write about how you will approach each of them to ask for this support.

Name	**How I Will Ask for Support**
_____	_____
_____	_____
_____	_____

e. *Spirituality.* Whether or not you're religious, recovery involves making changes in your values; people who include spiritual resources in recovery are usually more successful.

    (1) How will I address this component of my recovery?

_____

_____

    (2) What questions do I have about this, and whom can I ask for assistance?

_____

_____

f.   *Work.* Your job can be a major source of satisfaction, self-esteem, security, and, sometimes, great stress. Recovering people are prone to workaholism and burnout, either because we want to make up for lost time or because we aren't used to moderation.

(1) What will I do to keep my work within healthy, moderate limits?

_____

_____

(2) What will I do if something about my work is posing a risk to my recovery?

_____

_____

(3) How do I plan on dealing with stress related to work?

_____

_____

g.   *Legal issues.* Cleaning up any legal messes from our addictions is important—to be responsible, reduce stress, and gain self-respect. What am I doing in this area?

_____

_____

h.   *Finances.* This is a part of life with great impact on self-esteem and stress levels. Many newly recovering people are intimidated by financial problems when they get clean and sober, but with steady effort they can clear the difficulties up faster than expected.

(1) What financial problems do I have and what am I doing to resolve them?

_____

_____

(2) What is my long-term plan for financial stability?

_____

_____

i.   *Recreation.* Early recovery is a time to start having healthy fun, with activities you have enjoyed in the past or with new activities, to help you cope with stress and enjoy life.

(1) What old healthy recreational activities will I take up again?

_____

(2) What new activities will I try, and/or am I interested in learning more about?

_____

(3) What steps will I take to incorporate this into my weekly schedule?

_____

    j.   *Other areas of life.*

        (1) What other things do I see that I should focus on?

_____

_____

        (2) What is one step I can take today to make progress on one of these issues?

_____

    k.   *Crisis management.* Your plan must include steps to handle crises. Please list things you'll do to handle an unexpected (or expected) crisis without relapsing into addiction.

_____

_____

6.   Finally, please list activities you know you need to avoid, as they may lead to relapse. This may mean not going to certain places, seeing some people, or engaging in particular work or recreational activities.

_____

_____

_____

      Congratulations! You've laid a foundation on which to build, and created a reference that will come in handy when you're under stress and having trouble thinking clearly. By completing this exercise, you've done much of that thinking in advance.

Be sure to bring this handout back to your next therapy session, and be prepared to discuss your thoughts and feelings about the exercise and make modifications as needed.

WHAT DO I HAVE TO OFFER TO OTHERS?

GOALS OF THE EXERCISE

1. Agree to a verbal or written no-harm contract with the therapist.
2. Identify and change dysfunctional beliefs about self, others, and the world.
3. Reestablish a sense of purpose and future orientation.
4. Eliminate suicidal ideation and intent.

ADDITIONAL PROBLEMS FOR WHICH THIS EXERCISE MAY BE USEFUL

- Amputation, Loss of Mobility, Disfigurement
- Borderline Personality
- Depression
- Homesickness/Loneliness
- Posttraumatic Stress Disorder (PTSD)

SUGGESTIONS FOR PROCESSING THIS EXERCISE WITH VETERANS/SERVICE MEMBERS

The "What Do I Have to Offer to Others?" activity is designed to counter suicidal ideation by correcting cognitive distortion in a key area in the suicidal state of mind, the perception that one doesn't matter to anyone else and wouldn't be missed. This assignment asks the veteran/service member to identify how important people in his/her life will be affected if he/she commits suicide and to write brief letters to himself/herself from the post-suicide perspectives of those people. The goal is to help the veteran/service member develop an acute picture of how he/she is valued and how loved ones would be hurt by his/her loss. Although the assignment uses typical close relationships as examples, you should help the veteran/service member tailor it to his/her situation. Keep in mind that this will be a very emotional exercise for the veteran/service member and should be processed with the therapist as soon as possible after completion. Depending on level of risk, it may be safer to do this exercise verbally in session using the "empty chair" technique rather than writing letters. A safety plan must be in place before its start, and prompt follow-up must be provided. Follow-up will include discussion about the assignment, and can use bibliotherapy with books listed in Appendix A of *The Veterans and Active Duty Military Psychotherapy Treatment Planner*.

WHAT DO I HAVE TO OFFER TO OTHERS?

People thinking of suicide often wonder how their death would affect others. It's important to take your time and really think through how losing you would impact your friends and family. If at any time you feel this exercise is increasing your thoughts of suicide, stop immediately and contact your therapist; tell a friend, family member, or superior; call 911; or go to the emergency room.

1. To get a clear picture of this, we need to start in a different place. Please think of times family members, friends, comrades, or role models have done things that were helpful and important in your life. For three examples, please say who they were, what they did, and why it matters:

    a. _____

    b. _____

    c. _____

2. Now think of three people whose lives you've touched in a good way—again, say who they are, along with what you did that made a difference for them:

    a. _____

    b. _____

    c. _____

3. Picture yourself asking three people close to you "What are some ways I can help someone, and who could I help that way?" and then record the answers they would probably give you here:

    a. _____

    b. _____

    c. _____

4. Now please write a brief letter to yourself from each person listed. Write what you think they would want to tell you about the possibility of losing you:

    Person: Spouse / Significant Other

    Dear _____,

If you were no longer alive,

_____

_____

_____

_____

_____

Love, _____

Person: Father / Mother / Grandparent

Dear _____,

If you were no longer alive,

_____

_____

_____

_____

_____

Love, _____

Person: Child

Dear _____,

If you were no longer alive,

_____

_____

_____

_____

_____

Love, _____

Person: Friend

If you were no longer alive,

_____

_____

_____

_____

_____

Love, _____

Person: Other _____

If you were no longer alive,

_____

_____

_____

_____

_____

Love, _____

5. People close to you would want to help if they knew of your pain; how could they help?

    _____

    _____

6. Name three people who'd want to help. How can you ask them for their help?

    a. _____

    b. _____

    c. _____

    Please consider giving them the chance to be there for you. It is doing a good thing for them, a thing they'd want you to do and something they would wish for the rest of their lives you had done if you didn't. They'd feel the same way you would feel if the situation was reversed.

Be sure to bring this handout back to your next session with your therapist, and be prepared to discuss your thoughts and feelings about the exercise.

FINDING EMOTIONAL RELIEF AND SUPPORT

GOALS OF THE EXERCISE

1. Agree to a verbal or written no-harm contract with the therapist.
2. Identify and change dysfunctional and maladaptive beliefs about self, others, and the world.
3. Reestablish a sense of purpose and future orientation.
4. Decrease feelings of hopelessness and increase self-esteem.
5. Eliminate suicidal ideation and intent.

ADDITIONAL PROBLEMS FOR WHICH THIS EXERCISE MAY BE USEFUL

- Amputation, Loss of Mobility, Disfigurement
- Borderline Personality
- Depression
- Homesickness/Loneliness
- Posttraumatic Stress Disorder (PTSD)

SUGGESTIONS FOR PROCESSING THIS EXERCISE WITH VETERANS/SERVICE MEMBERS

The "Finding Emotional Relief and Support" activity is designed to counter suicidal ideation by correcting cognitive distortions in two of the key areas in the suicidal state of mind: the perception on the part of a suicidal person that he/she is emotionally isolated and that no one cares or understands his/her emotional pain, and the perception that there is no way to relieve that pain except by dying. This exercise is intended both to help the veteran/service member gain more control over his/her thoughts to reduce his/her risk of suicide, and to initiate relief of some of the emotional pain underlying suicidality and instill hope in the veteran/service member. Although the examples in this exercise are typical thoughts of suicidal people, it's important to help the veteran/service member identify his/her own unique thoughts leading to the suicidal ideation in order to target those specific dysphoric cognitive distortions. Please keep in mind that it is important to have a safety plan in place while doing this exercise and ensure prompt and consistent follow-up, which could include reporting back to the therapist on actions related to this assignment and their outcomes, as well as bibliotherapy using books suggested in Appendix A of *The Veterans and Active Duty Military Psychotherapy Treatment Planner*.

FINDING EMOTIONAL RELIEF AND SUPPORT

How we think about ourselves, others, and the situations we're in greatly influences how we feel. Unfortunately, when we're hurting or depressed, those thoughts get distorted so that things look even worse. We see ourselves, our situations, and our futures in the worst possible way; furthermore, we underestimate how much we matter to other people and lose the ability to see solutions to our problems. One man who survived a suicide attempt described it by saying, "All the doors in my mind slammed shut except the one that led to death, and I had to get out somehow." This is how the thought of suicide may develop. But it is not the only way to relieve the emotional pain—we can feel better by first testing our thoughts and replacing those that are dark distortions with more balanced and accurate ones. That, in turn, will let some of those doors in our minds start swinging open again as we regain our ability to see other solutions. In this exercise, you will develop more realistic alternatives to the negatively warped thoughts that are common when people's thinking is suicidal. Then you'll be asked to explore options other than hurting or killing yourself that you may be able to see more clearly by pushing through that distortion. If at any time you feel this exercise is increasing your thoughts of suicide, stop and contact your therapist; tell a friend, family member, or superior; call 911; or go to the emergency room.

1. Read through each of the hopeless, all-or-nothing negative thoughts below. For each, circle it if it's a thought you've been having; then think about evidence for and against it, and identify a positive and adaptive alternative thought that might be more true. After you finish this exercise practice doing this when you catch yourself thinking negative all-or-nothing thoughts.

   a. "This emotional pain is worse than I can stand."

      Alternative thought: _____

   b. "Nothing except dying can ease the pain I'm feeling."

      Alternative thought: _____

   c. "Nobody understands or cares about me."

      Alternative thought: _____

   d. "My family would be better off if I were dead."

      Alternative thought: _____

   e. "Things will never get better."

      Alternative thought: _____

f. "I can't do anything right—I'm useless."

Alternative thought: _____

g. "There's nothing good in my life—it's not worth living."

Alternative thought: _____

h. Personal negative thought: "_____."

Alternative thought: _____

i. Personal negative thought: "_____."

Alternative thought: _____

j. Personal negative thought: "_____."

Alternative thought: _____

2. Usually, when people think of suicide, they don't actually want to die—they want to stop feeling so much pain, and can't see any other way to do it. Is this part of what you've been thinking?

_____

3. Before taking the irreversible step of suicide, it makes sense to try another solution if one turns out to be available. Look at the alternative thoughts you listed for items 1.b., 1.c., and 1.e. If you thought carefully, you were probably able to identify possible alternatives and ways to ease your pain without dying. You most likely thought of people who would probably understand if you shared your thoughts and feelings with them and who care and would want to help. And you also probably found ways to help things get better. Drawing on these ideas, please describe some possible solutions that would involve gaining some emotional relief and support:

_____

_____

_____

_____

_____

_____

_____

4. Looking at item 1.f., you might want to consider that if you do find solutions and work through this time in your life, you would have a lot to offer other people who found themselves feeling the same way. You could potentially save lives and that good would ripple from those people through the others who care about them. Please record your thoughts and feelings about the idea that by overcoming the

crisis you're experiencing, you would be in a position to save other people's lives down the line:

_____

_____

_____

_____

_____

_____

5. Finally, if it would feel rewarding to you to be able to help someone else stay alive, please consider that your friends and family will almost certainly feel the same way if you give them the chance to help you stay alive. Briefly share your thoughts on this idea:

_____

_____

_____

_____

_____

_____

_____

Be sure to bring this handout back to your next session with your therapist, and be prepared to discuss your thoughts and feelings about the exercise.

CORRESPONDING WITH FALLEN FRIENDS

GOALS OF THE EXERCISE

1. Accept that loss is part of life.
2. View self as a fortunate survivor.
3. Reflect on the meaning of life.

ADDITIONAL PROBLEMS FOR WHICH THIS EXERCISE MAY BE USEFUL

- Bereavement Due to the Loss of a Comrade
- Depression
- Nightmares
- Posttraumatic Stress Disorder (PTSD)
- Spiritual and Religious Issues

SUGGESTIONS FOR PROCESSING THIS EXERCISE WITH VETERANS/SERVICE MEMBERS

The "Corresponding with Fallen Friends" activity addresses survivor's guilt by testing distorted cognitions and asking whether the standard the veteran/service member is using in self-judgment is reasonable. This is a three-step exercise. In step one, the veteran/service member writes a letter to a fallen friend, expressing thoughts and emotions about the death and his/her own survival. Step two is a written version of the "empty-chair" technique; the veteran/service member writes a reply he/she believes the friend would make to his/her letter. The third step asks the veteran/service member what he/she would want for the friend if he/she had died while the friend survived. Note: It is important to allow the veteran/service member freedom to write what he/she feels and thinks, but equally important to ensure key questions are addressed. The veteran/service member should consider why he/she feels guilty and think about what he/she could have been expected to do differently, given the circumstances. If appropriate, the veteran/service member may be guided to apologize or ask forgiveness if he/she feels he/she made a mistake that contributed to the death, while considering whether he/she would forgive the friend if the roles were reversed. Follow-up can include asking the veteran/service member to decide how he/she can honor the friend's memory and bibliotherapy with books listed in Appendix A of *The Veterans and Active Duty Military Psychotherapy Treatment Planner*.

CORRESPONDING WITH FALLEN FRIENDS

Many people who suffer from survivor's guilt wish they could tell the person who died how they feel and what they are thinking. In this exercise, you will have the chance to let your friend, family member, or comrade know how you feel about his or her death. First, we ask that you write a letter to the person who died and tell him/her whatever you wish you could say if you could talk with him/her again.

1. Please compose a short letter to the person who died, expressing your thoughts and emotions about what happened. Along with anything else you want to say, be sure you explain why you feel this death was your fault and what you believe you should have done differently, under the conditions and with the information you had at the time. If you believe you were at fault and wish to ask for his or her forgiveness for your role in the death, please do so.

Dear _____,

_____

_____

_____

_____

_____

_____

_____

_____

_____

_____

Sincerely,

When you've written your letter, please read it aloud and visualize the person to whom you're writing listening as you read it. When you've finished this reading, briefly describe your thoughts and emotions in reaction to the experience:

_____

_____

_____

2. Now we're going to ask you to move on to a step you may not have considered. Again, we'll ask that you picture the person you lost facing you, having heard you read the letter you just wrote to him or her. Now, do your best to look at yourself through his or her eyes. Please write another short letter, this time the one you believe your friend or loved one would be most likely to write to you in reply to the letter you just wrote. What would he or she think and feel—would your friend or loved one blame you?

Dear _____,

_____

_____

_____

_____

_____

_____

_____

_____

_____

_____

Sincerely,

3. Finally, we'll ask you to imagine a different outcome in which you had died while your friend or loved one had lived, and in which he or she was feeling guilty and responsible for your death. If that had happened, what would you have wanted for the other person? Imagine him or her writing a letter like the one you wrote in the first part of this exercise. What would you want to say in reply to that letter? Would you be angry at your friend or loved one for living, or would you be happy that they had survived even if you had been less fortunate?

_____

_____

_____

_____

4. Many people, when they think about this, decide that they would want their friends who had survived them to mourn and then let go, to move on with life and

be happy, perhaps to do some good things in their names. Does this sound like a wish you might have for someone close to you who had survived when you died? If so, what are some things you can do to make the world a better and more joyous place, in the name of the person you lost?

_____

_____

_____

_____

Be sure to bring this handout back to your next session with your therapist, and be prepared to discuss your thoughts and feelings about the exercise.

CARRYING THE LEGACY

GOALS OF THE EXERCISE

1. Accept that loss is part of life.
2. View self as a fortunate survivor.
3. Reflect on the meaning of life.

ADDITIONAL PROBLEMS FOR WHICH THIS EXERCISE MAY BE USEFUL

*   Bereavement Due to the Loss of a Comrade
*   Depression
*   Nightmares
*   Posttraumatic Stress Disorder (PTSD)
*   Spiritual and Religious Issues

SUGGESTIONS FOR PROCESSING THIS EXERCISE
WITH VETERANS/SERVICE MEMBERS

The "Carrying the Legacy" activity addresses survivor's guilt by probing the veteran's/ service member's cognitions regarding the death of a friend or loved one, asking him or her to consider whether the thoughts contributing to guilt and depression are reasonable. It presents the idea of cognitive distortion, asking the veteran/service member to weigh whether the guilt-producing thoughts seem valid or distorted and to supply a balanced and realistic alternative if the original cognition is distorted. The activity's second part asks the veteran/service member how he/she thinks the deceased friend or loved one would want his/her memory to be carried forward—with guilt and unending sadness, or with a period of mourning followed by a lifetime of gratitude for having shared time with him/her and with positive memories. It concludes by asking the veteran/service member to think of a way to make the world a better place as a living memorial. Follow-up can include bibliotherapy with books listed in Appendix A of *The Veterans and Active Duty Military Psychotherapy Treatment Planner* and/or video-therapy using films on "Death and Dying" and/or "Grief and Loss" recommended in *Rent Two Films and Let's Talk in the Morning*, 2nd ed., by John W. Hesley and Jan G. Hesley, published by John Wiley & Sons.

CARRYING THE LEGACY

Survivor's guilt occurs when a person believes he or she has done wrong by surviving a situation in which a friend or loved one has died, especially if the person feels he or she caused the death or should have prevented it but failed to do so. Survivors of combat, natural disasters, and accidents and friends and family of people who die by suicide sometimes feel this way. The problem is that the belief that causes the guilty feelings is often not accurate and people blame themselves for things over which they had little or no control, sometimes living under a cloud of grief and regret for the rest of their lives as a result. This exercise asks you to look at whatever beliefs underlie guilty feelings about a situation in which you lost someone close to you, and see whether those beliefs are reasonable. A loss is a loss no matter what, and no one has any business telling you how long or how short your period of grief over a loss should be. Your heart is your own. However, if you are punishing yourself for something of which you aren't really guilty, you're also taking something from all the other people, still living, who care about you. The goal here is to make sure that your understanding of what happened and your role in it is accurate.

1. To begin with, please rate the strength of your belief that you are at fault somehow in the situation in which your friend or loved one died and you lived, on a scale of 1 (least) to 10 (most) intense: _____ Now rate the strength of your negative emotions about yourself related to the same situation on the same 1 to10 scale: _____

2. Read through each of the self-blaming negative thoughts below. For each, circle it if it's a thought you've been having; then think about evidence for and against it, and identify a positive alternative thought that might be more realistic. Use 2.g. through 2.j. for any self-blaming thoughts you may experience that are different from those in 2.a. through 2.f. After you finish this exercise, practice doing this when you catch yourself thinking these kinds of thoughts.

    a. Self-blaming thought: "It is my fault he/she is dead."

    Alternative thought:

    _____

b. Self-blaming thought: "I should have done more to prevent it."
Alternative thought:

_____

c. Self-blaming thought: "Everyone blames me."
Alternative thought:

_____

d. Self-blaming thought: "My life can never be happy again. It would be disloyal of me to let go of this grief."
Alternative thought:

_____

e. Self-blaming thought: "I don't deserve to be alive since he/she is dead."
Alternative thought:

_____

f. Self-blaming thought: "He/she would blame me if he/she was still here."
Alternative thought:

_____

g. Self-blaming thought: "_____."
Alternative thought:

_____

h. Self-blaming thought: "_____."
Alternative thought:

_____

i. Self-blaming thought: "_____."
Alternative thought:

_____

j. Self-blaming thought: "_____."
Alternative thought:

_____

3. Please read the self-blaming thoughts and your alternate thoughts over again. Now we'll ask you to go back to question 1 and re-rate the strength of your belief that you are at fault and your negative emotions about yourself on that 1 to 10 scale. Have your ratings changed, and if so, how?

_____

4. Finally, we'd like to ask you to think about the person you lost, what he or she was like, and what would be the most fitting way to remember that person. It's common in our society for events to be held as memorials for people who have died. Think of those memorials, and whether it's more suitable for them to keep the focus on grieving the loss, or on celebrating what the person being remembered brought to the world. Once you had time to go through your own process of grief, which way would you want to be remembered, and what do you believe the person you've lost would want—more grief from now on, or healing and pleasure at their memory?

    _____

    _____

5. We would like to ask you to conclude by taking some time and thinking about what would be the best way to carry on the legacy of your friend or loved one in your life; perhaps there's a cause you could volunteer for in his or her name, or it might just be a matter of sharing that person's best qualities with the world by working to make them as strong in your own dealings with people as you can. Please think about this, and write the idea you choose here:

    _____

    _____

Be sure to bring this handout back to your next session with your therapist, and be prepared to discuss your thoughts and feelings about the exercise.

AVOIDING NICOTINE RELAPSE TRIGGERS

GOALS OF THE EXERCISE

1. Recognize internal triggers that lead to tobacco use.
2. Recognize external triggers that lead to tobacco use.
3. Develop adequate coping resources to refrain from all tobacco use.
4. Develop coping strategies to manage nicotine cravings.
5. Decide on and commit to a specific date to quit using tobacco.
6. Remove all tobacco paraphernalia from home, car, and workplace.

ADDITIONAL PROBLEMS FOR WHICH THIS EXERCISE MAY BE USEFUL

- Anxiety
- Opioid Dependence
- Performance-Enhancing Supplement Use
- Substance Abuse/Dependence

SUGGESTIONS FOR PROCESSING THIS EXERCISE WITH VETERANS/SERVICE MEMBERS

The "Avoiding Nicotine Relapse Triggers" activity is designed to help the veteran/service member plan for successful cessation of nicotine use. It is designed to be the veteran's/service member's own creation. This exercise works well for individual therapy but can also be useful for groups. The three larger tasks outlined in the exercise—getting prepared, setting up supports, and identifying alternative coping methods—can be broken into smaller segments and assigned over several sessions. Follow-up for this exercise can include keeping a journal and bibliotherapy using one or more of the books listed for this issue in Appendix A of *The Veterans and Active Duty Military Psychotherapy Treatment Planner*.

AVOIDING NICOTINE RELAPSE TRIGGERS

No one starts using tobacco because they want, or plan, to get addicted. Some don't think about it at all. Most people who use tobacco become addicted very quickly, and many deny that they are addicted. While everyone's experience is unique, there are both common physical factors (i.e., physical pleasure and cravings, biological processes), as well as social (i.e., what your peers see as normal) and psychological factors (i.e., relaxation, pleasure), that play important roles in maintaining the addiction. Giving up tobacco requires taking a realistic look at this addiction and why it is so hard to quit. You can gain useful information from attempts you may have already made to quit (what worked, what didn't?). This exercise will help you to plan the three basic components of a successful smoking/chewing cessation plan: (1) increasing your motivation, (2) finding and using supports, and (3) learning and using alternative coping skills.

PREPARATION/GETTING READY

1. What signs of addiction do you see in your use of tobacco (e.g., increased use, failed attempts to quit, tolerance, withdrawal, use despite negative consequences)?

2. What denial statements have you used to rationalize continuing to use (e.g., "Life is too stressful now," "I'm not mentally prepared to quit," "I'll probably fail if I try to quit now")?_____

   _____

3. What are the top three reasons you want to give up tobacco, as of today?

   a. _____

   b. _____

   c. _____

4. What family, social, and emotional challenges will you face in your recovery plan?

5. Part of every successful recovery plan is identifying your doubts and fears about quitting and to prevent setting yourself up for defeat even before you start. What are your doubts and fears about quitting?

6. If you've quit before, what worked for you, and what led to your return to using tobacco?

7. Please set a start date to begin carrying out your plan: _____

8. How and when will you tell your family, friends, and coworkers about your plan?

    _____

    _____

9. What triggers will you have to watch out for (e.g., certain people, places, situations, feelings, association with daily activities or habits, times of the day, events)?

    _____

    _____

10. Of these triggers, which can you avoid?

    _____

    _____

11. What is your plan to cope with the triggers you can't avoid?

    _____

    _____

12. Which of the following methods or sources of support will you use to deal with triggers and cues to smoke or chew tobacco?

a.	Self-help groups	e.	Publications and reading material
b.	Acupuncture	f.	Smoking cessation clinics and programs
c.	Medications	g.	Online support
d.	Hypnosis	h.	Other:_____

13. How will you handle cravings and other withdrawal symptoms? (Remember, they're temporary and will pass, and the longer you abstain, the more your withdrawal symptoms will lessen in both frequency and intensity.)

    _____

    _____

14. What rewards will you give yourself for abstinence, and when?

    _____

    _____

Be sure to bring this handout with you to your future therapy sessions, and be prepared to discuss your thoughts and feelings about the exercise as you begin your recovery plan.

USE OF AFFIRMATIONS FOR CHANGE

GOALS OF THE EXERCISE

1. Develop adequate coping resources to refrain from all tobacco use.
2. Develop coping strategies to manage nicotine cravings.
3. Use cognitive-behavioral techniques to assist with tobacco cessation.
4. Practice stress management and relaxation skills to reduce overall stress levels and attain a feeling of comfort.
5. Develop healthy strategies to neutralize cravings for tobacco use.

ADDITIONAL PROBLEMS FOR WHICH THIS EXERCISE MAY BE USEFUL

*   Anxiety
*   Opioid Dependence
*   Performance-Enhancing Supplement Use
*   Substance Abuse/Dependence

SUGGESTIONS FOR PROCESSING THIS EXERCISE WITH VETERANS/SERVICE MEMBERS

The "Use of Affirmations for Change" activity is an evidence-based activity, relying on two cognitive principles—first, that when people are presented with information repeatedly, they are likely to accept it as correct, altering their cognitions more each time they're exposed to it; and second, that when people find their actions in conflict with their cognitions, it causes cognitive dissonance, which is usually resolved in turn by modifying the behavior rather than the belief system, especially if the belief system continues to receive reinforcement. In this activity, this process is used with the aim of shifting the veteran/service member's cognition and behavior. This exercise empowers the veteran/service member, guiding him/her through a first use of a structured stress-management meditation, with the veteran/service member choosing the goal and designing his/her own affirmation. Follow-up can include keeping a journal and reporting back to the therapist/therapy group after 3 to 4 weeks about changes brought about as a result of consistent daily use of affirmations, as well as reading assignments from Appendix A of *The Veterans and Active Duty Military Psychotherapy Treatment Planner*.

USE OF AFFIRMATIONS FOR CHANGE

All of us have negative beliefs about ourselves, often because of painful experiences or things others have said to us. When we talk to ourselves, silently or aloud, what we say is often negative. One way to know this is going on is to notice when you say something to yourself that's harsher than anything you'd say to a friend. This negative self-talk molds our thoughts, feelings, and actions. Overcoming it takes work. However, when we do that work, we learn to think of ourselves in ways that are more balanced, that support our feelings of self-worth, and that help us stop self-destructive behaviors. This exercise will help you identify harmful messages you give yourself and replace them with positive self-talk.

1. We all talk to ourselves as we go through the day, aloud or silently in our thoughts. Over the next week, pay attention to the things you say to yourself, about yourself, and your actions. Also, notice when anyone else gives you messages about yourself (e.g., your boss, coworkers, family members, or friends). When you find yourself saying negative things in your self-talk, or when others are negative or critical to you, note here what negative messages you repeat to yourself or hear from others most often. Then rewrite them to express your desired situation and self-view in reasonable but positive terms.

Negative Self-Statements	**Positive Self-Statements (in Present Tense)**
Ex.: I can't stay sober.	I like being clean and sober.
Ex.: I'm weak and this is too hard.	I am learning new skills and getting better.
_____	_____
_____	_____
_____	_____
_____	_____

2. Think about a situation in your life that bothers you. List the negative self-statements that accompany this situation, then describe your feelings when you think about these negative statements. Create positive self-statements to replace those negative messages.

Situation: _____

Negative Statement	Feelings	Positive Replacement Statement
_____	_____	_____
_____	_____	_____
_____	_____	_____

3. Does this situation seem more manageable to you after doing this? If so, what's different?

_____

_____

4. Here's a specific way to use positive self-statements to solve a problem or make a change in your life, such as quitting smoking. This is based on two scientific principles. The first is that if we hear something over and over, we start to believe it—why do you think negative messages have so much power? If this wasn't true, advertisers wouldn't spend their money to make sure we hear their messages again and again. The second principle is that when there is a mismatch between our actions and what we believe, it makes us uncomfortable and we tend to change our actions to match our beliefs. This activity is designed to change your beliefs about a situation in your life so your actions will change to match the new beliefs. Name a problem or change you'd like to make here.

_____

5. Now think about the way you want things to be in this situation, and describe it in one short sentence. Use the present tense, and use only positive terms—talk about what will be going on, instead of what won't be. For our example of quitting smoking, the sentence could be something like "I love living smoke free and breathing fresh air." Write your sentence here.

_____

6. Now create a mental picture to go with that sentence, which is called an affirmation. For our example, you might picture yourself strolling along a beach taking deep breaths of clean salty air, or in a pine forest in the mountains. Close your eyes, picturing this mental scene as clearly as you can for 10 or 15 seconds, and repeat your affirmation sentence in a quiet voice. What is this like for you—what feelings and thoughts come up?

_____

_____

7. Now write your affirmation on index cards or sticky notes and put them where you will see them several times a day—places like your bathroom mirror, your wallet or purse, your car's dashboard, your desk, your refrigerator, and so on. For one

month, make it part of your routine to stop what you're doing 10 times a day for 30 seconds each time to close your eyes, visualize your mental picture, and repeat your affirmation to yourself softly. You may even want to write it out before or after you do this. This will only take five minutes out of your day, and you can do it almost anywhere, so it won't be hard. Don't try to use more than two affirmations in the same month, or they won't work very well.

8. Answer this question after a month of testing your affirmation: What changes do you see in your behavior from the time you started using this affirmation until now?

_____

_____

_____

Be sure to bring this handout back to your next therapy session, and be prepared to discuss your thoughts and feelings about the exercise.

Appendix

ADDITIONAL ASSIGNMENTS FOR PRESENTING PROBLEMS

Anger Management and Domestic Violence

Antisocial Behavior in the Military

Anxiety

Attention and Concentration Deficits

Bereavement Due to the Loss of a Comrade

Borderline Personality

Brief Reactive Psychotic Episode

Chronic Pain after Injury

Combat and Operational Stress Reaction

Conflict with Comrades

Depression

Diversity Acceptance

Financial Difficulties

Homesickness/Loneliness

Insomnia

Mild Traumatic Brain Injury

Nightmares

Opioid Dependence

Panic/Agoraphobia

Parenting Problems Related to Deployment

Performance-Enhancing Supplement Use

Phobia

Physiological Stress Response — Acute

Post-Deployment Reintegration Problems

Posttraumatic Stress Disorder (PTSD)

Pre-Deployment Stress

Separation and Divorce

Sexual Assault by Another Service Member

Shift Work Sleep Disorder

Social Discomfort

Spiritual and Religious Issues

Substance Abuse/Dependence

Suicidal Ideation

Survivor's Guilt

Tobacco Use

ABOUT THE CD-ROM

INTRODUCTION

This appendix provides you with the information on the contents of the CD that accompanies this book. For the latest and greatest information, please refer to the ReadMe file located at the root of the CD.

SYSTEM REQUIREMENTS

- A computer with a processor running at 120 Mhz or faster
- At least 32 MB of total RAM installed on your computer; for best performance, we recommend at least 64MB
- A CD-ROM drive

Note: Many popular word processing programs are capable of reading Microsoft Word files. However, users should be aware that a slight amount of formatting might be lost when using a program other than Microsoft Word.

USING THE CD WITH WINDOWS

To install the items from the CD to your hard drive, follow these steps:

1. Insert the CD into your computer's CD-ROM drive.
2. The CD-ROM interface will appear. The interface provides a simple point-and-click way to explore the contents of the CD.

If the opening screen of the CD-ROM does not appear automatically, follow these steps to access the CD:

1. Click the Start button on the left of the taskbar and then choose Run from the menu that pops up. (In Windows Vista and Windows 7, skip this step.)
2. In the dialog box that appears, type d:\setup.exe. (If your CD drive is not drive d, use the appropriate letter in place of d.) This brings up the CD interface described in the preceding set of steps. (In Windows Vista or Windows 7, type d:\setup.exe in the Start > Search text box.)

USING THE CD WITH A MAC

1. Insert the CD into your computer's CD-ROM drive.
2. The CD-ROM icon appears on your desktop, double-click the icon.
3. Double-click the Start icon.
4. The CD-ROM interface will appear. The interface provides a simple point-and-click way to explore the contents of the CD.

WHAT'S ON THE CD

The following sections provide a summary of the software and other materials you'll find on the CD.

Content

Includes all 78 homework assignments from the book in Word format. Homework assignments can be customized, printed out, and distributed to clients in an effort to extend the therapeutic process outside the office. All documentation is included in the folder named "Content."

Applications

The following applications are on the CD:

OpenOffice.org

OpenOffice.org is a free multi-platform office productivity suite. It is similar to Microsoft Office or Lotus SmartSuite, but OpenOffice.org is absolutely free. It includes word processing, spreadsheet, presentation, and drawing applications that enable you to create professional documents, newsletters, reports, and presentations. It supports most file formats of other office software. You should be able to edit and view any files created with other office solutions. Certain features of Microsoft Word documents may not display as expected from within OpenOffice.org. For system requirements, go to www.openoffice.org.

Software can be of the following types:

- Shareware programs are fully functional, free, trial versions of copyrighted programs. If you like particular programs, register with their authors for a nominal fee and receive licenses, enhanced versions, and technical support.
- Freeware programs are free, copyrighted games, applications, and utilities. You can copy them to as many computers as you like—for free—but they offer no technical support.
- GNU software is governed by its own license, which is included inside the folder of the GNU software. There are no restrictions on distribution of GNU software. See the GNU license at the root of the CD for more details.
- Trial, demo, or evaluation versions of software are usually limited either by time or functionality (such as not letting you save a project after you create it).

TROUBLESHOOTING

If you have difficulty installing or using any of the materials on the companion CD, try the following solutions:

- **Turn off any antivirus software that you may have running.** Installers sometimes mimic virus activity and can make your computer incorrectly believe that a virus is infecting it. (Be sure to turn the antivirus software back on later.)
- **Close all running programs.** The more programs that you're running, the less memory is available to other programs. Installers also typically update files and programs; if you keep other programs running, installation may not work properly.
- **Reference the README file.** Please refer to the README file located at the root of the CD for the latest product information at the time of publication.

USER ASSISTANCE

If you have trouble with the CD-ROM, please call the Wiley Product Technical Support phone number at (800) 762-2974. Outside the United States, call 1 (317) 572-3994. You can also contact Wiley Product Technical Support at http://support.wiley.com. John Wiley & Sons will provide technical support only for installation and other general quality control items. For technical support of the applications themselves, consult the program vendor or author.

To place additional orders or to request information about other Wiley products, please call (800) 225-5945.